ADVANCE PRAISE FOR

Chants of Christological Continuity

"This work is an important contribution to the field of contextual Christology from a sub-Saharan African perspective. Dr. Ehinack has skillfully used oral materials from the popular religious songs to construct a Christology in light of African anthropology and ecclesiology. In doing so, he has demonstrated a thorough understanding of African worldview and practices. I do not know of any comparable works to his in the field of Christology."

—Anh Tran, PhD, Associate Professor of Systematic and Historical Studies at Jesuit School of Theology Santa Clara University

"Dr. Ehinack skillfully explains complex Christology and Mariology concepts in simple and easy to read manner. This work showcases a glimpse of the divine richness of Christ and Mary in the lived expression of our faith within the context of the African culture in beloved songs. This is a must read for anyone seeking examples of the universality of our catholic faith in the African cultural and traditional contexts."

—Dr. Mathilda K. Fienkeng, Author and Public speaker

Chants of Christological Continuity

Bible and Theology in Africa

Knut Holter
General Editor

Vol. 33

Benedict B. Ehinack

Chants of Christological Continuity

African Anthropology, Christology, and Patristic Dialogue

PETER LANG

New York · Berlin · Bruxelles · Chennai · Lausanne · Oxford

Library of Congress Control Number: 2024917871

Bibliographic information published by the Deutsche Nationalbibliothek.
The German National Library lists this publication in the German
National Bibliography; detailed bibliographic data is available
on the Internet at http://dnb.d-nb.de.

Cover design by Peter Lang Group AG

ISSN 1525-9846 (print)
ISBN 9781433190827 (hardback)
ISBN 9781433190834 (ebook)
ISBN 9781433190841 (epub)
DOI 10.3726/b18663

© 2025 Peter Lang Group AG, Lausanne, Switzerland
Published by Peter Lang Publishing Inc., New York, USA
info@peterlang.com - www.peterlang.com

All rights reserved.
All parts of this publication are protected by copyright.
Any utilization outside the strict limits of the copyright law, without the permission of the
publisher, is forbidden and liable to prosecution.
This applies in particular to reproductions, translations, microfilming, and storage and
processing in electronic retrieval systems.

This publication has been peer reviewed.

DEDICATION

To

My Dad, (Joseph Behina) and my Mom, (Marie-Salome Behina)

&

to

All who daily answer the question that God asked Cain:

"Where is your brother, Abel?" (Gen.4: 9)

CONTENTS

Acknowledgments   xiii

General Introduction   1
Research Questions   3
Scope and Limit of This Work   3
Methodology   4
Literature Review   5
Significance of the Study   6
Description of Chapter Content   7

Chapter 1   Anthropological and Philosophical Frameworks of Patristic Christology: Insights from the Christological Controversies of Nicaea (325) to Chalcedon (451)

     Introduction   15
     Christology of the School of Alexandria   16
         Philosophical and Anthropological Framework   17
         Cyril of Alexandria's Christology: The *hypostatic* Union   18
     Christology of the School of Antioch   21
         Philosophical and Anthropological Framework   21

		Nestorius of Constantinople's Christology:	
		The *Prosopic* Union	22
		Chalcedonian Christology Examined: Probing the Dual	
		Nature of Christ	25
		Explaining Foundational Theological Concepts	26
		When Humanity Meets Divinity: The Mode of	
		Union of Christ's Natures	28
		Heresies and the Chalcedonian Debate: The Struggle	
		for Doctrinal Purity	29
		Chalcedonian Theology Revisited: An African Perspective	36
		Conclusion	41
	Chapter 2	Transitioning Worlds: From Anthropology to Christology	
		Introduction	43
		African Anthropology: Major Characteristics	44
		The Three Instances of the Human Person	45
		The Body	47
		The Heart of Ubuntu Philosophy: Probing	
		Its Core Tenets	50
		When Faith Meets Culture: Toward a Theology	
		of Inculturation	53
		Conclusion	58
	Chapter 3	Ecclesiology and Christology in Africa: Reflections	
		on the Sociopolitical Dynamics	
		Introduction	59
		Colonization and Evangelization: Untangling the African	
		Church's Story	60
		Historical unfoldment of Modern Evangelization	
		Periods in Africa	69
		Church Identity in Africa: Exploring a Major African	
		Ecclesiological Model	70
		Key Issues Framing the Discourse in the African Church	78
		Anthropological Poverty	78
		HIV/AIDS	79
		Political, Social, and Psychological Vulnerability	81
		Conclusion	82

Chapter 4	Who Do You Say That I Am?' In Africa: An Exploration of Christological Models	
	Introduction	85
	Christ as Master of Initiation	86
	Christ as Healer	90
	Christ as Liberator	96
	Christ as Chief	100
	Christ the Ancestor	106
	Conclusion	119
Chapter 5	African Religious Chants: Unveiling a Lived Christology through Melodies – A Theological and Pastoral Perspective	
	Introduction	121
	Melodic Expressions of Christ: West African Popular Gospel Songs	122
	"*Only You Jesus*" by Ada Ehi of Nigeria: A Window into a Christology of Supreme Strength and Unparalleled Power	122
	"*Jesus Dey for Your Corner*" by Glory Drops from Cameroon: Christology of Proximity in Focus	127
	Focus – *Jesus Dey for Your Corner*	128
	A *Golgotha* by Le Rossignol De New-Deido – Cameroon: Unveiling the Redeeming Christ in a Christology of Sacrificial Innocence	133
	Victory by Eben of Nigeria: Presenting Divine Triumph in a Christology of Ultimate Victory	136
	Melodic Expressions Christ: East African Popular Gospel Songs	140
	Hoziana by the Ambassador Choir, Rwanda: Introducing the Significance of Regal Christology	140
	Amenitendeya (He Has Done It for Me) by the Mwamba Children Choir, Uganda: Displaying Divine Abundance with Christ the Generous Giver	146
	Unikumbuke (Remember Me) by Christina Shusho, Tanzania: In Sync with Human Plight with Christ as the Merciful Listener	148
	Conclusion	152

Chapter 6	African Religious Chants: Unveiling a Lived Mariology through Melodies – A Theological and Pastoral Perspective	
	Introduction	153
	African Motherhood in Mary: A Mariological Perspective	154
	Portraits of Mary: West African Popular Gospel Songs	158
	Maria, Maa-Nfor (Mary, Queen-Mother), Cameroon: Divine Maternity: Mariology in the Concept of "Maa-Nfor" (Queen-Mother)	158
	A Nna Maria (O Mother Mary) by Gervais Mendo Ze – Cameroon Mary the Active Mother: Toward a Dynamic Mariology	162
	Hail Full of Grace by Aloysius Fonkeng, Cameroon Radiant Joy: Exploring Mariology and the Resplendence of Mary's Presence	166
	Portraits of Mary: East African Popular Gospel Songs	168
	Ayi Omutima gwa nyaffe Maria (Oh Heart of our Mother Mary), Uganda Mary's Eternal Faithfulness: Analyzing Vows in the Heart of Mariology	168
	Ewe Mama Maria (Yes, Mother Mary), Tanzania Divine Motherhood: Mary's Significance in Mariological Reflection	172
	Mama Maria, Mother of All Mothers (Mother Mary, Mother of All Mothers), Kenya Liberating Love: Toward a Mariology of Liberation	174
	Conclusion	177
General Conclusion		179
	Bibliography	183

ABOUT THIS BOOK

Chants of Christological Continuity
African Anthropology, Christology, and Patristic Dialogue
Dr. Benedict B. Ehinack

In the crucible of a new religion (Christianity) interacting with Greek civilization, the Church Fathers utilized their Hellenistic anthropological framework to forge a Christology that became normative and entrenched as doctrinal orthodoxy. Similarly, Sub-Saharan African Christology, relying also on an underlying anthropology, leads us to ponder how the Christian faith is articulated and lived within its present anthropological and sociopolitical context.

Drawing from my rich cultural heritage and utilizing a robust, multifaceted methodological approach—encompassing hermeneutic, descriptive, and narrative techniques—I explore how foundational anthropological perspectives, specifically Patristic Hellenistic dualism and Africa's inherently pluralistic anthropology, have sculpted their respective Christological narratives. This exploration reveals how contemporary African Christological frameworks align seamlessly with both Scripture and Church Tradition, finding lived expression in widespread daily gospel songs.

This book delves into Christological and Mariological themes embedded in these songs, unveiling a culturally pertinent Christology characterized by concepts like Christology of Proximity, Functional Christology, and Mariology of liberation. Mary is revered not only as the Queen-Mother with unique access to the divine but also as a proactive agent of liberation. These songs, which resonate deeply within African life, bring to light the profound lived experience of Christology in the continent, underscoring Sub-Saharan Africa's vital contributions to theological discourse and the New Evangelization. This dialogue between Hellenistic and African Christologies enhances our understanding and appreciation of how anthropology profoundly influences and enriches Christology and ecclesiology in Africa. In this context, the Church, deeply rooted in the familial ethos of *ubuntu*, addresses its communal challenges through a theology that is both informed and shaped by its unique anthropological insights.

Without prejudice to the supracultural dimension of Christology and Mariology, it is clear that no single historical reality can exhaust the richness of Christ or Mary. This explains why no Christological or Mariological model conferred on Christ or Mary can be absolutized. This research not only adds impetus to Africa's voice in Christological matters but also illuminates the dynamic interplay between anthropology, Christology, ecclesiology and Mariology in Africa. It acts as a catalyst for articulating God's eternal word via ever-evolving expressions to ensure its relevance in our times.

ACKNOWLEDGMENTS

A very deep appreciation goes to Dr. Anh Q. Tran, SJ., and Dr. Eduardo C. Fernandez, SJ., for their practical advice and constructive remarks which propelled me to see the big picture as well as the minor details of this work. Without their goodwill, this work would never have materialized.

I give great thanks to Dr. Bienvenu K. Mayemba, SJ., chair of African theology at the Jesuit Institute of Theology in Abidjan, Ivory Coast. His wise counsel and unbridled encouragement and input contributed immensely to sharpening my theological vision and the success of this research. I also thank Dr. Thomas Cattoi and Dr. Gabriel Mmassi SJ., for their strong support and mentorship at the initial stage of this research.

I thank Dr. Mathilda K. Fienkeng for her unwavering and steadfast commitment to offering invaluable suggestions and revisions to this research. Her insightful comments generously contributed nourishment to the intellectual refinement of this endeavor.

Getting through this writing required more than academic support, and I have many, many people to thank for listening to and, at times, having to tolerate my ways. I would like to thank the Parishioners of St. Lawrence O'Toole, especially Ms. Sellman C. and Ms. Watkins, and St. Benedict Parishes,

Oakland, for their support toward my spiritual, moral, and academic growth during the time of my studies in Berkeley, California.

I would be amiss if I did not thank all my friends in Michigan, the San Francisco Bay Area, and Minnesota (especially the Tubuo, Doh, and Akosa families). Without their assistance and dedicated involvement in every step throughout the process, this "Patristico-African journey" would never have been accomplished. Thank you very much for your support and understanding over these past years. To my CamBay family, I say "thank you." To the 1995 Batch of Bishop Rogan Minor Seminary for their fraternity and presence, I extend love and appreciation. Special salutation to Frs. Sama Muma, Noel-Jean Fogang, Jean-Robert Fankam, Angelbert Chikere, Robain Lamba, Tegha Afunwi, Tony Famave, Wilson Enow, and deacon Sunny Offorjebe, and to my agile brother, Prime Bella. To you reading this book, I say "merci beaucoup."

To my parents (Joseph & Marie-Salome Behina) and my siblings – Stella, Veronique, Michael, Jean, Angela & Micheline – this research stands as a testament to your unconditional love and encouragement. May God keep and bless you.

Ekenedere Chukwu (thanks be to our God) to whom I owe my life and blessings. "Amen, blessing and glory and wisdom and thanksgiving and honor and power and might, be to our God forever and ever. Amen" (Rev 7:12).

GENERAL INTRODUCTION

The theological and pastoral atmosphere in Africa rests on the following two poles: the "missionary pole" and the "cultural pole." In the "missionary pole," the faith and method of evangelization, brought by the early missionaries, are used indiscriminately to spread the gospel, while the "cultural pole" favors an exclusive emphasis on the local culture. Many of the local diocesan priests in Africa were taught either by European missionaries or by people who went through a European philosophical and theological training. This Western-training imposed on the local Christians a European mindset that encouraged a "theology of repetition."[1] On the other hand, in reaction to this approach, some Christians and pastors chose to embrace an exclusive "cultural pole" approach. They completely abandon the rich theological heritage of our

---

1 "Theology of Repetition" is a phrase used by George Flovovsky to refer to a blind, uncritical rehashing of past theology. It is a repetition that dissociates itself from the day-to-day realities of human life. It is a disconnect between the ontological and the historical dimensions of faith. It pays no attention to cultural adaptation of any sort, but rehearses indiscriminately what was done in the past. It is an imitative theology. See George Flovovsky, "St. Gregory Palamas and the Traditions of the Fathers," in https://www.bulgarian-orthodox-church.org/rr/lode/florovsky1.pdf, accessed on February 2, 2018.

apostolic faith, in favor of the local culture. This latter group sees little or no pastoral or theological contribution from the Early Church.

My personal experience of the Church and my seminary formation in Cameroon imposes upon me the task of avoiding a theological flaw that not only had a cancerous effect on African theology and Christian living, but has also stood in the way of a full understanding and integration of the Gospel into the lives of Africans. I want to avoid a "theology of repetition" which has failed to let cultural riches help in the understanding of the doctrinal statements arrived at during the early councils. This would be like doing everything to theologize like Athanasius, using his language and images, without regard to the people to whom the Gospel is preached, or like considering humanity as one whole, in a way that negates individual or group cultural identity.

With the available philosophical understanding and cultural resources of their time, the Early Church Fathers from the second to the fifth century articulated a Christology that has become normative throughout Christian traditions. In the face of a new religion (Christianity) interacting with Greek culture, the Early Church Fathers, from both the Alexandrian and Antiochene schools of thoughts, struggled with how to understand and present Christian doctrines using their own Hellenistic, cultural prisms.[2] In response to the questions on the person and nature of Christ, the Early Church thinkers from these two schools of thoughts had a unique anthropological lens. Their theological views largely contributed to their understanding and articulation of Christology.

Given the contemporary setting, I would like to consider what Patristic Christology can offer to us living in Africa today and how African Christology can achieve its relevance in the lived expressions of the African people.

Contemporary African theologians, like the Church Fathers of the early days of Christianity, attempt to articulate Christological expressions using the categories from their sociocultural settings. I argue that being consistent with Patristic Christology, African Christology is expressed through the process of inculturation of Christ's representations, in a variety of conceptual models and popular religious songs. Furthermore, given the African cultural setting and the primordial place of motherhood, African Christology cannot be separated from a lived Mariology. The integration of Christology and Mariology through popular gospel songs will be examined closely.

---

2 Hellenistic dualism as championed by Plato and other thinkers was the dominant influence on Patristic theology. It made a sharp distinction between visible corporeal reality and an intelligible corporeal world of ideas.

Research Questions

The dialogue between Patristic and African Christologies brings out a common trend at the level of methodology, precisely in their use of anthropological understanding in articulating Christology. This leads to the question, "What are the theological and pastoral implications of a dialogue between Patristic and African Christologies?" This question is crucial for this research because it brings out the role of anthropology in Christology and prepares the ground for understanding how Christology is lived daily in the life of ordinary African Christians. It also brings us to attempt a response to the question, "How is Christology lived and expressed within the present Anthropological, cultural heritage and socio-political context of Africa through major African Christological models and songs?" Given that in Africa, one cannot effectively talk of a child without referencing the mother, what is the unique, indispensable place of Mariology in the lived expressions of the people? What Mariology stems from African songs about Mary?

Scope and Limit of This Work

The scope of this work is black Africa, or sub-Saharan Africa, which ranges from Sierra Leone in the West to the Nuba Mountains in the East, and down to the Cape in the South.[3] This precision is necessary, given the extensive and diverse nature of the African continent.

One difficulty in undertaking this research was the "guilt" of speaking about Africa and Africans in general, or of the African culture in a pure state. This "guilt" stems from my full awareness of the fact that Africa enjoys a rich, complex diversity in the face of deep current mutations. Despite its diversity, black Africa shares many cultural trends that add to its unity. In fact, like Efoé Julien Penoukou, I am of the conviction that "Black Africa does exhibit certain constant data and represents a more and more precise cultural and historical entity."[4] In this light, whenever I used African culture, traditions, or values in this book, I employed it with all the reserves of usage applied in such an unscientific generalization.

---

3 Eduard G. Parrinder, *African Traditional Religion* (Westport: Greenwood Press, 1976), 12.
4 Efoé Julien Penoukou, "Christology in the Village," in *Faces of Jesus in Africa*, ed. by Robert J. Schreiter (Maryknoll, NY: Orbis, 1991), 29.

Methodology

Despite the fact that some theologies still claim to represent "a form of thought which does not regard itself as contextual,"[5] for most theologians, the contextual nature of theology has nowadays become axiomatic[6] for "contextualization is part of the very nature of theology itself."[7] Without contextualization, the Christian message remains foreign and sterile. With contextualization comes transformation, understanding, and full participation.

The Church in Africa seeks not only to have a voice in Christological reflections but also to make that voice heard in its various manifestations. This imposes on this book an interdisciplinary and multidimensional methodology which is at the same time hermeneutic, descriptive, and narrative. By hermeneutic, I will interpret theological concepts, titles, and notions in articulating a relevant Christology. By narrative, I will relate relevant cultural histories and traditions that help in explaining various representations of Christ. By descriptive, I will shed light on or explain theological notions, traditions, and representations that help to facilitate the dialogue between African and Patristic theologies.

This hermeneutic, descriptive, and narrative methodology will provide a window to the African sociocultural and political context of that lived Christology, giving space not only for the culture to flourish and be enriched, but also for the Christian identity to be strengthened and renewed in the process. Far from being a literal word-for-word translation from Patristic to African Christology, this approach will go a long way to correct the outdated, fantastical notion that there exists a word-for-word correspondence from language to language all over the world.

This book took into consideration the four main sources of African Christology proposed by John Mbiti. They include the Bible, the theology of the Older or ancient Churches, the traditional African concepts, and the living experiences of the Church in Africa.[8] These sources provide a framework for

---

5 John Hall Douglas, *Thinking the Faith: Christian Theology in a North American Context* (Minneapolis, MN: Fortress Press, 1991), 69. Robert Jenson, commenting on the inherent contextual nature of theology, argues that, "recent clamor for 'contextual' theology is, of course empty, there never having been any other kind." See Robert W. Jenson, *Systematic Theology*, vol. 2 (New York: Oxford University Press, 1997), 1.
6 Donald A. Carson, *The Gagging of God: Christianity Confront Pluralism* (Grand Rapids, MI: Zondervan, 1996), 97.
7 Stephen B. Bevans, *Models of Contextual Theology* (Maryknoll, NY: Orbis, 1996), 1.
8 John Mbiti, "Some African Concepts of Christology," in *Christ and the Younger Churches*, ed. by Georg F. Vicedom (London: Society for Promoting Christian Knowledge, 1972), 51,

the different ways of reflecting on Christ in Africa. The main point of departure for my analysis is my own experience of the Church and its various ways of a lived Christology and Mariology, the African culture, and the Gospel in Africa. I will draw from my culture and my life in the Church. In this light, I will use major Christological models, narratives, and popular gospel songs to illustrate and explore the lived expressions of Christology in contemporary African Christians.

While most African Christians do not doubt that Jesus is human and co-substantial with the Father, as evident in their songs and major Christological models, I will seek in this writing not only to look at how Jesus' consubstantiality with the Father and with humanity can be relatable to the average African in a way that would be most meaningful but also how this divine-human unity is played out in concepts and popular gospel songs. I will look here at images/titles similar to the Christological titles of the Early Church that could be meaningful enough to Africans, to the point of spurring a response. This response, which may take different and varied forms, can be in the form of deeper devotion, or of justice, peace, hope, and love.[9]

Literature Review

Many scholars have studied and articulated how African Christology stems from the culture of the people. Charles Nyamiti and Benezet Bujo, for instance, have done extensive work on situating the gospel within the context of African realities by developing the Ancestor Model in Christology. They engage extensively with Patristic theology vis-à-vis African cultural realities. In his, *Christ as Our Ancestor: Christology from an African Perspective*, Charles Nyamiti focuses on Christ as the brother-ancestor showing how relevant this model is in the context of Africa.[10] Bénézet Bujo, in this same light, portrays Christ as the proto-ancestor.[11] Also, Uchenna A. Ezeh, in his *Christ the Ancestor, An*

---

quoted by Uchenna A. Ezeh, *Christ the Ancestor, An African Contextual Christology in the Light of the Major Dogmatic Christological Definitions of the Church from the Council of Nicaea (325) to Chalcedon (451)* (Berne: Peter Lang AG, European Academic publishers, 2003). 264.
9 I will use titles like Jesus the Ancestor, Jesus the Healer, Jesus the Liberator, Jesus the Chief, and Jesus the Master of Initiation.
10 Charles Nyamiti, *Christ as Our Ancestor: Christology From an African Perspective* (Gweru: Mambo Press, 1984).
11 Benezet Bujo, *African Theology in Its Social Context*, trans. by John O'Donohue (Eugene, OR: Wipf & Stock Publishers, 2006).

African Contextual Christology in the Light of the Major Dogmatic Christological Definitions of the Church from the Council of Nicaea (325) to Chalcedon (451) engages African ancestral Christological model with major Christological councils of the Patristic era. In his article *African Christianity: Its Scope in Global Context*, Caleb O. Oladipo treats aspects of the Christian faith in Africa by highlighting unique characteristics of Christianity in Africa. He argues that Christianity in Africa has come to stay because it is anchored on the culture. While Oladipo touches on the strong sense of community (*ubuntu*) as one of the major characteristics of Christianity in Africa, he does not deal with the issue of Christological expressions through songs.[12]

While all these works largely contribute to theology and highlight Africa's voice to the table of theological endeavors, they neither address the role of anthropology in these theologies nor bring out how these models are lived and expressed daily through an important tool like songs.

This work puts an emphasis not only on Africa's unique voice in articulating Christology in the universal Church but also on how African Christology is consistent with Patristic thoughts and Scriptures, and how it is lived and expressed in popular daily hymns and songs of the people. This work uniquely seeks to articulate a Christology in light of an African anthropological and sociopolitical cultural context. Since within the context of African culture, one cannot speak of an important figure without mentioning the mother and also, taking into account the popularity of Marian devotions in Africa, this work examines and integrates a Mariological perspective, showing how Mary is articulated in songs. My aim is to create space for a theological and pastoral exchange between Patristic and African Christologies.

Significance of the Study

Vatican II with all its reforms emerges the need for a burgeoning Christianity, that neither stifles nor makes people reject their cultures in the process of becoming Christians.[13] The Early Church Fathers, though distant in time, are really part and parcel of our Christian heritage. Given their own culture,

12 Caleb O. Oladipo, "African Christianity: Its Scope in Global Context" in *Development, Modernism and Modernity in Africa*, ed. by Augustine Agwuele (New York & London: Routledge, 2012).
13 This research meets the needs of present-day scholarship in Africa. It falls within the broader initiative which encourages African theologians to gain fresh understanding of how the Christian faith engages contemporary African realities through interdisciplinary

heritage, and sociopolitical setting, they succeeded in making their voices heard in articulating concepts and images that have become normative for Christology. Because these Christological concepts/images do not always connect with the African setting, we, therefore, have a task to re-interpret them from our various cultural paradigms that can suit the African contextual setting. I use the word "re-interpret" here in the sense of explaining in a way that is lucid and helpful to the African cultural context. This book illuminates the dynamic and reciprocal relationship between culture and theology, demonstrating that the understanding and expression of Christian doctrines are deeply influenced by the cultural contexts in which they are articulated and lived. The insights derived from the African context, particularly through the medium of popular gospel songs, shows that theology is not a static, universal monolith but a living, breathing dialogue that evolves and adapts to meet the spiritual needs of its adherents.

This hermeneutic, descriptive, and narrative dialogue between Patristic and African Christologies is important not only because it increases the voice of contextual Christology but also in the fact that it brings out how African Christology is lived in the daily lives of the people. It makes the relevant connection with the Early Church while bearing in mind the supracultural dimension of Christology.[14]

Overall, the significance of this study lies in its ability to bridge the gap between academic theological research and practical Christian living. It invites scholars, clergy, and lay Christians alike to rethink Christology in a way that is both deeply rooted in traditional doctrinal frameworks and profoundly responsive to the cultural and social realities of contemporary African life.

Description of Chapter Content

Although an exhaustive analysis of the historico-theological background of Patristic Christology is beyond the scope of this research, in Chapter 1, I will address Patristic Christology in its anthropological and philosophical context

> research. (See Tite Tiénou, "Christian Theology: African Realities and African Hope," *International Bulletin of Mission Research 4*, vol. 41, (2017): 294.)
>
> 14 "Supra-cultural dimension of Christology" is a phrase used by Stephen Bevans in his *Models of Contextual Theology*, to denote the fact that there exist certain contents in Christology that must be held even if their preservation goes against and is destructive of a particular culture. Contents such as "Jesus Christ is Divine" would be a good illustrative example.

by looking at how the two schools of Alexandria and Antioch not only used their dualistic anthropological lens to articulate a relevant Christology but also how their theologies opened doors to some Christological heresies and dogmas.[15] I will examine the broader Christological controversies, explaining conciliar dogmatic responses to each of them, clarifying terms such as *ousia*, *hypostasis*, *phusis*, and *prosopon* as used during these controversial debates and examining the mode of union between the human and the divine natures of Christ.[16] Because this chapter aims to espouse the philosophical background of Patristic Christology,[17] which of course takes flesh in the two schools of thoughts and finds its most solemn expressions/definitions in Chalcedon, I will briefly examine the African theologians – John Pobee's[18] criticism of Chalcedonian Christology and what Africa has to do with Chalcedon, thus setting the groundwork for Chapter 2.

In the same way as Chapter 1 shows how anthropology shaped Christology, Chapter 2 of this work examines not only the African pluralistic anthropology as presented by the Jesuit philosopher and theologian Meinrad P. Hebga, in his *La Rationalité d'un Discours Africain sur les Phénomènes Paranormaux*, but also the concept of *Ubuntu*, meaning a person is a person only through, with, and for the community. The identity of a person is defined by his or her relationship to the community.[19] He notes that Hellenistic dualism constitutes a real

15 A reading of both the Alexandrian and the Antiochene Traditions reveals their many points of agreement. Among these agreements are the fact that they both hold to the idea of cosmic Christ, both believe in the idea of personal continuity and say that the divine logos, while being incarnate, remain all that he was, etc.
16 In his *The Philosophy of the Church Fathers I: Faith, Trinity, Incarnation, His Structure and Growth of Philosophic Systems from Plato to Spinoza*, vol. I (Cambridge, MA: Harvard University Press, 1956), 385. Harry Austryn Wolfson notes five ways in which two realities could unite according to ancient Greek Church Fathers.
17 With the intention of engaging in dialogue with African Christology.
18 The Ghanaian theologian, John S. Pobee, very critical of Chalcedonian Christology, undermined the legitimacy of Nicene/Chalcedonian Christianity as reference point for Christological discourse and contends that our intellectual indebtedness to Greco-Roman culture has predisposed us to keep on discussing Christology in metaphysical terms. In his *Towards an African Theology* (Nashville, TN: Abingdon, 1979), 82, Pobee notes that any Christological proposal which uses the Chalcedonian Creed as a point of departure lacks authenticity – whether in Africa or elsewhere in the Christian world (p. 83). Pobee argues that Jesus' divinity is deduced from his day-to-day works and actions. He advocates a functional divinity rather than the Chalcedonian ontological divinity.
19 Michael J. Battle, *Reconciliation: The Ubuntu Theology of Desmond Tutu* (Cleveland, OH: Pilgrim Press, 2009). Also see Michael J. Battle *Ubuntu, I in You and You in Me* (New York: Seabury Books, 2009).

difficulty in understanding African anthropology and that transitioning "*du dualisme au pluralisme*" (from dualism to pluralism)[20] is the main key that opens the door to understanding African anthropology. I will also show how that African pluralistic anthropology and the concept of *ubuntu* help in the understanding and articulation of an African Christology. In Africa, a human being is not limited to biological features but also includes the community, *ubuntu* aspects. This will go a long way toward helping us understand the philosophical foundations and presuppositions of African Christological models and its lived expressions. In other words, understanding African anthropology is an indispensable gateway to appreciating both the African Christological models and its lived daily expressions.

Chapter 3 will discuss African ecclesiology, setting the context in which Patristic and African Christologies will dialogue. I will describe the effects of colonialism on the life of the Church in Africa, dwelling precisely on how colonialism has shaped and affected the continent, superimposing a colonial mindset that encouraged a mentality of repetition, which assailed the pastoral, social, and political lives of the people in Africa. I will argue that Christianity, like colonialism, was gradually implanted into the culture of the African people and is still prevalent in today's Africa.[21] In this chapter, I will look at the colonial undertone of the missionary enterprise, and how it still affects the reception of the Gospel message by Africans; I agree with the Nigerian historian, Emmanuel A. Ayandele that there are many reasons to conclude that missionary activities in Africa were the "spiritual wing of secular imperialism."[22] I will critically analyze Adrian Hastings' four periods of evangelization in Africa.[23]

---

20 En même temps, on veut laisser entendre que chaque instance n'est pas une partie de la personne, mais la personne tout entière perçue sur un angle particulier Meinrad P. Hebba, *La Rationalite d'un Discours Africain Sur les Phenomenes Paranormaux* (Paris: Harmattan, 1998), 26.
21 In the words of John Mbiti, "... the image that Africans received, and to a great extent still hold, of Christianity is much colored by colonial rule and all that was involved in it. We are still too close to that period to dissociate one from the other." See John Mbiti, *African Religions and Philosophy* (London: Heinemann, 1969), 231.
22 Emmanuel Ayandele et al., *The Growth of African Civilization: The Making of Modem Africa*, vol. 2 (London: Longman, 1968), 135.
23 In his *Church and Mission in Modern Day Africa* (New York: University Press, 1967), Adrian Hastings presents the modern evangelization, distinguishing four periods of evangelization with each period having specific characteristics, methods of evangelization, and sociopolitical situations. An analysis of these periods of evangelization is very pertinent because

By identifying this important concept, the Church in Africa situates itself under the recognition that the same blood of the ancestors circulates in the veins of all members from generation to generation, upholding human dignity and promoting life, even for those yet to be born. I will engage extensively with John Paul II's *Ecclesia in Africa*,[24] Benedict XVI's Post-Synodal Apostolic Exhortation *Africae Munus*,[25] and a prominent African ecclesiologist – Agbonkhianmeghe E. Orobator[26] so as to trace the stages of modern evangelization in Africa and some major sociocultural and political issues affecting the Church in Africa today including "Anthropological poverty,"[27] HIV-AIDS, Political, Social and Psychological Vulnerability. According to Engelbert Mveng, one of the problems that assail the Church in Africa and the continent as a whole is anthropological poverty. Anthropological poverty captures the predicament of the whole continent; a predicament that hinges on human and material poverty brought about through the mechanism of foreign domination, exploitation, and dependence.

---

    it provides us with a window into the historical *locus operandi* of African ecclesiology on which *Ecclesia in Africa*, *Africae Munus*, and African ecclesiologists function.

24 John Paul II's *Ecclesia in Africa* or the Church in Africa, is a September 1995 document that captured the reflections of the 1994 synod of Bishops for Africa. The image of the Church as God's family has gained roots because in Africa, human relatedness forms a central pillar of life and worth. During this synod, African bishops adopted the concept of family as the most eloquent expression of what it means to be Church in Africa. The notion of family serves as the organizing principle that regulates our relationship not only with Christ's humanity and divinity but also with one another and all other socio-cultural, political and economic concerns within the Church.

25 Pope Benedict XVI published the Post-Synodal Apostolic Exhortation *Africae Munus* (Africa's Commitment) on November 19th, 2011. Building on *Ecclesia in Africa*'s theme of "Church as Family of God," he describes the family as a place of belonging, dialogue, solidarity, human respect and dignity; a place that propagates the "culture of forgiveness, peace and reconciliation" (*Africae Munus*, 43). *Africae Munus* challenges the Church in Africa to look deep within itself to find and embrace elements within its culture that serve as pillars of reconciliation, justice and human dignity.

26 Orobator uses the model of Church as family that emerged from the 1994 African Synod of Bishops. According to him, the African family is a "heuristic paradigm" that gives insights into a renewed vision of Church. A. E. Orobator, SJ., *The Church as Family: African Ecclesiology in Its Social Context* (Nairobi: Paulines Publications Africa, 2000), 138.

27 Engelbert Mveng, "Impoverishment and Liberation: A Theological Approach for Africa and the Third World," in *Paths of African Theology*, ed. by Rosino Gibellini (Maryknoll, NY: Orbis, 1994), 156. For Mveng, anthropological poverty is a kind of poverty which mainly affects the very being, essence, and dignity of the human person.

In Chapter 4, entitled "'Who do you say that I am?' in Africa: An exploration of Christological Models," I will analyze five major African Christological models as viewed by African theologians who have reflected extensively on these models. I will analyze Christ as Master of Initiation with Bishop Anselm Sanon from Burkina Faso,[28] who holds that in the same way as the initiation process uses symbols as vehicles to higher values of the community, so does the image of Christ as Master of initiation leads us on through symbols, especially the sacraments. Sacraments therefore in the African context are seen to reach their perfection and fulfilment in the life of the Christian community. The second Christological model will be the Christ as Healer model by Cece Kolie from Guinea.[29] Cece Kolie dwells on the concept of Jesus the traditional healer, basing himself from the Kpele and Logoma ethnic groups of Guinea to derive an ethos of healing which might have ramifications for understanding Jesus Christ as Healer. The third is Christ as Liberator,[30] a model that has been discussed extensively by African theologians like Englebert Mveng, Jean-Marc Ela, Laurenti Magesa, and Mercy Amba Oduyoye. The fourth model is the Christ as Chief model particularly seen in the writings of François Kabasélé.[31]

---

28 The "Christ as Master of Initiation" image has had particular emphasis in the work of Bishop Anselm Sanon. See *Enraciner l'évangile: Initiations africaines et pédagogie de la foi* (Paris: Cerf, 1982).

29 The Christological title of Christ as Healer which resonates well with the Gospels narratives opens a way for the universal Church to rediscover who Jesus is for us today. See Cece Kolie "Jesus as Healer" in *Faces of Jesus in Africa*, ed. Robert Schreiter (Maryknoll: Orbis, 1991) 128–50. Another African theologian who has written extensively on the image of Jesus the Healer is the Jesuit theologian and exorcist, Meinrad Hebga. See Meinrad Hebga *Sorcellerie et prière de délivrance* (Abidjan: Présence Africaine, 1986.)

30 Christ as Liberator image is very much present in many African theologians, (See Englebert Mveng, *L'Afrique dans l'Eglise, Paroles d'un Croyant* (Paris: L'Harmattan, 1985)); Also see "Impoverishment and Liberation: A Theological Approach for Africa and the Third World," in *Paths of African Theology* (Maryknoll, NY: Orbis, 1994), 154–65. Jean-Marc Ela, sees a "prophetic" dimension to the Jesus the Liberator image. (Jean-Marc Ela, *African Cry* (Maryknoll, NY: Orbis, 1986)); *My Faith as an African* (Maryknoll, NY: Orbis, 1988). Jesus' liberation also includes the liberation of women. Mercy Amba Oduyoye, a Methodist originally from Ghana, has done extensive work on the liberation of women in Africa, (See *Daughters of Anowa: African Women and Patriarchy* (Maryknoll, NY: Orbis, 2003); *Hearing and Knowing: Theological Reflections on Christianity in Africa* (Maryknoll, NY: Orbis, 1986).)

31 Christ as Chief concept has particularly gained grounds because of the unique, important place that chiefs occupy in the smooth running of the village community. Francois Kabasélé in his work "Christ as Chief" elaborates this concept very deeply. See Francois Kabasélé Lumbala, *Celebrating Jesus Christ in Africa: Liturgy & Inculturation* (Maryknoll,

Jesus as Chief not only because he has triumphed over Satan, and defends and protects His people but also because he is the child of the Chief (of God) – the Chief's Emissary. The last Christological model is the Christ as Ancestor, evident in the works of the Ghanaian John S. Pobee, the Congolese Bénézet Bujo, and the Tanzanian theologian Charles Nyamiti.[32] The purpose of this chapter is to espouse the major African Christological images with reference to Patristic Christology and to assess the strengths and weaknesses of this Christology[33] in terms of their continuity with Patristic Christology and their consistency with Scripture. It also highlights Africa's voice in Christological matters, paving the way to Chapters 5 and 6 which touch on the lived experiences of these Christological models, evident through songs.

There are many expressions of a lived Christology in Africa such as proverbs and rituals, but music particularly stands out and constitutes the focus of analysis in this research because it permeates all aspects of African life. In fact, today, music is so deeply rooted in African culture to the point that manual work, recreational periods, grinding, pounding, building, hunting, ploughing, tapping, fishing, suffering moments, weddings, driving, soccer games, and village meetings are often punctuated with music. It reveals life. It is life itself. Africans believe that, in as much as sowing and reaping are important parts of life, human beings must do more than sow and reap; words and songs must be added to it, for indeed, they contain the indispensable material necessary for the corn seed to germinate and grow, the cow to produce milk, and the carpenter to transform his handiwork into a masterpiece, thus making the world a better place. With Alex Asigbo, we stress that "contrary to popular opinion....

NY: Orbis, 1998). It is treated by F. Kabasélé, "Le Christ comme chef," in *Chemins de la Christologie africaine*, ed. F. Kabasélé, J. Doré, and R. Luneau (Paris: Desclée, 1986) 109–25.

32 African theologians have presented Christ's ancestorship in varied ways. We see this in the works of John S. Pobee, who portrays Jesus as the *Nana*, "the Greatest Ancestor." (See John Pobee, J. S. *Skenosis: Christian Faith in an African Context* (Gweru: Mambo Press, 1992)), the Congolese, Bénézet Bujo, says Christ is the proto-ancestor, (See Benezet Bujo, *African Theology in Its Social Context*, trans. by John O'Donohue (Eugene, OR: Wipf & Stock Publishers, 2006)). The Tanzanian theologian Charles Nyamiti, refers to Christ as the brother-ancestor. (See *Christ as Our Ancestor: Christology from an African Perspective* (Gweru, Zimbabwe: Mambo Press, 1984). The Congolese theologian, François Kabasélé, refers to Christ as an elder brother-ancestor. (See "Christ as Ancestor and brother" in *Faces of Jesus in Africa*, ed. by Robert Schreiter (Maryknoll, NY: Orbis, 1991)).

33 The concepts of Ancestor, Healer, Liberator, and traditional Head cannot be applied to Christ in a literal, non-metaphorical way. Qualifying these terms helps avoid misunderstandings that come with limitations of these Christological titles.

Oral performance can indeed redirect an earring society, be a tool for moral and ethical regeneration and in fact, serve as a vanguard for socio-cultural change."[34]

Chapter 5 is titled *African Religious Chants: Unveiling a Lived Christology through Melodies – A Theological and Pastoral Perspective.* It presents four songs from West Africa and three from East Africa in their original lyrics (and translations where necessary), with a Christological analysis of each song. It is noteworthy that this lived Christology also expresses concrete responses to anthropological poverty; HIV/AIDS; and political, social, and psychological vulnerability that assails the continent.

Given that "To become human is to become the child of a mother,"[35] Chapter 6,

African Religious Chants: Unveiling a Lived Mariology through Melodies – A Theological and Pastoral Perspective, focuses on analyzing West and East African popular Marian songs, bringing out an African Mariology as lived daily by the people, through songs. The importance of highlighting the place of Motherhood in Africa in relation to Mary is because it represents an effort (conscious or otherwise) to achieve two related goals. First, it helps to retrieve the female/mother experience and its value in the Incarnation. Second, it gives expression to a recurring theme, namely, incorporation of motherhood in God, emphasizing Christ's human and divine characteristics that resonate with African values.

Talking about a Christology in which Motherhood is prioritized, Lynette Jean Holness notes:

> A Christology from "within," in which motherhood is a core image, can have profound relevance in the African context. Since motherhood is an integral (perhaps the most basic) part of the reality of most women's lives on this continent, the fact that Christ emerged from the body of a woman accords dignity to this state. Mary's designation as *Theotokos*, bearing in mind the full meaning of the title, can then be understood as a recapitulation of motherhood. . . .[36]

---

34 Alex C. Asigbo, "Re-Inventing the Wisdom of the Ancients: Moral Signposts in Mike Ejiagh's Akuko N'Egwu," in *A Bountiful Harvest. Festschrift in Honour of Very Rev. Msgr. Prof. J. P. C. Nzomiwu*, A. B. C. Chiegboka, I. Okodo, I. L. Umeanoluue, Ed. (Nimo: Rex Charles and Patrick, 2012), 696.
35 Hans Urs Von Balthasar, *The Threefold Garland: The World's Salvation in Mary's Prayer* (San Francisco: Ignatius Press, 1982), 30.
36 Jean Holness Lynette, "Christology from Within: A Critical Retrieval of the Humanity of Christ, with Particular Reference to the Role of Mary," (Doctor of Philosophy Dissertation, University of Cape Town, 2001), 234.

Theotokos symbolizes the participation, not only of one Galilean girl but also of motherhood as a whole. Mary's role as the *theotokos* in some way situates motherhood in the ambit of redemption, thus helping to mediate a Christ relevant to African pastoral contexts, where motherhood is violated daily. Mary, as the Mother of God – the God who suffered the excruciating pain of the cross, makes her more relatable to African women. This is particularly true in contexts of hardship and female oppression with which many African women identify. It would be problematic for African Catholics to discuss Jesus in isolation from Mary, for she mediates Christ's humanity, and constitutes the locus of meeting between the human and the divine person of Jesus.

The Mariology songs are carefully drawn from different sub-Saharan cultures and languages within the Catholic tradition. In the same way, as Patristic anthropology informed the articulation of a Christology that has become normative in Christian circles, these songs reveal the anthropological undertones that inform African Christological models. Because Christology is not the exclusive domain of any *one* Christian denomination, I have included and analyzed Christological songs from different Christian denominations and expressions in their original languages, thus enriching the ecumenical, multilingual, and multidenominational outlook of this work.

· 1 ·

ANTHROPOLOGICAL AND PHILOSOPHICAL FRAMEWORKS OF PATRISTIC CHRISTOLOGY: INSIGHTS FROM THE CHRISTOLOGICAL CONTROVERSIES OF NICAEA (325) TO CHALCEDON (451)

Introduction

In his article "Patristic Exegesis and Theology: The Cart and the Horse," Donald Fairbairn argues for the position that the Alexandrian school possesses platonic philosophical presuppositions that originate from Philo's allegorical work on Scripture.[1] Among these presuppositions is the platonic dualistic anthropology. It is important to note that the period of antiquity, very much characterized by anthropological dualism, largely informed the theology of both Alexandrian school and the Antiochene school. Hellenistic dualism, as it is often called, explains everything along dualistic lines. Plato made a sharp distinction between visible corporeal reality and an intelligible corporeal world of ideas. He argued that every human person has two components: a visible, corporeal, and perishable body, and an invisible, incorporeal, and imperishable soul. From a platonic perspective, the human person is a rational soul which

---

1 Donald Fairbairn, "Patristic Exegesis and Theology: The Cart and the Horse," *Westminster Theological Journal* 69, no. 1 (Spring 2007): 2.

has a prior existence as a spirit in the world of ideas and only assumes a human body because of a spiritual fall. The body, being the inferior part, is the "tomb" of the soul. This dualism seems to have dominated and influenced many subsequent philosophical and theological reflections. It is important to note that anthropological dualism has not been without contention as to the relationship or separateness between the corporeal and the incorporeal natures.

Anthropological Dualism informed the theological discourse of the fourth and fifth centuries, especially when it came to answering the questions about the person and nature(s) of Christ. How many persons and natures does Christ have? How do they interact with each other? What is the mode of the union? Where do the natures unite? These questions opened the gateway to a series of Christological controversies which culminated at Chalcedon in 451.

In this chapter, I argue that to fully understand the Chalcedonian Christological formulation one needs to understand the theological backgrounds of the major disputes which essentially were based on different anthropological assumptions. It is worth emphasizing that the period leading to Chalcedon was marked by intense theological disputes that often reflected the clashes of personalities and, of course, different schools of thoughts. I shall examine these disputes in their proper theological and anthropological contexts, underlining how their anthropological view informed their Christology. I will highlight the anthropological undertones of the two major schools of Antioch and Alexandria which eventually contributed to the Christological doctrine of Chalcedon, which solemnly defined that Christ is fully God and fully human. I will also analyze the council of Chalcedon, from an African perspective thus introducing Africa's voice and contribution to the table of Christological discourse. I will conclude this chapter by attempting to answer the question: What has Africa to do with Chalcedon?

Christology of the School of Alexandria

Alexandria distinguished itself by a Christology informed by a hermeneutical system that sought to uncover allegorical symbolism. For the purpose of this research, I shall present the philosophical and anthropological context of the school of Alexandria as a gateway to understanding the Christology of Cyril of Alexandria, a major Alexandrian theologian. I shall limit this to the period of 428–33 because it was during the Nestorian crisis, that Cyril developed his Christology which greatly influenced Chalcedon. It is worth mentioning briefly the Christological conflict between Cyril and Nestorius at Ephesus to highlight the Christologies of each of them, revealing the dualistic anthropological philosophies embedded in each of them.

Philosophical and Anthropological Framework

At the end of the second century, there arose a theological school in Alexandria led by Clement of Alexandria (150–215) and Origen (185–254), both of whom had significant influences on Christian hermeneutics and theology in the region. It was a very organized entity, patronized and supervised by the local bishop.[2] In a bid to appeal to the mind of the growing Hellenistic intellectuals and following the platonic philosophical presuppositions that originate from Philo's allegorical work on Scripture,[3] the Alexandrian fathers placed a big emphasis on spiritual and abstract interpretations[4] which largely made use of allegories to explain the close relationship between Jewish theology and pagan philosophy. For them, each word in the biblical text was chosen for a precise reason[5] which could be hidden from the surface level. In fact, they believed: "All theologians, barbarians and Greeks, hid the beginnings of things and delivered the truth in enigmas and symbols, allegories and metaphors, and similar figures."[6]

With little regard for politics, law, or any domain that directly dealt with the practical human affairs, theologians at Alexandria focused on metaphysical speculations.[7] Platonism was the lens through which reality was seen,[8] and abstract philosophical speculation was the *modus operandi*. Cyril, an Alexandrian theologian, influenced by platonistic dualism, started attempting Christological questions about the nature of Christ. Cyril himself notes that he discerns his Christian view of God by drawing inspirations from Plato, his

---

2 Manlino Simonetti, *Biblical Interpretation in the Early Church: An Historical Introduction to Patristic Exegesis*, trans. John A. Hughes and ed. Anders Bergquist and Markus Bockmuehl (Edinburgh: T&T Clark, 1994), 67.
3 Donald Fairbairn, "Patristic Exegesis and Theology: The Cart and the Horse," 2.
4 Simonetti, *Biblical Interpretation in the Early Church*, 32–35.
5 Ibid., 35.
6 Karlfried Froehlich, *Biblical Interpretation in the Early Church* (Philadelphia: Fortress Press, 1984), 15.
7 Thomas H. Olbricht, "Greek Rhetoric and the Allegorical Rhetoric of Philo and Clement of Alexandria," in *Rhetorical Criticism and the Bible*, ed. Stanley E. Porter and Dennis L. Stamps, *Journal for the Study of the New Testament Supplement*, no. 195 (2002): 29–31.
8 Simonetti, 2–7.

disciple Plotinus (AD 205–70) who is the founder of Neoplatonism, and from his disciple Porphyry.[9]

Cyril of Alexandria's Christology: The *hypostatic* Union

To explain Cyril's Christology, we need to understand not only how the divine and the human unite in Christ but also the single-subjectivity of the Incarnation. Cyril posits the locus of the union of the human and the divine during the Incarnation at the level of person, not nature. As in the doctrine of the Trinity, there are neither three Gods (tritheism) nor one nature and one person in three different modes (modalistic monarchianism). The divine nature does not overwhelm the human nature, and the human and divine natures are not juxtaposed. This unique mode of union is called the *"hypostatic* union." Lewis S. Chafer explains the meaning of *Hypostatic* Union:

> The term Hypostatic is derived from hypostasis, which word, according to the Standard Dictionary, means "The mode of being by which any substantial existence is given to any independent and distinct individuality." Thus, it follows that a union of hypostasis is a union of natures that are within themselves independent and distinct. The expression Hypostatic Union is distinctly theological and is applicable only to Christ in whom, as in no other, two distinct and dissimilar natures are united.[10]

Here, Cyril's words are worth quoting at length:

> The natures, however, which combined unto this real union were different, but from the two together is one Godthe Son, without the diversity of the natures being destroyed by the union. For a union of two natures was made, and therefore we confess One Christ, One Son, One Lord. And it is with reference to this notion of a union without confusion that we proclaim the holy Virgin to be the mother of God, because God the Word was made flesh and became man, and by the act of conception united to Himself the temple that He received from her. For we perceive that two natures, by an inseparable union, met together in Him without confusion, and indivisibly. For the flesh is flesh, and not deity, even though it became the flesh of God: and in like manner also the Word is God, and not flesh, though for the dispensation's sake He made the flesh His own. But although the natures which concurred in forming the union are both different and unequal to one another, yet He Who is formed from them both is only One... we affirm that Christ Jesus is One and the

---

9 Meijering, "Cyril on the Platonists and the Trinity," in *God, Being, History: Studies in Patristic Philosophy* (Amsterdam/Oxford: North Holland Publishing 1975), 116.
10 Lewis S. Chafer, "Trinitarianism: Part 7," *Bibliotheca Sacra*, no. 98 (1941): 265.

Same, acknowledging the distinction of the natures, and preserving them free from confusion with one another.[11]

According to Cyril, the union of the two natures in the one person makes it possible to say that before the incarnation, the second person of the Trinity was called God, but after the incarnation, he could be called Man and mediator. The hypostatic union is a union of Godhead and manhood, that is, the Godhead and the manhood took place dynamically so that only one individual presided over them both, the person of Christ.

The hypostatic union makes it possible to give divine qualities to the single person of Christ or human qualities to the single person of Christ. In this light, Mary could rightly be called *theotokos* (God bearer) because far from being the mother of the Godhead who sustains all creation and called the earth into form, she was the vessel or instrument through whom the only begotten Son, the Logos of God, was made human. In other words, Mary should be called *theotokos* because the body of Christ, the Logos-made-flesh, came not from heaven above but from Mary here below. She bore Jesus. This opens the way for what Cyril calls "two births," that is, the eternal generation of the Son before the foundation of the world, and the incarnation of the same Son through a woman, Mary of Nazareth.[12]

Cyril was the first to propose the idea of *hypostasis* of the Logos as the locus of the union between the divine and human natures of Christ. This means that Christ's personal unity is sustained by the Logos of God as the divine *hypostasis*, in which subsists the divine and human natures. His divine and human natures are united in the single divine *hypostasis*. The Logos of God is "hypostatically united to the flesh" in Christ.[13] This is union by nature. After the Incarnation, Christ's human nature and divine nature are preserved in his single divine *physis*, which Cyril describes as "natural unity."[14] This is union by nature. We note that for Cyril, *physis* and *hypostasis*, are synonymous and they mean individual concrete reality.

---

11 Cyril of Alexandria, "Commentary on Luke" (Online edition, Trans. by Roger Pearse, 1996), Lk. 2:1–7, http://www.tertullian.org/fathers/cyril_on_luke_01_sermons_01_11.htm#C1.
12 Cyril of Alexandria, "Five Tomes Against Nestorius" (Online edition, Trans. by Roger Pearse, 2005), Vol. 47, http://www.tertullian.org/fathers/cyril_against_nestorius_00_intro.htm.
13 Cyril of Alexandria, "Third Letter of Cyril to Nestorius," para. 5, in McGuckin, 269.
14 Cyril of Alexandria, "Festal Letter 17," in *Festal Letters 13-30*, trans. Philip R. Amidon (Washington D. C.: The Catholic University of America Press, 2013), 68.

According to Cyril, the Logos becomes the locus of the union of the natures at the incarnation. Inspired by Philippians 2:6‑8 which expresses how God emptied himself, assuming the status of a slave and taking human form,[15] Cyril notes that because the Logos took flesh through *kenosis*, the Logos and human flesh thus have a strong, inextricable relationship which one another plays a crucial role in redemption. Neither changed into human nor transformed into a perfect man with soul and body, the divine Logos appropriates human nature in the Incarnation within the divine economy, retaining its proper nature.[16] Therefore, with Cyril, we note that, in an ineffable and incomprehensible manner, by divine economy the Logos united itself to flesh animated with rational soul, thus becoming human, the Son of Man.[17] In this union of the divine and human, each retains their characteristics and attributes, which explains why at Calvary, Christ experienced real suffering, even though by virtue of his divinity, he was incapable of suffering and death. In *A Defense of the Twelve Anathemas against Theodoret*, Cyril states his awareness of the impassibility of the Word by arguing:

> For he made the passible body his very own, the result of which is that one can say that he suffered by means of something naturally passible, even while he himself remains impassible in respect of his own nature; and since he willingly suffered in the flesh, for this very reason he is called, and actually is the Savior of all.[18]

Cyril says that the Logos suffered impassibly[19] to underline the solid connection between the human and divine natures in Jesus. This connection gives room for the mixing, or confusion of the two natures and from both of them is one Jesus Christ.[20] In the *Second Letter of Cyril to Succensus*, Cyril emphasizes that after the union, we conceive of only one incarnate nature of the Logos.[21]

In a nutshell, Cyril of Alexandria makes the distinction between the full divinity and full humanity of Christ and explains the form of the union

---

15 Cyril of Alexandria, "Cyril's Letter to the Monk of Egypt," para. 13, trans. John A. McGuckin, in McGuckin, 252.
16 Cyril of Alexandria, "Scholia on the Incarnation of the Only Begotten," ibid., 307.
17 Cyril of Alexandria, "The Second Letter of Cyril to Nestorius," para. 3, ibid., 263.
18 Cyril of Alexandria, "A Defense of the Twelve Anathemas against Theodoret," trans. Daniel King, in Daniel King, *St. Cyril of Alexandria: Three Christological Treatises* (Washington, D.C.: The Catholic University of America Press, 2014), 129
19 Cyril of Alexandria, "Scholia on the Incarnation of the Only Begotten," para. 35, in McGuckin, 332.
20 Ibid., 319.
21 Cyril of Alexandria, "Second Letter of Cyril to Succensus," para. 2, ibid., 359.

between the two natures in order to save the personal unity of Christ. On the issue of single-subjectivity, we have seen how Cyril fits the two natures together in a single subject – the divine Word. In order to explain the union, Cyril introduced the theory of the *hypostatic* union while Nestorius, based on his Antiochene traditional background of interpreting reality (which is the subject of the next section), proposed the theory of *prosopic* union.

Christology of the School of Antioch

In this section, I will analyze the Christology of a major Antiochene theologian, Nestorius, and present the philosophical and anthropological context from which he derived his theology.

Philosophical and Anthropological Framework

The theological school of Antioch distinguished itself from that of Alexandria in that it focused on the literal meaning of scriptural texts. Gerald Bray argues that for the Antiochene method of interpretation, "the spiritual sense (*theoria*) of Scripture was not allegorical, but was to be sought in the literal sense itself."[22] According to the Antiochene theologian Diodore of Tarsus,[23] one of the advantages of the Antiochene methodology is that it actually "frees us, on the one hand, from a Hellenism which says one thing for another and introduces foreign subject matter; on the other hand, it does not yield to Judaism by forcing us to treat the literal reading of the text as the only one worthy of attention and honor."[24] The Antiochene methodology does not mean that all interpretation is limited to the surface literal sense. Diodore cautions that "[o]ne thing to be watched, however: *theoria* must never be understood as doing away with the underlying sense; it would then be no longer *theoria* but allegory."[25]

---

22 Gerald Bray, *Biblical Interpretation: Past and Present* (Downers Grove, IL: Intervarsity Press, 1996), 106. I have to mention emphatically that "*theoria*" is a platonic idea but was later redefined in the school of Antioch in a way that contradicts the Alexandrian allegorical methodology.
23 According to Simonetti, Diodore of Tarsus should be considered the true founder of the Antiochene interpretive method. See Simonetti, 59.
24 Froehlich Froehlich, Karlfried, *Biblical Interpretation in the Early Church* (Philadelphia: Fortress Press, 1984), 86.
25 Ibid., 82.

One other important characteristic within Antiochene exegesis was its emphasis on the ancient concept of *historia*. *Historia* is concerned with the chronological succession of God's redemptive actions in the past; a closer look at the historical context.[26] Summarizing the philosophical tenets of the Antiochene school, Adam M. Schor writes:

> First in works of exegesis, these authors declared an interest in the "literal" (*katalexin*) and the "historical" (kath' historian) meaning of Scripture. Second, in the same commentaries, the authors attacked "allegory" and expressed skepticism about figurative interpretations. Third, these authors pointed to biblical typologies, links between the "prototypes" of Old Testament characters and the "reality" (*alētheia*) of Jesus or the "types" of the Christian sacraments and the "reality" of future salvation.[27]

The Antiochian school was characterized by a methodology that ascribed to the literal, the historical, and the typological. Its hermeneutical roots can be found at least in part in both Judaism and Greek philosophy. Even though the Jews in Antioch were of considerable size, they were not influenced by Philo, a Platonist. Antioch is more in line with Aristotle,[28] a faithful disciple of Plato, who denied the possibility of knowing the world apart from the things that are available to our senses. The blending of Aristotelian elements in addition to the more literal approach from Judaism informed the exegetical style of Antioch.

Nestorius of Constantinople's Christology: The *Prosopic* Union

Even though the Nestorian controversy was fundamentally Christological, Mary the mother of Christ was the focus of the dispute between Cyril and Nestorius. Nestorius, belonging to the Antiochene, had undoubtedly been

---

26 Charles Kannengiesser confirms, "The rhetorical and philosophical culture of Antioch inspired the local masters of biblical exegesis with a sense of the value of historical Old Testament narratives, which was different from the treatment of such narratives taught to Christian exegetes on the basis of Philo of Alexandria's legacy." See Charles Kannengiesser, "A Key for the Future of Patristics: The 'Senses' of Scripture," in *In Dominico Eloquio—In Lordly Eloquence: Essays on Patristic Exegesis in Honor of Robert Louis Wilken*, ed. Paul M. Blowers et al. (Grand Rapids, MI: Eerdmans, 2002),) 101–2.
27 Adam M. Schor, "Theodoret on the 'School of Antioch': A Network Approach," *Journal of Early Christian Studies* 15, no. 4 (Winter 2007): 520–21.
28 Richard A. Norris, *Manhood and Christ: A Study in the Christology of Theodore of Mopsuestia* (Oxford: Clarendon Press: 1963), 250.

influenced by Theodore of Mopsuestia who believed that Christ has a complete human nature (with flesh and spirit) inhabited by the divine Word. He likened the unity of Christ to the "one flesh" of husband and wife, with each spouse distinct, though they both form a single person.

While Cyril proposed the *hypostatic* union to explain how the divine and the union came together, Nestorius, on his part, inspired by the Antiochian tradition, which emphasized a clear distinction of the divinity and the humanity in Christ, proposed the *prosopic* union, which means the *prosopon* of God and the *prosopon* of the human make one *prosopon* in Jesus Christ because he has the *prosopon* of God as his own *prosopon*. Nestorius explicates his idea of *prosopic* union in *The Bazaar of Heracleides*. According to Aubrey Vine, for Nestorius, *prosopon*, which means the self-revelation and self-manifestation of a particular *ousia*, consists of the underlying individuality and the manifestation of that individuality.[29] *Prosopon* is the manifestation of an *ousia* according to its nature, for there can be "no *prosopon* without an underlying *ousia* to give it a ground of existence" and "the *prosopon* of an *ousia* is as necessarily related to it as is its nature."[30] Thus, each *prosopon* has its own nature. Hence, the union of *ousia* necessarily involves the union of nature, and the union of *ousia* and natures involves the union of *prosopa*.[31] There is, therefore, the human *prosopon* and the divine *prosopon* that coexists in one *prosopon* of Christ. We thus encounter "unity as well as diversity in the single concrete figure of 'the Christ.'"[32] This one common *prosopon* is designated as "Christ, Only Begotten, Son, or Lord."[33]

Nestorius believed that a correct Christology with good soteriological implications had to consider both the humanity and divinity of Christ. Divinity, according to him, meant the absence of suffering, pain, change, and any form of limitation.[34] For him, it's impossible for God to suffer, grow, or change. To be fully human, on the other hand, means:

> One must be ready to attribute to Christ the full panoply of human characteristics, excepting sin, which is not a "humanising" characteristic or even a defining human

---

29 Aubrey R. Vine, *An Approach to Christology: An Interpretation and Development of Some Elements in the Metaphysic and Christology of Nestorius as a Way of Approach to an Orthodox Christology Compatible with Modern Thought* (London: Independent Press, 1948), 99–100.
30 Ibid., 105.
31 Ibid.
32 John McGuckin, *St. Cyril of Alexandria: The Christological Controversy*, 152.
33 Ibid.
34 Ibid., 130.

attribute in any case. He must have a human mind, a human soul with human feelings choices and limitations, both mental and physical, involving him in a range of testing situations (the temptations of the Lord) which proved and refined his virtue as a man, and which involved him inexorably in all the suffering consequent on being human.[35]

Nestorius did everything to avoid the tendency to dissolve, absorb, or evaporate the humanity of Christ into his divinity, because "a theory of incarnation that wiped away the human reality in the advent of the deity constituted not only a failure of revelation theology, but an inability to value the extraordinary role which the Christian Gospel gave to human experience in its conception of God's redeeming work."[36] He referred to this as an "absorption theory," which reduced theology to mythology. Any form of mixture of the *phusis* or natures implied a change or even a complete annihilation of the specific mixed elements.[37] Nestorius considered Christ to be one person (*prosopon*) in two natures (*phusis*), human and divine. So, when Cyril notes that at the incarnation, the human and divine realities became one through *kenosis*, Nestorius saw it as a revamp of Apollinarism.[38]

For Nestorius, answering the question of how the human and the divine come together in the person of Christ leaves us with only two alternatives. The first is to posit two distinct but related natures, and the second, which, of course, is conflating the two natures into a hybrid. In other words, the incarnation could not be a transformation, for then, God would cease to be God in order to become a created reality, or the human nature would be suppressed by the divine reality, or even a *tertium quid*, that was neither truly human nor truly divine, and would be formed by the intermingling of the two.

It is important to note that in the *prosopic* union, one *prosopon* can make use of another *prosopon* for its self-manifestation. In such a case, one *prosopon* can dwell in another *prosopon*, and vice versa. The divine *prosopon* of the Logos can dwell in the human *prosopon* for its self-manifestation, and the human *prosopon* of Jesus can dwell in the divine *prosopon* and show himself as a real human. In brief, the *prosopa* can inter-dwell and make use of one another.

Nestorius, holding on to the Antiochian traditional distinction of the divinity and the humanity in Christ, postulates that the one Christ must be fully divine and also fully human which means that on the one hand, the Logos

---

35 John McGuckin, St. Cyril of Alexandria: The Christological Controversy, 130–31.
36 Ibid.,131.
37 Ibid.
38 Ibid., 132.

of God must be impassible, immortal, and eternal because it is consubstantial with the Father,[39] and on the other hand, Christ has to be mortal, passible, created, possessing a human mind and body. The divine nature corresponds to the divine *prosopon* while the human nature corresponds to the human *prosopon*. Both are united in the one common *prosopon* of Jesus Christ.[40]

Like Cyril, Nestorius thinks that by the process of *kenosis*, the Logos of God humbled himself, became a human being, suffering death on the cross, by the use of his human *prosopon*, who died and was crucified and exalted. The *prosopon* of the Logos has the divine nature. The human *prosopon* has the human nature in terms of dying on the cross and being exalted. Christ has two natures, the likeness of God and the likeness of a servant. Nevertheless, Christ has one *prosopon* of two natures because there is only one name which is more excellent than all names.[41]

Nestorius denies the communication of idioms but explains that the two *prosopa* are united with one another in a natural union.[42] This *voluntary union* consists in the connection through love, adoption, and acknowledgment between God and the human in Christ.[43]

Chalcedonian Christology Examined: Probing the Dual Nature of Christ

In *The Fathers on Christology: The Development of Christological Dogma from the Bible to the Great Councils*, Pieter Fran Smulders notes that, far from solving all the theological problems of the time, the council at Ephesus left behind a tragedy. This tragedy, due largely to the overwhelming influence of Cyril at the Council of Ephesus, was that the genuine and complete humanity of Jesus Christ again appeared to be violated.[44] The years between Ephesus (431) and Chalcedon (451) were controversial and determinant in the shaping of orthodox Christology by providing a conducive atmosphere for those on both sides of the *theotokos* debate to grapple more with the question of the most appropriate language not only for speaking about the unity and distinction between

39 McGuckin, 172.
40 Ibid.
41 Ibid., 57.
42 Ibid., 38.
43 Ibid., 54–55.
44 Pieter Fran Smulders, *The Fathers on Christology: The Development of Christological Dogma from the Bible to the Great Councils* (De Pere, WI: St. Norbert Abbey Press, 1968), 5.

Christ's divinity and humanity but also how it affects human salvation. At the end of the Council of Ephesus, John of Antioch and Cyril of Alexandria were charged with the task of coming up with a compromise formula of union which stressed the union while reiterating the two natures, talked of the one person of Christ, and used the title of *theotokos* to refer to Mary. Both sides had to accept some compromises: Cyril had to agree to the use of "two natures" in reference to Christ, while many Antiochenes accepted the use of *theotokos*.

While the majority was satisfied with the formula, some on both sides were not pleased at all. Eutyches (378–454) was so supportive of Cyrilian Christology against Nestorianism that he became an extreme Cyrilian, who emphasized one nature in the incarnation. One thing to note about Cyril's Christology, as we have seen above, is that, when he uses the phrase "two natures" or before the union, he did not mean that before the incarnation, there were two separate existing natures. In fact, the divinity existed separately but the humanity did not yet exist in Christ.[45] It seems, according to Eutyches, that, the human nature, which existed alongside the divine nature before the incarnation, was consumed by the divine nature at the incarnation. As Leo Davis describes, Eutyches believed and taught that "before the incarnation, Christ was of two natures, but after it, there was one Christ, one Son, one Lord, in one hypostasis and one *Prosopon*."[46]

The Eutychian controversy led to the convening of the council of Chalcedon in 451. In this section, I will situate the theological context of Chalcedon, examining relevant terms used to explain the mode of union and elucidating the heresies that it opposed, thus creating solid grounds to examining the relation that Chalcedon has with Africa.

Explaining Foundational Theological Concepts

In the Christological controversy at Chalcedon, unlike any other theological dispute in the ancient Church, there was a great deal of obscurity because of the technical terms that were employed. In his letter to Eusebius, the scholastic Severus briefly defines the terms *ousia* and *hypostasis* briefly.[47] *Ousia* signifies

---

45 Stephen W. Need, *Truly Divine & Truly Human: The Story of Christ and the Seven Ecumenical Councils* (Peabody: MA: Hendrickson Publishers, 2008), 95.
46 Leo D. Davis, *The First Seven Ecumenical Councils (325–787): Their History and Theology* (Collegeville, MN: Liturgical Press, 1990), 171.
47 Severus, "Letter to Eusebius" (Online edition), accessed May 22, 2017, http://www.newadvent.org/fathers/3502.htm.

that which is common, and *hypostasis* that which is particular. The name God, for instance, is common to the Father, the Son, and the Holy Spirit. "The Father is God; He is beyond time and eternal. So is the Son; and so is also the Holy Spirit." The Father is unbegotten; the Son is begotten; the Holy Spirit proceeds from the Father. In this way each of them, while being fully God, is different from the other two. *Ousia* is the reality which, when individuated, gives rise to particular objects or hypostases.

Ousia is the essence of a particular thing and "the ultimate ground of its existence."[48] *Ousia* is "the thing as it is in itself independently of being known."[49] For example, the *ousia* of a stone exists "independently of our knowledge of it and possesses properties and qualities independent of our interpretation of them."[50] Therefore, in the context of ancient Christology, *ousia* means the "essence, substance, being, genus, or nature" of being.[51]

Physis meant "nature, inborn quality, property or constitution of a person or a thing."[52] Thus, the *physis* of *ousia* is "the sum total of its qualities and properties." The *physis* of any particular *ousia* includes every known and unknown property or constitution about that thing such as the shape, size, weight, color, texture, and any other properties that would transcend the limits of our knowledge.[53]

For example, the *physis* of water is "clear liquid, tasteless, and odourless."[54] An *ousia* is manifested by its *physis*. An *ousia* cannot be perceived or known except as it is revealed in its *physis*, and there cannot be a *physis* without an *ousia* to ground its existence.[55] In the Christology of the fifth and sixth centuries, *ousia* and *physis* became interchangeable because both terms came to mean commonality of being, while *hypostasis/prosopon* meant individual existence.

Hypostasis means the concrete reality of a thing, the underlying essence. In earlier Christian thought, *hypostasis* was the synonym of *physis*. For example, in the New Testament, *hypostasis* is equivalent to *physis* or *ousia* (Heb. 1: 3).

---

48 Vine, *An Approach to Christology*: 65.
49 *Ousia* is "a noun derived from the feminine participle *einai*, which means 'to be.'" Aristotle, defines it as "the essence of any particular thing, the thing in itself absolutely, *to ti esti* (what it is)." Vine, 65.
50 Vine, 65.
51 McGuckin, 138.
52 Vine, 65–66.
53 Ibid., 66.
54 Ibid.
55 Ibid.

Origen uses this word to denote actual existence. In his commentary on John, he repudiates those who distinguish Father and Son only in thought (*epinoia*), not in *hypostasis*, actual concrete reality.[56] He mentions that there are three *hypostaseis*, the Father, the Son, and the Holy Spirit.[57] Thereafter, *hypostasis* indicates the individual divine person of Christ in Cyril's Christology. In the neo-Chalcedonian Christology, *hypostasis* comes to mean individual existence, which exists by itself and sustains the union of the two natures.

Prosopon originally means "face or countenance." It has to do with the external, when applied to a person, not the inner ego or personality.[58] In Cyril, *prosopon* becomes synonymous with *hypostasis*, which is the individual concrete reality. In the Christological context, this signifies the "who" of Christ as well as *hypostasis*. Other theologians, like Nestorius, used *prosopon* to mean the self-manifestation of *ousia*, not individual reality. Therefore, after the Council of Chalcedon, the term *hypostasis* eventually replaced *prosopon* as "individual existence" to avoid this confusion.

When Humanity Meets Divinity: The Mode of Union of Christ's Natures

How do the two natures unite? What is the relationship between the human and the divine nature? In what sense can we affirm that the two natures are "unconfusedly, unchangeably, indivisibly, and inseparably."[59] According to Harry Austryn Wolfson, there are five ways in which two realities could unite according to ancient Greek Church Fathers: first, *union of composition*, in which the elements are united as an aggregate of constituents in perceptible juxtaposition; second: *union of mixture* (the first type), in which two elements become a third one (*tertium quid*) after the union, though it can be dissolved into its constituents; third, *union of mixture* (the second type), in which the union is not a third one but an aggregate of its constituents in juxtaposition. It can be dissolved into its constituent parts, but the constituents are imperceptible; forth,

---

56 Origen, "Comm. John 10. 37," in *Origen, Commentary on the Gospel according to John, Books 1–10*, trans. Ronald E. Heine (Washington D.C.: The Catholic University of America Press, 1989), 212.
57 Ibid.
58 G. R Driver and Leonard Hodgson, "Commentary to Nestorius, Bazaar of Heracleides," in *The Bazaar of Heracleides*, ed. and trans. G. R. Driver and Leonard Hodgson (Oxford: The Clarendon Press, 1925), 402.
59 Richard Price and Michael Gaddis, *The Acts of the Council of Chalcedon* (Liverpool: Liverpool University Press, 2007), 59.

union of confusion, in which the union is a third one, but it cannot be dissolved into its constituents; fifth, *union of predominance*, in which one smaller element is dominated by another, greater element. Nevertheless, the smaller is not completely destroyed but is related to the greater as matter to form.[60]

Wolfson notes that many ancient Church Fathers prefer the union of predominance when they speak of the relationship between the divine and human natures of Jesus Christ (e.g., Tertullian, Gregory of Nyssa, Augustine, Nemesius of Emessa, John Damascus, and so forth).[61] In his *De Principiis*, Origen uses the analogy of "fire" and "iron."[62] If one puts iron into the fire, the iron will be ignited and united with fire, but the iron will retain its essence. This is an example of a union of predominance.

The Chalcedonian formula used the terms, "unconfusedly, unchangeably, indivisibly, and inseparably." The term "unconfusedly" regulates the position on the union of mixture and the extreme version of the union of predominance which can either fall into a form of Monophysitism (two becomes one either by being dissolved/absolved into the other or by forming an entire third single reality). The word "unchangeably" drives home the point that when the divine Logos becomes incarnate, it is not changed or interchanged into or with human flesh. This change or interchange would unavoidably lead to a third substance, which is neither God nor human. Third, the terms "indivisibly and inseparably" regulate an extreme position on the union of composition. The union of composition, in a less extreme form, appears to be the most appropriate reflection of the Chalcedonian definition. We can thus say the human and the divine natures of Christ are united by composition in such a way that the union dissolves none of the natures.

Heresies and the Chalcedonian Debate: The Struggle for Doctrinal Purity

At Chalcedon, the synod fathers were seeking a common declaration against Christological heresies that would be in accord with Nicaea, Constantinople, and Ephesus. Oftentimes, those declared heretics were people with good

---

60 Harry Austryn Wolfson, *The Philosophy of the Church Fathers I: Faith, Trinity, Incarnation*, vol. I, His Structure and Growth of Philosophic Systems from Plato to Spinoza (Cambridge, MA: Harvard University Press, 1956), 385.
61 Ibid., 387–406.
62 Origen, *De Principiis*, ed. for New Advent by Kevin Knight (Buffalo, NY: Christian Literature Publishing Co., 1885), II. 6. 6, http://www.newadvent.org/fathers/0412.htm.

intentions who wanted to be consistent with Christ in their articulation of their theology. That is why Lynn H. Hough explained that "a heresy is usually a genuine hunger eating the wrong fruit."[63] Explaining these heresies go a long way to serve as a guide as I analyze, in chapter four, major African Christological models and dialoguing them with Patristic Christology.

Here, I would like to examine the creed from Chalcedon, and deduce from it the different heresies that affected the Church at that time. In the Chalcedonian definition, Jesus Christ is

> the same perfect in Godhead and the same perfect in manhood, truly God and the same truly man, of a rational soul and body, consubstantial with the Father in respect of the Godhead, and the same consubstantial with us in respect of the manhood, like us in all things apart from sin, begotten from the Father before the ages in respect of the Godhead, and the same in the last days for us and for our salvation from the Virgin Mary, the Theotokos, in respect of the manhood, one and the same Christ, Son, Lord, Only-begotten, acknowledged in two natures [en dyo physesin] unconfusedly [asynchtōs], unchangeably [atreptōs], indivisibly [adiairetōs], and inseparably [achoristōs] (the difference of the natures being in no way destroyed by the union, but rather the distinctive character of each nature being preserved and coming together into one person and one hypostasis), not parted or divided into two persons, but one and the same Son, Only-begotten, God, Word, Lord, Jesus Christ, even as the prophets from of old and Jesus Christ himself taught us about him and the symbol of the fathers has handed down to us.[64]

The creed of the Council of Chalcedon reveals heresies that were common in the days of the council. From the above statement, it is possible to note a refutation of eight different heresies: Sabellianism, Docetism, Arianism, Adoptionism, Ebionism, Gnosticism, Apollinarianism, and Nestorianism. The underlined phrases in the creed above reveal how the creed expressed the refutation of the heresies.

Sabellianism, also known as modalism, modalistic Monarchianism, or Modal Monarchism, asserts that the one God manifests himself in three ways: as Creator, Redeemer, and Sanctifier.[65] As a result, Jesus is merely a *manifestation* of the Father in his role as "Redeemer." He is not, nor does he possess a distinct divine Person. It attributes no distinction in personality within the

---

63 Lynn Harold Hough, *Athanasius: The Hero* (Cincinnati, OH: Jennings and Graham, 1906), 44.
64 Richard Price and Michael Gaddis, *The Acts of the Council of Chalcedon*, 59.
65 David E. Wilhite, *The Gospel According to Heretics: Discovering Orthodoxy through Early Christological Conflicts* (Ada, MI: Baker Academic, 2015), 92–93.

Trinity. It is essentially monotheistic. The Father, the Son and Holy Spirit are different *modes* or *aspects* of one God, as perceived by the believer, rather than three distinct persons in God *Himself*.[66]

Sabellianism as a teaching is often described by many other words such as modalism, monarchianism, and patripasianism. Scholars often use two terms to describe Monarchianism: dynamic monarchianism and modalistic monarchianism. "The dynamic kind protects the oneness of God by claiming that Jesus was simply called God and thus became the Son of God. In other words, dynamic monarchianism is the same as Adoptionism."[67] Modalistic Monarchianism has as its starting point the first "mode" in which God was known: Father (creator, shepherd, King). Next God is known as son, born of the Virgin Mary. This son finally descended into heaven so is present to us only in the form of spirit. This shows one God (monarchianism) known in three different ways of being (Modalism). Modalism is a sought of God changing costume.

The Chalcedonian creed contradicts this teaching when it says that the "the same perfect in Godhead and the same perfect in manhood." The Sabellians, in declaring that Jesus is only a mode or manifestation of the Father, essentially deny the divine Personhood of the Word in Jesus Christ. In saying that the Son is "perfect in Godhead," the council affirms the full divinity and Personhood of the Son in opposition to this heresy.

Docetism comes from the Greek *dokeo*, "to seem." This heresy asserts that God did not actually become human in Jesus Christ. Instead, he only *appeared* to take on human flesh, and Jesus only *appeared* to die on the cross, thus reducing the humanity of Christ nothing more than a phantasm. Docetists found it difficult to reconcile Christ's divinity to his physical birth.[68] Docetism is dealt with in the creed when it states that "perfect in Godhead and perfect in manhood, very God and very man, of a reasonable soul and body." In other words,

---

66 David E. Wilhite, *The Gospel According to Heretics*: 92.
67 Ibid.
68 Henry Wace, *A Dictionary of Christian Biography and Literature to the End of the Sixth Century A.D., with an Account of the Principal Sects and Heresies* (Peabody, MA: Hendrickson Publishers, 1994), 272. Prominent Docetists such as Marcion, and his follower Apelles, replaced the incarnation doctrine with the idea that Jesus came without birth but directly from heaven. Saturninus on his part noted that "the Saviour was without birth, without body, and without figure, and appeared a man in phantasm, not in truth." Valentinus theorized that Jesus' "body passed through Mary as through a channel" and said he was "born of the mother ... by a shadow." (John Arendzen, "Docetae," *The Catholic Encyclopedia* (New Advent, Online edition), accessed May 12, 2017, http://www.newadvent.org/cathen.)

Jesus Christ is just as fully human as he is fully God. Of course, this strikes at the heart of Docetism, which, in stating that Jesus only *appeared* to be human and to die, denies his real and complete humanity.

Arianism, named after Arius, a priest from Alexandria is certainly the most insidious of all the other heresies. Arius was strongly Aristotelian in his intellectual position.[69] God, for Arius, was transcendent who remains forever in Himself, and to Himself, and by Himself.[70] God is distant; He could not be revealed.

Arius adhered to subordination. The "Son" for him implied an act of pro-creation, which means that before such an act there was not a Son, neither could God properly be called "Father." There was a time when God was not a father; afterwards, He became a Father.[71] The Son, therefore, is not co-eternal, but begotten of the will of the Father, begotten out of nothing, begotten before time. He is a creature, "created and made." The Father is the only one without a beginning, and "there was a time when the Son was not."[72] Only the Father was seen as eternal with no beginning. The son is "begotten." Based on this premature understanding of the Trinity and in reference to Scripture passages (Prv 8:22; Col 1:15), Arius concluded that the "begotten" must have been created. In Arius' own words, and contrary to Origen,[73] there was "once when He was not."[74]

Arius believes in a certain superiority of the Son to the rest of Creation. He was the firstborn of all creatures; he was made and created first and alone. The son is the medium through whom all things might thereupon be brought to be. For Arius, the Son was as like God as it was possible to be, the highest

---

69 Adrian Ignat, "The Spread Out of Arianism. A Critical Analysis of the Arian Heresy," *International Journal of Orthodox Theology* 3, no. 3 (2012): 108.
70 Rufus M. Jones, *The Church's Debt to Heretics* (London: James Clarke & Co. Limited, 1925), 88.
71 Athanasius, "Orationes Contra Arianos," in *Nicene and Post Nicene Fathers*, ed. Philip Schaff and Henry Wace, vol. IV, 2nd (Grand Rapids, MI: Eerdmans Publishing Co, 1975), 5. These "Orations" are the primary source for the views of Arius and the Arian party, since little of their literature is extant.
72 Millard J. Erickson, *The Word Became Flesh: A Contemporary Incarnational Christology* (Grand Rapids, MI: Baker Books, 1906), 48. Preceding school of influence was the Christology of Origen who vaguely introduced the idea of Christ's different essence and subordination to the Father. The primacy of the Father was taught in defense of the monotheistic teachings of the Old Testament ('Monarchianism').
73 Wace, *A Dictionary of Christian Biography and Literature to the End of the Sixth Century A.D., with an Account of the Principal Sects and Heresies*, 42.
74 H. D. McDonald, "Development and Christology," *Vox Evangelica* 51, no. 9 (1975): 11.

of all creatures, the architect of the universe, but not equal to God: "One equal to the Son, the Superior is able to beget; but one more excellent, or superior, or greater, He is not able."[75]

As the first and the greatest of all the creatures, the Son is a sort of demiurge who mediates between God and all creation. The son is not of the same substance (*homoousios*) but of similar substance with the Father (*homooisios*). The issue of Christ's divinity had been treated at Nicaea in 325, and Chalcedon only reaffirms this when it states that the Son, Jesus Christ, is "consubstantial with the Father in respect of the Godhead." This goes a long way to tell us that the Son is of the same divine essence as the Father. Thus, the Father and the Son are both equally God, and Arianism, which make the Son only a creature, is contradicted.

Adoptionism, with its founder Theodotus, preaches a doctrine that declares that Jesus was just an ordinary man until his baptism by John. It was only at baptism that Jesus was adopted and became the Son of God.[76] It asserts a double sonship in Jesus Christ. As "Divine, Christ is the Son of God by generation and nature, but as human, he is the Son of God by adoption and grace."[77] The doctrine holds that there was a time when Jesus was *not* God, and his sonship is not unlike our own, when God adopts us through baptism.

In a very lucid way, Chalcedon affirms the fact that the Son was "begotten from the Father before the ages in respect of the Godhead."[78] Jesus' sonship does not come in time, or at a certain point in his human life. It is eternal and timeless, for it is predicated of him in virtue of his union with the Word, who was begotten before the ages.

Ebionism, derived from the Hebrew word for "poor," denied the divinity of Christ and his Virgin Birth. They believed that Jesus was the greatest prophet, but he was still just a prophet, and he was born like every other human. According to Origen, "Ebionism" was at first a general expression for Christians with Jewish background who believed that Jesus was sent only to the nation of Israel. They taught that Jesus was a mere man who by his scrupulous obedience to the Law was justified and thereby became the Messiah.[79] His becoming the messiah

---

75 Athanasius, "De Synodis," in *Nicene and Post Nicene Fathers* (Buffalo, NY: Christian Literature Publishing Co., 1892), ii, 24, http://www.newadvent.org/fathers/2817.htm.
76 Ben Quash and Michael Ward, *Heresies and How to Avoid Them: Why It Matters What Christians Believe* (Peabody, MA: Hendrickson Publishers, 2007), 51.
77 Ibid., 50.
78 Richard Price and Michael Gaddis, 59.
79 Bruce L. Shelley, *Church History in Plain Language* (Dallas, TX: Word Publishing, 1995), 50.

did accord him divine status.[80] Another Ebionistic Jewish group called "Nazarenes" disagreed with the Ebionites proper in acknowledging the miraculous virgin birth of Christ.[81] They denied Jesus' birth from a virgin and regarded him as a mere human.

Chalcedonian creed deals with the issue of Ebionism by reaffirming the teaching of the Council of Ephesus, that Mary is *theotokos*, "Virgin Mary, the *Theotokos*."[82] Of course, if Mary is the Mother of God, and Jesus is her son, then Jesus is God.

Gnosticism is so broad that it is difficult to narrow it down to one set of beliefs. Its origins can be found in Hellenistic thinking and to some extent also in Judaism even before the Christian period.[83] Gnosticism derives its name from the Greek word "gnosis" meaning knowledge. Generally, most Gnostic sects share the belief that matter and the created world are evil, and all things, including "Jesus" and "Christ" and "the Word," either come from or are themselves one of at least 30 *aeons*, or divine powers emanating from the *Propator*, the "first father" of the *Pleroma*. The Gnostics distinguish between their god, who is utterly transcendent and naturally unknown, and the Demiurge, the creator of the world and the God of the Old Testament. They believe in a radical dualism between spirit and matter, and the redemption, thanks to a revealed, superior knowledge. Christ is considered the Redeemer from above who brought this superior knowledge.

Chalcedon contradicts gnostism by declaring that he who was born of the Virgin Mary is "one and the same Son, Only-begotten, God, Word, Lord, Jesus Christ, even as the prophets from of old and Jesus Christ himself taught us about him and the symbol of the fathers has handed down to us."[84] In other words, "Christ" and "Son" and "Lord" are not themselves distinct *aeons* of the *Propator*. Instead, Jesus is at the same time Christ, Son, and Lord. Furthermore, he is not one of many begotten of the Father. He is the "*only*-begotten."

Apollinarism, named after his founder, the bishop of Laodicea Apollinarius, claims that the human soul, intellect, and will were subsumed by the divine nature upon the union of the two natures in Jesus Christ. The Logos supplants these human distinctions and fuses, or mixes, directly with the flesh of Jesus.

---

80 Bruce L. Shelley, *Church History in Plain Language*, 50.
81 Charles Hodge, *Systematic Theology*, vol. 2 (Peabody, MA: Hendrickson Publishers, 1999), 399.
82 Richard Price and Michael Gaddis, 59.
83 Wilson R. McL., *The Gnostic Problem* (London: A.R. Mowbray & Co. Limited, 1958), 68.
84 Richard Price and Michael Gaddis, 59.

As a result, Apollinarianism tends toward Monophysitism, or the belief that Jesus only had one nature – the divine nature. The nature of the flesh is not altered by its union with the Godhead, and on the other hand, the nature of the Godhead is not changed by its participation in the body of flesh.[85] Like a slave, Christ emptied himself while retaining his divine essence. He, therefore, remains at the same time unaltered and undiminished.[86] According to Apollinarius, this is the only feasible way to preserve the distinction between divinity and humanity in the person of Christ. Apollinarius referred to Christ as "the human being from heaven."[87] He is not an ordinary human but rather a special divine-human, who is an incarnate divine intellect. and possesses a divine "life-giving Spirit."[88] According to Apollinarius, the human spirit and intellect are completely replaced by the divine spirit and intellect in the Incarnation because human spirit and intellect cannot affect human salvation.[89] If the divine Logos had not assumed the human intellect and spirit, the human subjectivity would not be redeemed.

Chalcedon blatantly overrules this when it states that "in two natures [en dyo physesin] unconfusedly [asynchtōs], unchangeably [atreptōs], indivisibly [adiairetōs], and inseparably [achoristōs]. The difference of the natures is in no way destroyed by the union,"[90] but rather the peculiar property of each nature is preserved and united in one Person and subsistence. In Christ, the divine nature does not overshadow the human nature; rather, the union of both natures is harmoniously preserved, ensuring that each remains fully intact and unimpaired.

Nestorianism, taught that there were two *prosopa*, or "persons" in Jesus Christ. The human *prosopon* is separate from the divine *prosopon* (their union being of only a "moral" or "psychological" kind), and what is predicated of one cannot be predicated of the other, or of the two when working together.

---

85 Apollinarius of Laodicea, "On the Union in Christ of the Body with Godhead," 7, in *The Christological Controversy*, trans. and ed. Richard A. Norris Jr. (Minneapolis: Fortress Press, 1980), 105.
86 Apollinarius of Laodicea, "On the Union in Christ of the Body with Godhead," para. 7, 105.
87 Apollinarius of Laodicea, "Fragment 25," in *The Christological Controversy*, trans. and ed. Richard A. Norris Jr. (Minneapolis, MN: Fortress Press, 1980), 108.
88 Apollinarius of Laodicea, "Fragment 89," in ibid., 110.
89 Later, however, Gregory Nazianzen would counter: "What he (the *Logos*) has not assumed, he has not healed." Gregory of Nazianzen, "Letter to Cledonius," in *St. Cyril of Alexandria: The Christological Controversy*, trans. John A. McGuckin, 393.
90 Richard Price and Michael Gaddis, 59.

Nestorius separates the divine nature from the human nature in Christ and avoids any kind of "'mixture' or 'confusion' of the divine and human spheres of reality in Christological discourse."[91] For Nestorius, God assumed the human Christ "distinguished from other men in whom God dwelt, only by the plenitude of the divine presence, and the absolute control of the divine over the human."[92]

The Chalcedonian creed underlines the idea that "the distinctive character of each nature being preserved and coming together into one person and one *hypostasis*, not parted or divided into two persons,"[93] There is one Person in Jesus Christ—the Word, the Son, the Second Person of the Blessed Trinity—and in him the two natures of Christ are united.

The very last major heresy that Chalcedon spoke out against was that of Eutyches, one of the first monophysites. *Monophysitism* is the teaching that Christ has only one nature.[94] Eutyches, who came to the lamplight in the heat of the controversy between Nestorianism, Apollinarianism, and the Cyrilians believed that Nestorianism posed a big threat to the sanity of the Church. He misinterpreted Cyril's formula "one nature (*physis*) incarnate of God the Word" and ended up slipping into a form of monophysitism that denied the oneness of Christ. He held to Cyril's *mia physis* doctrine as did Apollinarius, and interpreted it to such a degree that it was interpreted as having heretical overtones. *Physis*, in the Alexandrian sense, means concrete existence.

Chalcedonian Theology Revisited: An African Perspective

The council pronounced that Christ is one person, his two natures preserved in one *prosopon* and *hypostasis* (hypostatic union). Both natures, divine and human, are unimpaired, perfect, consubstantial with God and human, and born of the Virgin. The distinct natures are fully God and human, thus securing salvation by a saving God and a human being.

The definition of Chalcedon affirmed uncompromisingly both the duality of natures and the unity of persons. Thus, Aloys Grillmeier, a modern

---

91 McGuckin, 131.
92 Charles Hodge, *Systematic Theology*, 401.
93 Richard Price and Michael Gaddis, 59.
94 Wilhite, 172.

historian of Chalcedon, sums up the significance of the Chalcedonian definition as follows:

> If the person of Christ is the highest mode of conjunction between God and man, God and the world, the Chalcedonian "without confusion" and "without separation" shows the right mean between monism and dualism, the two extremes between which the history of Christology also swings. The Chalcedonian unity of person in the distinction of natures provides the dogmatic basis for the preservation of the divine transcendence, which must always be a feature of the Christian concept of God. But it also shows the possibility of a complete immanence on which the biblical doctrine of the economy of salvation rests. The Chalcedonian definition may seem to have a static-ontic ring, but it is not meant to do away with the salvation-historical aspect of biblical Christology, for which, in fact, it provides a foundation and deeper insights.[95]

The council of Chalcedon was a dogmatic council. It seems to me that it was a statement by Fathers who were first and foremost pastors of the truth of tradition, having, first of all, listened carefully to the proven witnesses of that tradition. This means therefore that their formula was more the result of a firm intuition of the faith than a product of scholarly analysis. The words were well chosen, but their meaning was not clearly defined. This, of course, has invited much theological labor and attention since 451. Many theologians see the formula not in a static-ontological sense but as a dynamic historical proclamation of Christology which provides both a foundation and source for further insight. In this sense, Chalcedon is, in the words of Karl Rahner, not merely an end but a beginning; not only a beginning where the truth of Christ's divinity and humanity was stated but also as a beginning or departure point of theological endeavors.[96] Referring to Chalcedon, he says:

> The clearest formulations, the most sanctified formulas, the classic condensations of the centuries-long work of the Church in prayer, reflection and struggle concerning God's mysteries: all these derive their life from the fact that they are not end but beginning, not goal but means, truths which open the way to the ever-greater truth.[97]

In this section, I will present the council of Chalcedon from an African perspective. I will briefly look at one African theologian John Pobee who, over the years, have been very clear in their critical thoughts about the council of

---

95 Aloys Grillmeier, *Christ in Christian Tradition: From the Apostolic Age to Chalcedon (451)*, 2nd ed., vol. I (Louisville, KY: Westminster John Knox, 1975), 491.
96 Walter Kasper, *Jesus Christ*, trans. V. Green (Mahwah, NJ: Paulist Press, 1977), 17.
97 Karl Rahner, *Theological Investigations*, vol. I (Baltimore, MD: Helicon Press, 1961), 150.

Chalcedon. His view on Chalcedon indeed gives us a path to his theological methodology, making us understand the lens from which he develops his Christology, thus introducing us to what Africa has to do with Chalcedon.

The Ghanaian theologian John S. Pobee was very critical of Chalcedonian Christology because he believed that Chalcedon, as well as the other earlier ecumenical councils, are so indebted and influenced to Greco Roman culture that it has lost its practical relevance. In his *Towards an African Theology*[98] Pobee challenges the metaphysical terms used during the Early Church councils. Without questioning the faith propagated by the creed, he considers the language and concepts that were used during the councils to be completely irrelevant for today. He writes:

> Who today, theologian and philosopher included, normally uses terms such as "substance" or "person" or "hypostases" in their technical Chalcedonian sense? The creed was, indeed, an attempt to translate the biblical faith into contemporary language and thought forms. In order words, so far as it concerns us, the issue is to get behind the creed to the biblical faith. And so, whatever we evolve should be tested against the plumb line of the biblical faith.[99]

Biblical faith is, therefore, the measuring rod for the authenticity of any theology. This explains why Pobee went on to construct a theology from his Akan cultural background that aligns with biblical faith and is devoid of the metaphysical language of Patristic theology. He says:

> Metaphysical speculations about the relation within the Godhead are absent (in the bible), Even the fourth gospel, which declared the "Word was God," nowhere speculates on how the word was God. Indeed, it soon leaves the heavenlies and comes down to earth with the tremendous affirmation: "The Word became flesh and dwelt among us, full of grace and truth; we beheld his glory." (John 1:14)[100]

He rejects using Chalcedon as the reference point of Christology. Pobee contends that any Christological proposal which uses the Chalcedonian Creed as a point of departure lacks authenticity – whether in Africa or elsewhere in the Christian world.[101]

According to him, humanity and divinity are the two non-negotiables of any authentic Christianity.[102] He hinges his Christology on the humanity and

---

98 John S. Pobee, *Towards an African Theology* (Nashville, TN: Abingdon, 1979).
99 John S. Pobee, *Towards an African Theology*, 82.
100 Ibid.
101 Ibid.
102 Ibid.

the divinity of Christ without discussing them in terms of the Nicene and Chalcedonian Creed. Pobee begins by explaining the meaning of the humanity of Christ for the Akan people by exploring the Akan anthropology. He says, "The evidence of Jesus' humanity settles down to his anthropological makeup of being spirit, flesh, and body; his finitude in terms of his knowledge and power and his deep consciousness of total dependence on God."[103] After exploring the Akan anthropology, Pobee finds a place for Jesus therein and develops a Christology rooted in Scripture.

In response to the question of "who is Jesus Christ?" Pobee holds that Jesus is fully God and fully human but notes that Jesus' divinity is deduced from his day-to-day works and actions in his community. For him, in contrast to Chalcedonian Christology that upholds Christ as being *perfect in Godhead or homoousios* with the Father, Jesus is a full embodiment of God. He advocates a functional divinity, rather than the Chalcedonian ontological divinity. Speaking from an Akan point of view, Pobee argues that the metaphysical terms drawn from the Graeco-Roman cultural context are not useful in today's world. He prefers functional terms, ignoring Patristic Christological developments.

In discussing the divinity of Christ in relation to his sinfulness, Pobee leans principally on the Akan concept of community. Sin is understood to have both a horizontal and a vertical dimension. It can be horizontal when it involves actions that harm others and vertical when it has to do with transgressing God's law and breaking fellowship with him. The horizontal dimension of sin is emphasized in the Akan society, even though culturally both of them exists.

> In Akan society, the essence of sin is an anti-social act. It is not an abstract transgression of law; rather it is a factual contradiction of established order. Further, thus contradiction or fault sometimes does harm to others – e.g. jealousy, murder, rape, incest – and is considered to involve ill will to the other person. The contradiction thus fractures the interpersonal relationships centred on the ego.[104]

Sin does not contribute to the welfare of the community. Instead, it detracts from fellowship and separates children of God's family.[105] Jesus' sinlessness, which also has a vertical dimension, is evident in the horizontal sense because he was a man of love – "which alone produces the harmony, peace, and

---

103 Pobee, 84.
104 Ibid., 92.
105 Ibid., 118.

cohesion of society. . . . (and) Jesus' life was one story of perfect loving of fellow men."[106] Jesus' sinlessness, according to Pobee, does not in any way make Jesus less human. On the contrary, it points to the need to affirm his divinity as well as his humanity.

Without going into any details, it is worthwhile to note emphatically that the councils before 451 played a significant role in shaping the theology of Chalcedon, and that the contribution of North Africans in the Early Church toward these councils was crucial. It suffices for us to focus on contemporary times in this research. In this vein, we can ask: If contemporary Africa brought her whole, unbridled self into the council, would it still be recognizable by the universal Church? In other words, if Africa lets her anthropological understanding inform her Christology, in the same way as the Early Church fathers used their anthropology to articulate a Christology that has become normative for the universal Church, would it be acceptable by all?

Chalcedon helped the Church to move forward in its mission. It also helped to curtail the power play dynamics that were very prevalent at the time. Its solemn definitions and its normative character provided, for those who took the Gospel to new missionary lands, palpable materials from which to draw understanding and meaning. Mark Noll provides a good picture of what Chalcedon did:

> Chalcedon was a threefold triumph: a triumph of sound doctrine over error in the Church, a triumph of Christian catholicity over cultural fragmentation, and a triumph of discriminating theological reasoning over the anti-intellectual dismissal of philosophy, on the one hand, and over a theological capitulation to philosophy on the other.[107]

There is no gainsaying the fact that Chalcedon is the apex of the Christological formulation in a multi-cultural Church that enjoys a long history. In the words of Karl Rahner:

> The Church and its faith are indeed always the same throughout their history, for otherwise there would only be desperate events in an atomized history of religion, but not the history of a single Church and of a single faith, which is ever the same. But since this single and identical Church has had a history, and still has a history, the ancient formulas of the Church are not merely the end of a very long history of faith and dogma.[108]

---

106 John S. Pobee, *Towards an African Theology*, 92.
107 Mark Noll, *Turning Points: Decisive Moments in the History of Christianity* (Grand Rapids, MI: Baker Books, 1997), 67.
108 Rahner, *Theological Investigations*, vol. I (Baltimore, MD: Helicon Press, 1961), 211.

For Rahner, Chalcedon is an end because it settled the theological disputes in the Church during that time. Chalcedon is also a beginning. It is a beginning in the sense that one can refer back to it and re-articulate its doctrinal truth in a different historical or cultural context. According to Rahner,

> Chalcedon is "the starting point of a spiritual movement of departure and return which is our only guarantee or better, hope of having understood the ancient formula. For no understanding is possible anywhere if what is understood remained fixed and frozen and is not launched into the movement of that nameless mystery which is the vehicle of all understanding."[109]

Chalcedon's definition of Christ as true God and true human, without mixture and separation, against the views of Eutyches, could be seen as a sort of Christological *perichoresis*. Joseph Pohle defines *perichoresis* as "the mutual in-existence of the two unmixed natures (the divine and the human) by reason of the hypostatic union with the person of the logos."[110] *Perichoresis* has to do with how the elements combine in the one substance. While in the Trinity, the persons are in one nature, in Christology the two natures are in the same person. Being the starting point, Chalcedon not only enriches the terminology, highlighting the supracultural dimension of Christology, but it also creates an atmosphere in which the divine and human natures of Christ can be looked at through the African anthropological cultural lenses.

Conclusion

We have looked at the anthropological background of the two schools of Alexandria and Antioch, showing how their dualistic understanding played a crucial role in understanding the natures of Christ. This also led us to examine not only the mode of union between the human and the divine natures of Christ but also the heresies that ensued, how the council of Chalcedon dealt with them, and how an African theologian, John Pobee, approaches Chalcedon from his unique perspective. Understanding all these further expands our knowledge of Christ and prepares us to better understand how Africa's unique

---

109 Karl Rahner, *Theological Investigations*, vol. IV (Baltimore, MD: Helicon Press, 1961), 106.
110 Joseph Pohle, *Christology: A Dogmatic Treatise on the Incarnation* (London: Herder, 1946), 180–81.

anthropology informs her Christology. In the next chapter, I will underline the primordial place of anthropology in Christology and present the basis of the African understanding of the human person so as to facilitate our understanding of how it informs its Christology.

· 2 ·
TRANSITIONING WORLDS: FROM ANTHROPOLOGY TO CHRISTOLOGY

Introduction

I have seen how the Early Church fathers' view of anthropology influenced their articulation of a Christology that has become normative in Christian circles, thanks to the early ecumenical councils from Nicea to Chalcedon. This chapter highlights the role of anthropology in the articulation of any Christology and demonstrates how the African view of the human person informs African Christology. In 1981, the International Theological Commission, reflecting on the complex relationship between Christology and anthropology, published a document highlighting the need for a better study of anthropology toward an understanding and articulation of Christology in today's world. In fact, the Commission warned of the danger of ignoring anthropology in the study of Christ, the God-made-human.

> The context of Christology includes the human desire for and the knowledge man has of God, the revelation of the Triune God, and the image of man in contemporary anthropology and in the Incarnation of Jesus Christ. If these basic elements are not first treated adequately, Christology itself is placed in danger.[1]

---

1 The International Theological Commission, "Theology, Christology, Anthropology," 1981, http://www.vatican.va/roman_curia/congregations/cfaith/cti_documents/rc_cti_1982_teologia-cristologia-antropologia_en.html. Accessed on September 3, 2017. It is headed by the

In the third chapter of this work, I will examine the anthropological context, so as to better understand an articulation of an African Christology. To do this, I will analyze major characteristics of African anthropology (instances of the human person and the concept of *ubuntu*) and examine the dynamics between Christian faith and culture, noting the ways that can be used to articulate a correlation between them.

African Anthropology: Major Characteristics

Given the vast and diverse nature of both the European and the African continents, can one talk of a Western anthropology or of an African anthropology, and still hold claim to truth? The Cameroonian-born Jesuit Meinrad P. Hebga advocates diverse anthropologies, as well as diverse systems of thought:

> Occidental or Western thought is usually used to refer to a collection of philosophical, theological, scientific and literary works of North America and recently, even as far as Israel and Japan.[2]

In his *L'unité Culturelle de L'Afrique Noire*, Cheick Anta Diop gives some insight into the particularities of the African continent, which opens the way for a more independent study of the distinct cultural realities of the continent:

> To explain the common characteristics of Africans, I started from the material conditions, from domestic life to the life of the nation, including its ideological structure, its successes, failures and technical decline. This led me to analyze the structure of the African and Indo-European family and to try to show that the matriarchal base on which the former rests is not universal, as it may seem. I then tackled the notions of state, kingdom, moral, philosophy, religion and arts and consequently literature and esthetic. In each of these various domains, I tried to bring forth the common denominator of African cultural in contrast to the Northern Aryan... this work will

---

Cardinal Prefect of the Congregation for the Doctrine of the Faith, comprised of theologians of various schools and nations who are outstanding in the science of theology and fidelity toward the magisterium of the Church. The members are appointed by the Supreme Pontiff.

2 Il est aussi d'usage d'appeler pensée occidentale l'ensemble des oeuvres philosophiques, théologiques, scientifiques, littéraires de l'Amérique du Nord, et meme dépuis peu, d'Israel et du Japon. Meinrad P, *La Rationalite d'un Discours Africain Sur les Phenomenes Paranormaux* (Paris: Harmattan, 1998), 26.

contribute in reinforcing the positive sentiments thus proving our organic cultural entity.[3]

In the first chapter of this work, I discussed how the dualistic Platonist anthropology informed the various schools of thought in their articulation of Christological dogma and agree with Hebga that "Platonic dualism continues to be found in catechisms, homilies and the popular prayers of the Roman Church."[4] In this sub-section, I am going to present the cultural, socio-economic, and political understanding of the human person in Africa by examining Hebga's three dimensions of the human person and the concept of *Ubuntu*. This understanding will go a long way to providing an anthropological context in which African Christology will be based.

The Three Instances of the Human Person

In Africa, a human person is composed of at least three dimensions, which make up both an invisible and a visible unity. Multiple unities exist especially in the invisible domain. In Rwanda, for instance, the human person is composed of the material aspect, the non-material and perishable aspect, and the non-material and imperishable aspect.[5] The material component, known as body, is the locus of perception, which, far from encompassing the whole of the human person, ceases to exist after death. The immaterial and perishable aspect, called the *Igicucu*, is like the shadow of the individual. Like the shadow of any object, the result of an obstruction of light exists wherever and whenever the person exists and follows the human body around, intimately linked

---

3 J'ai essayé de partir des conditions matérielles pour expliquer tous les traits culturel commun aux Africains, depuis la vie domestique, jusqu'à celle de la nation, en passant par la structure idéologique, les succès, les échec et régression techniques. J'ai donc été amené à analyser la structure de la famille Africaine et aryenne et a tenter de démontrer que la base matriachale sur laquelle repose la première, n'est point universelle malgré les apparences. J'ai abordé la notion d'Etat, de royauté, la morale, la philosophie, la religion et l'art par conséquent, la littérature et l'esthétique. Dans chacun de ces domains si variés, j'ai essayé de dégager le dénominateur commun de la culture africaine par opposition à la culture nordique aryenne... puisse ce travail contribuer à renforcer le sentiment des biens qui ont démontré ainsi notre identité culturelle organique Cheikh Anta Diop, *L'Unite Culturelle de L'Afrique Noire*, 2nd ed. (Paris: Presence Africaine, 1982), 7. This is my translation.
4 Hebga, *La Rationalite d'un Discours Africain Sur Les Phenomenes Paranormaux*, 56."C'est le dualism platonicienqui continue d'être convoyé dans les catéchismes, les homélies et les prières populaires de l'église romaine."
5 Ibid.

to it. To try to harm someone's shadow is a direct attack on the individual person. *Ubuzima* is life or health and exists only as long as the person is alive. *Ubwenge*, translated as "knowledge," exists in a human person only as long as the person is alive with all his/her cognitive faculties. This means that a person loses his/her *Ubwenge* if he/she is sick with a condition that causes loss of cognitive abilities or performance. The non-material and non-perishable aspect is often referred to as *Mutima* or heart. Far from being that muscular organ in all human beings and most animals, which pumps blood to the blood vessels by repeated, rhythmic contractions, the heart refers to the human person in his/her affective or intellectual life. It is what makes the human personality, and this distinguishes one person from another.[6]

The Yoruba people of Nigeria, like the Rwandans, hold a threefold conception of the human person. These three can be subdivided into seven elements. The material element alone, for the Yoruba, is comprised of three aspects; the body, the soul, and the inside of the body (interior body). The body is an integral part of the person. It is thanks to the body that one can be physically and visibly present in the world. It is subject to natural needs, like nutrition, and it returns to the dust from which it was made after death. The shadow is like the companion of the body. It is referred to in Yoruba as "*o jiji*." According to Louise Vincent, the *o jiji*, is directly linked to the person and ceases to exist when the person dies.[7] The interior of the body, called the *ikpin-i-jeun*, is the perishable center for the distribution of food.

The perishable non-material element, called *Iye*, is Spirit. It is located at the back of the head but is different from intelligence. According to the Yoruba people, a person can lose his/her *Iye* if mentally ill. The imperishable and non-material elements, like the material element, is composed of three aspects: the head, the breath, and the heart. The head is not the physical upper part of the body that contains the brain, the skull, and sense organs, but it is an imperishable, spiritual part that incarnates into a newborn child from the ancestors. It is called the *Ori* or *Olori*. The breath, also called *Emin*, is a blowing force that gives movement to the body. It leaves the body as soon as the person dies to return to the abode of the Supreme Being, where it belongs. The heart, called *Kon*, is the most distinguishing aspect of the person. It is considered to be the *locus par excellence* of the individual value of the human person.

---

6   Dominique Nothomb, *Un Humanisme Africain: Valeurs et Pierres Dattente / Dominique Nothomb*, 1st ed. (Bruxelles: Editions Lumen Vitae, 1965), 24.
7   Louis-Vincent Thomas and René Luneau, *La Terre Africaine et Ses Religions* (Paris: Larousse, 1975), 8.

From the above descriptions, it is evident that the African conception of humanity is not dualistic but pluralistic. The richness and particularities of each African culture only add to the depth and beauty of African thought. Different countries and cultures basically have different names to denote the same pluralistic anthropological view.

In a nutshell, in Africa, the human person is thought of being composed of three elements. The material element (body) is the perishable; the non-material element, which accompanies the person throughout his/her life, and leaves that person after death (Shadow); and the non-perishable and non-material element, which is the soul. The body, soul, and shadow, therefore, comprise the human person in Africa. Hebga, refers to these three as the "instances of the human person." According to him, to understand the African conception of the human person, we have to make that indispensable passage *"du dualisme au pluralisme"* (from dualism to pluralism).[8] A human being is therefore not just body and soul but body (*corps*), breath or soul (*souffle*), and shadow (*l'ombre*). He calls these the "the triadique schema" (*schema triadique*).[9] It is worthwhile to note that, with Hebga, each of these "instances" is not an element of the whole, but each constitutes a whole person. Hebga notes: "At the same time, we understand that each of these instances is not a part but an entire whole person seen from a particular angle."[10]

The Body

Far from being a thing, the body (*corps*) is a manifestation of the person during his/her life here on earth. In Cameroon, the Bassa, Douala, and Ewondo tribes refer to it as *nyuu*, *nyolo*, and *nyol*, respectively. It is the only instance of the person that is subject to the senses. The body is the epiphany of the person, the center of the exteriority of the person.[11] It is the "outside" of the person which

---

8   En même temps, on veut laisser entendre que chaque instance n'est pas une partie de la personne, mais la personne tout entière perçue sur un angle particulier Hebga, *La Rationalite d'un discours Africain Sur les Phenomenes Paranormaux*, 26.
9   Hebga, *La Rationalite d'un discours Africain Sur les Phenomenes Paranormaux*, 155.
10 Ibid.
11 For Merleau-Ponty, (*Phénoménologie de la perception* (Paris: Librairie Gallimard, 1945)), the human body reveals the entire human person. For Merleau-Ponty, we are our bodies (p. 75). Far from advocating a physiological reductionism, Merleau-Ponty sees the body as it is lived and not as a separate part. The body, as it is lived, is an experiential body, a body that opens onto a world and allows the world to be for us. Lived experience in the world permits me to realize I am my body and the other person is his/her body. The French Christian existentialist, Gabriel Honoré Marcel (1889–1973), along the same line, views the human

only death can take away. The African conception of body as the subject is very much embedded in African thought and culture.

The body, therefore, is not an image of the human person; it is the person. For the Bassa, Ewondo and Duala people of Cameroon and for the Fon in Benin, the word "why" is literally translated as "body what?" as if the body possesses in itself the metaphysical capacity to explain the reason for an action or its finality. Also, "for me" is translated as "to my body," which makes one identify the person with his/her body. For the African, the body can also be used to refer to the exterior part of the person (skin).

The Breath (Soul)

The breath (*souffle*) is not to be confused with the air we breathe. The air we breathe is a sign which represents the presence of the vital breath. According to Hebga: "The vital breath is not the breath of the nostrils; instead, it is a sign. Life is not subjected to the senses but to a series of signs, which announces rather than show. It can be inferred rather than seen."[12]

From the Greek *psyche*, the Latin *anima* means breath, light wind. In the same sense, the Greek *pneuma* and the Latin *spiritus* first denotes the breath of respiration, the wind, and, in a certain sense, spirit. Hebga explains that the word that translates breath for the Bassa people of East Cameroon, West Africa, is *mbuu*; in Ewondo, *evundi*; in Douala, *mudi*, and in Baluba, (a tribe from the Democratic Republic of Congo) *moyo*, meaning to persevere in life, or to last long. The person as breath is manifested through a mastery of a phenomenon, such as movements and reproduction. It is the vital breath, breath that gives life. It is important to note that *breath* is very different from the body, and will never replace the body, but co-exists with it.

Shadow (Spirit)

Like breath, the *shadow* is also an invisible dimension of the human person. Shadow is not a reflection of an object resulting from an obstruction of light

---

body not as an object or instrument, like in the Cartesian sense (Gabriel Marcel, *Du refus à l'invocation* (Paris: Gallimard, 1940), 29). When Gabriel Marcel says "my body," he is not referring to the body that "I have," advocated by the Cartesian rationalism, but to the body that *I am*.

12 Le souffle de narines n'est pas le souffle vitale; il en sera plutôt le signe. La vie ne tombe pas formellement sous les sens, mais à travers une série de signes qui l'annoncent plutôt qu'ils ne la montrent. Elle se laisse deviner plus qu'elle ne se fait voir. Hebga, *La Rationalite d'un Discours Africain Sur les Phenomenes Paranormaux*, 107–8.

from a particular direction.[13] According to Hebga, the shadow is a dynamic reality that acts independently of the body. When considering the functional status of the shadow, one notes that it does not just envelope the body, but it has the capacity of actually going beyond, or transcending the body, and acts independently.[14] In Africa, the body constitutes one aspect of the person among others. Worthy also of note is the fact that each of these instances is inseparable, because the human person is one whole.

The words *mbuu, mudi,* and *nsisim* for soul or breath for the Bassa and Douala, and shadow for the Ewondo, coexist with the body, and together with the body, form a substantial unity. It is invisible, indivisible, and immortal. Christian theology has attributed substantiality to shadow and breathe; a substantiality that it did not have in the original Bantu culture.[15] Instead of referring directly to a person as body, the Western influence has preferred to use adjectival mediation, such as "the body *of,* the breath *of,* the soul *of . . . .*" A common case is the prayer: "May the *souls of the faithful* departed through the mercy of God rest in peace," instead of "May the *faithful departed,* through the mercy of God rest in peace."

In Africa, the body of the person is that person; the shadow (Spirit) of the person is that person; the breath (soul) of the person is that person, and each of these dimensions is distinct and constitutes the whole person. It is also understood that the body, being material, degenerates or decays after "death." Death in the Bantu culture has a broader sense than the English word "death." It has to do with disappearing, vanishing. Death is, therefore, a definitive separation of the constitutive elements of the person. After death, the body is subjected to the ground through a process of decay but is not annihilated or wiped out into nothingness. In other words, death dilutes the body into the soil, thereby enriching and reinforcing it.

We have mentioned above that the dualistic and the pluralistic conceptions neither oppose nor contradict one another. With this in mind, it is still necessary to indicate, at least succinctly, what runs at the back of an African mind when the word "person" is used. Added to these biological entities are the sociocultural aspects of the human person.

---

13   Hebga, 56.
14   Ibid., 115.
15   Ibid., 137.

The Heart of Ubuntu Philosophy: Probing Its Core Tenets

A proper understanding of the human person in Africa is found not only in his/her material (body) and immaterial dimensions (breath/soul, shadow/spirit) but also in his/her sociocultural aspects. The philosophy/concept that captures this sociocultural dimension of African anthropology is the concept of *ubuntu*. The Danish Scholar, Christian Gade outlines five stages in which the *ubuntu* concept has been defined. Stage one, 1846–1962, refers almost exclusively to humanity in its goodness; Stage two, 1962–1975, refers to a philosophy or ethics that promotes the common good; Stage three, 1975–1990s, identifies it as an African humanism in which aid, giving, sympathy, care, sensitivity to the needs of others, respect, consideration, and patience are the order of the day; Stage four, 1990s–2000s, exposed *ubuntu* as the worldview through which Africans understand reality.[16] According to Desmond Tutu, this fourth stage characterized the South African society when they chose forgiveness instead of demanding retribution. In the fifth stage, 2000–till date, *ubuntu* started being identified with interconnectedness; hence, the "I am because we are."[17] *Ubuntu*, being a sociocultural African, is strongly based upon traditional values, beliefs, and practices acquired from childhood to adulthood, and transmitted from one generation to the next through oral means, such as fables, proverbs, storytelling, myths, and riddles.

The African concept or philosophy of *ubuntu*, which is very difficult to render into a western language, is derived from a Nguni[18] dictum: *Umuntu Ngumuntu Ngabantu*, which states that a person is a person because of or through others.

> The proverb means that 1) to be human is to affirm one's humanity by recognizing the humanity of others and, on that basis, established humane relation with them. 2) If and when one is faced with a decisive choice between one's own wealth and the preservation of the life of another being, then one should opt for the preservation of life. 3) The king owes his status, including all the powers associated with it, to the will of the people under him.[19]

---

16 The Danish scholar, Christian B. N. Gade, in his 2011 article published in the *South African Journal of philosophy*, vol. 30, no 3, titled "The Historical Development of the Written Discourses o *Ubuntu*" noted that the term *Ubuntu* has frequently appeared in writing since at least 1846 and gone through a series of phases (p. 303–29).
17 Desmond Tutu, *No Future Without Forgiveness* (New York: Doubleday, 1999), 31.
18 The Ngunis are a group of Bantu people who speak the Nguni language.
19 Mogobe B. Ramose, *African Philosophy through Ubuntu* (Harare: Mond Books, 1999), 308.

Reflecting on the interdependence of human beings in *ubuntu*, Michael Battle notes:

> We say a person is a person through other persons. We don't come fully formed into the world. . ... We need other human beings in order to be human. We are made for togetherknlness, we are made for family, for fellowship, (for community) to exist in a tender network of interdependence.[20]

According to Mogobe B. Ramose, the word *ubuntu* consists of two words: the prefix *nbu* and the stem *ntu*.[21] *Ntu* has to do with the notion of *be-ing* in general, which manifests itself in the concrete mode of the existence of a particular entity.[22] In this sense, the *nbu* is always oriented toward *ntu*, affirming their indivisibility, oneness, and wholeness which goes a long way to establish *ubuntu* as a verbal noun.[23] Desmond Tutu describes *ubuntu* as

> "the very essence of being human": it is not, "I think therefore I am." It says rather: "I am human because I belong. I participate, I share." A person with *ubuntu* is open and available to others, affirming of others, does not feel threatened that others are able and good, for he or she belongs in a greater whole and is diminished when others are humiliated or diminished, when others are tortured or oppressed, or treated as if they were less than who they are.[24]

Far from being a mere human quality with positive value in the African culture, in the sense of culture as a reality that encompasses the entire way of life of a society, such as its values, practices, symbols, institutions, and human relations,[25] it should be noted that *ubuntu* constitutes the very essence of the human being in Africa. It has to do with how one thinks, speaks, talks, acts, values, and arrives at the destinies of life. According to Johann Broodryk, *ubuntu* is the African art of being a true human being through other true human beings – *umuntu nganuntu ngabantu*.[26] It could be seen as the sum

---

20 Michael Battle, *Reconciliation: The Ubuntu Theology of Bishop Desmond Tutu* (Cleveland, OH: Pilgrim's Press, 1997), 65.
21 Ramose, *African Philosophy Through Ubuntu*, 50.
22 Mluleki Mnyaka and Mokgethi Motlhabi, "The African Concept of Ubuntu/Botho and Its Socio-Moral Significance," *Black Theology* 3, no. 2 (2005): 215–37.
23 Ramose, 51.
24 Desmond Tutu, *No Future without Forgiveness*, 31.
25 Samuel P. Huntington, "Culture Matters. How Values Shape Human Progress," in *Cultures Count* (New York: Basic Books, 2000), XV.
26 Johann Broodryk, *Ubuntu: Life Lessons from Africa* (Pretoria: Ubuntu School of Philosophy, 2002), 11.

total of human behavior, impressed on the individual person by the society, via established traditional structures over time. It means that to be human is to affirm one's humanity by recognizing the humanity of others and, on that basis, establish human relations with them.[27]

One other aspect about *ubuntu* is that, even though it is deeply rooted in African culture and its history, and is at the center of most African cultures,[28] its values are those of humanity in general; they are universal. One can confidently say that *ubuntu* is African in its conception, roots, and history but universal in its embodiment. The words of Desmond Tutu summarize succinctly the characteristics of the *ubuntu* concept which, in addition to the "three instances of the human person," make up African Anthropology:

> [*Ubuntu*] means the essence of being human. You know when it is there, as you know when it is absent. It speaks about humanness, gentleness, hospitality, putting yourself out on behalf of others, being vulnerable; it embraces compassion and toughness. It recognizes that any humanity is bound up with yours. It means not nursing grudges, but willingness to accept others as they are and being thankful for them. It excludes grasping competitiveness, harsh aggressiveness, being concerned for oneself, abrasiveness. Thus, *Ubuntu* is more than just a facet of individual acts. It is an essential humanistic orientation towards one's fellow men. Human relations therefore are the alpha and the omega of the concept.[29]

Like any acquired virtue, *ubuntu* can be lost. When anyone engages in inhumane practices such as rape, xenophobia, or racism, one is said to have lost their *ubuntu*. Because *ubuntu*, in its basic manifestation, engages and involves others, its loss automatically affects in a negative way, not only the person but also the wider community. Other characteristics of *ubuntu* include justice, forgiveness, and interdependence. In *ubuntu* philosophy, unforgiveness is solved with forgiveness so that the person can regain his/her *ubuntu*. It has to do with expressing compassion, reciprocity, dignity, harmony, and humanity for the sake of building and maintaining the community. It is a lived expression of the adage "Your pain is my pain, my wealth is your wealth, your salvation is my salvation."

We note that the African view of the human person is not just biological but extends to and is rooted in the community. The African view of personhood

---

27 Ramose, 52.
28 Augustine Shutte, *Ubuntu: An Ethic for a New South Africa* (Pietermaritzburg: Cluster Publications, 2001), 2.
29 Martha Bonn, "Children's Understanding of *Ubuntu*," *Early Child Development and Care*, 177, no. 8 (November 2007): 863.

denies the fact that a person can be described solely in terms of physical and psychological properties. This is because it is with reference to the community that a person is defined, hence, the saying, "A person is born for the other." Interdependence between self and community is a crucial aspect of it.

The *ubuntu* philosophy represents an African conception of human beings and their relationship with the community that embodies the ethics which defines Africans and their social behaviors. The survival of a human being is dependent on other people – the community and society.

When Faith Meets Culture: Toward a Theology of Inculturation

Having espoused an understanding of African anthropology in view of explaining how it shapes the articulation of an African Christology, it is indeed necessary to evaluate, at this juncture, the important question of faith and culture. Evaluating the dynamics of faith and its interaction with culture goes a long way in aiding us understand Christ from an African cultural perspective, so as to later show how that understanding is lived concretely in the daily lives of African Christians.

It is important to note at the very beginning that the question between faith and culture is not new. It goes as far back as the first century when the Early Church was faced with the tricky question of the condition of admissibility of the gentiles into the Christian community (Acts 15). In the early centuries, with the work of Patristic Apologists such as Justin Martyr, the issue of how faith interacts with culture was tackled with even greater focus, as the Church forged her way from a Hellenistic culture into a largely Jewish matrix. The great work of the early apologists, notwithstanding, did not completely settle the issue. The same question haunts the Church today as she makes her painful way from being a predominantly European reality to being a world Church.[30]

In order to evangelize fruitfully, what Pope Paul VI calls the "drama of our time," (*Evangelii Nuntiandi*, 20.) that is, the big divide between the proclamation of the Gospel and the exigencies of culture must be tackled with proper attention to avoid a neglect of one over the other.

---

30 Dermot A. Lane, *Religion and Culture in Dialogue: A Challenge for the Next Millennium* (Dublin: The Columba Press, 1993), 11.

> What matters is to evangelize man's culture and cultures (not in a purely decorative way, as it were, by applying a thin veneer, but in a vital way, in depth and right to their very roots) ... always taking the person as one's starting-point and always coming back to the relationships of people among themselves and with God. The Gospel, and therefore evangelization, are certainly not identical with culture, and they are independent in regard to all cultures. Nevertheless, the kingdom which the Gospel proclaims is lived by men who are profoundly linked to a culture, and the building up of the kingdom cannot avoid borrowing the elements of human culture or cultures. Though independent of cultures, the Gospel and evangelization are not necessarily incompatible with them; rather they are capable of permeating them all without becoming subject to any one of them. (EG, 20)

In a letter creating the Pontifical Council for Culture, Pope John Paul II noted: "I have considered the Church's dialogue with the cultures of our time to be a vital area, one in which the destiny of the world at the end of this twentieth century is at stake."[31] This is not simply because of the multiplication of cultures in today's world but also because modernization has created a situation where there is an increased acceleration of cultural mutation to a pace that is difficult to accommodate. In examining the relationship between Christian faith and culture, I will focus on Richard Niebuhr's models on how culture can interact with the person of Christ, noting the implications of each model.

In his book *Christ and Culture*, Niebuhr articulates the relationship between Christ and culture by proposing five models: Christ against culture; Christ of culture; Christ above culture; Christ and culture in paradox; and Christ and the transformer of culture.[32] Who is Jesus Christ and what is Culture? How do the two interact with each other?

Niebuhr notes that no one title can exhaust the totality of who Jesus is, for any one definition given of him would be inadequate because they are culturally conditioned. He, however, holds that individual biblical titles referring to Christ are adequate, for the purpose of meeting Him.[33] Culture for him is a pure product of the environment created by human beings, which encompasses the areas of "language, habits, ideas, beliefs, customs, social organization, inherited artifacts, technical processes, and values."[34]

The first model is the Christ-against-culture paradigm, which "affirms the sole authority of Christ over culture and resolutely rejects culture's claims to

---

31 Pope John Paul II, Letter to Agostino Cardinal Casaroli, creating the Pontifical Council for Culture, *Osservatore romano* (English edition), June 28, 1982, 7.
32 Richard Niebuhr, *Christ and Culture* (New York: Harper and Row, 1975).
33 Niebuhr, *Christ and Culture*, 14.
34 Niebuhr, 32.

loyalty."[35] To be a good Christian, it is necessary not only to make a radical break from one's culture but also to out rightly "reject" the culture, that is, reject participating in and endorsing activities and systems that are inherently sinful.[36] Niebuhr considers the third-century Patristic Latin theologian Tertulian and the nineteenth-century Russian writer Leo Tolstoy as good examples of this paradigm, which considers culture as the main residence of sin, and recommends that all believers withdraw from it.

The merits of this paradigm are in the resilience that those who adhere to it manifest, for the people who reject the world "have not taken easy ways in professing their allegiance to Christ. They have endured physical and mental sufferings in their willingness to abandon homes, property, and the protection of government for the sake of his cause."[37] It demonstrates drawing the often-difficult distinction between what belongs to God and what belongs to Caesar.

The problem with this paradigm lies in the fact that the separation between the culture and Christ or between the world and Christianity has never actually been achieved at any time. Also, to think one can actually avoid sin by escaping from culture is not practicable.[38] Niebuhr himself criticizes this model by adding that the "rejection of culture is easily combined with a suspicion of nature and nature's God: ... ultimately they are tempted to divide the world in the material realm governed by a principle opposed to Christ and a spiritual realm governed by the spiritual God."[39]

Opposed to the Christ against culture paradigm is the second model: the Christ of culture paradigm which views Christ as being in "agreement."[40] with culture. Culture is interpreted through Christ and vice versa resulting in a harmonization of the two. This model sees "no great tension between Church and world, the social laws and the Gospel ... the ethics of salvation and the ethics of social conservation or progress. On the one hand, they interpret culture through Christ, where those aspects that are most like Jesus are given, most honor. On the other hand, they interpret Christ through culture, selecting from his teaching that which best harmonizes with the best in civilization."[41]

---

35 Niebuhr, 45.
36 Ibid., 47.
37 Ibid., 66.
38 Ibid., 78.
39 Ibid., 81.
40 Ibid., 41.
41 Ibid., 83.

Jesus is considered to be "the Messiah of their society, the fulfiller of its hopes and aspirations, the perfecter of its true faith, the source of its holiest spirit."[42] It is a sort of "radically embracing this world without denying the other world" and filling the gap between both worlds.

One can credit this model on grounds that, historically, some people have come to Christ because of the "harmony of the Christian message with the moral and religious philosophy of their best teachers."[43] This model challenges those in the Christ against culture position which holds that it is only by refusing to adapt to culture that one can influence culture in a positive way. Being part of the society, one stands a better chance to influence and impact the lives of other people. The main problem with this paradigm is that the true historical and biblical Jesus ends up being distorted, and one is left with an image of Jesus that is far from reality because it is so tailored to the prevailing culture. This results in a situation where loyalty to a culture far exceeds loyalty to Christ.

In Christ above culture paradigm, God orders culture, and culture is neither good
nor bad. Here,

> [M]an is obligated in the nature of his being to be obedient to God. . . . [T]his obedience must be rendered in the concrete, actual life of natural, cultural man. In his sex life, in eating and drinking, in commanding and obeying other men, he is in the realm of God by divine ordering under divine orders. [44]

Even though sin is always expressed in cultural terms, it does not in any way render culture bad, because the grace of God sustains it. Culture and God are related. Niebuhr notes:

> They cannot separate the works of human culture from the grace of God, for all those works are possible only by grace. But neither can they separate the experience of grace from cultural activity; for how can men love the unseen God in response to His love without serving the visible brother in human society?[45]

One can credit this Christ above culture paradigm on grounds that it proposes achieving the balance between Christ and culture by portraying Christ as part of the culture and, at the same time, is outside of culture. Putting Christ

---

42 Niebuhr, 83.
43 Ibid., 103.
44 Ibid., 118.
45 Ibid., 119.

TRANSITIONING WORLDS: FROM ANTHROPOLOGY TO CHRISTOLOGY   57

as part of the culture on the one hand and above culture on the other drives home a clear message that for the good functioning of society, there is an indispensable need for direction from God – the sustainer of culture. This position posits the necessity of the Church and its spiritual role in ensuring respect for divine laws. On the other hand, one can decry this paradigm on grounds that when pushed to its limits, it unavoidably leads to the institutionalization of Christ and the gospel, thereby driving people away from eternal hope and from the goal of the Christian in favor of the temporal embodiment in a "man-devised form."[46] Moreover, this model does not confront or face up to the radical evil present in all human work and culture.[47]

One difficulty with this paradigm is that, given the dynamic nature of culture, it becomes difficult to lay its foundations in tandem with those of Christ. Doing this necessitates a constant reevaluation of their relationship and dialogue so that it does not become antiquated, drifting into irrelevance.

The third paradigm is the "Christ and culture in paradox" paradigm which puts culture and Christ at loggerheads with each other, with both having conflicting demands. Far from being a conflict between God and humans in general, it is a conflict between God and us as individuals.[48] The person is called upon to obey both God and culture because not only is Christ present in the culture, but he has also given power and authority to culture. It is "loyalty to Christ and responsibility for culture" that sustains this model.[49] The "paradox" and "conflict" in this model that exists between Christ and culture is due to the sin in culture. In dialoguing Christ with culture, we see both sin and grace at play. It is a sort of being in the world but not of it, a form of dual citizenship, a kind of model inspired by the biblical tension situation of Christians in their relationship with the world. A human being is "under law, and yet not under law but grace; he is sinner, and yet righteous...," recipient of "divine wrath and mercy."[50] For this ethic, "life must be lived precariously and sinfully, in the hope of a justification which lies beyond history."[51] Far from being a static rejection or an acceptance of culture like the other models above, this model presents a dynamic process. The downside of this approach lies in the fact that,

---

46 Niebuhr, 147.
47 Ibid.,148.
48 Ibid., 150.
49 Ibid., 149.
50 Ibid., 157.
51 Ibid., 43.

being in both worlds, one falls into the tendency of not making any meaningful contribution to anyone of them.

Christ the transformer of culture has a more "hopeful view toward culture."[52] Culture can be "a transformed human life, in and to the glory of God through the grace of God."[53] In this view, God has a heavy positive influence on culture and human activities. The sin inherent in culture is not permanent. It can be transformed or redeemed through Christ. Here, sin is defeated, not by escape but by confronting it with the redeeming and transforming power of the gospel.

I would prefer to consider the Christ of culture paradigm, which puts Christ in "agreement" with culture as the model that fits African Christology. It takes culture more seriously, and interprets and harmonizes it with Christ. It shakes off the culture or theology of repetition imposed by Western colonial-evangelizer who gave no room for African culture to interact freely with Christ and his message. It brings Christ into the African culture, bearing in mind that (without prejudice to his divinity) Christ came from a culture and his teachings were shaped by it.

Conclusion

I have explored how and to what extent anthropology constitutes an indispensable gateway to Christology by showing how African anthropology not only informs African Christology, but it also leads to a better understanding of the latter. With African anthropology, we understand the extent to which a person is defined, not only by his natural biological characteristics but also by his sociocultural environment. Thus, one can say that a person is not only three-dimensional but is also *ubuntu* by virtue of the fact that community life is part and parcel of human existence. In the next chapter, I will examine the sociopolitical context of African Christology – the Church in Africa, presenting how an African ecclesiology (the context and main channel through which the Gospel is preached) is anchored in African anthropology. This will set the ground for an understanding of African Christology vis-à-vis anthropology in Chapter 4.

---

52 Niebuhr, 191.
53 Ibid., 196.

· 3 ·

ECCLESIOLOGY AND CHRISTOLOGY IN AFRICA: REFLECTIONS ON THE SOCIOPOLITICAL DYNAMICS

Introduction

In the previous chapters, I elaborated how an anthropological understanding has shaped Christology in both the Patristic and African settings. In this chapter, I will discuss the sociopolitical context in which the transition from African anthropology to African Christology takes place. In discussing the sociopolitical context of African ecclesiology and Christology in this chapter, I will delimit the geographical scope of Africa that has very much changed over time, because of historical and cultural factors. I will look at the life of the Church in Africa from a historical-theological perspective and the role colonialism played, and still plays, in the Church in Africa, and will touch on the link between colonialism and the Gospel. Understanding how colonialism influenced the Church or how the former interacted with the latter will shed light on the theology of repetition that is still very existent in the continent. I will also examine African ecclesiology from the point of view of one major African ecclesiological model, that is, the Church-as-family model, which seems to relate more to African sensitivity. Lastly, I will look at a few problems that the Church faces in its mission to bring the Good News of Jesus Christ to every corner of the world.

Colonization and Evangelization: Untangling the African Church's Story

The Berlin Conference of 1884, called by the then German chancellor, Otto Von Bismarck, played a very important role in the colonial scramble for Africa. It gave a leeway to major European powers to colonize and divide any African territories of their choice. These powers, whose main objective was exploitation, under the guise of commerce, civilization, and Christianity,[1] superimposed their domains on the African continent, shaping the then politico-geographical map into a permanent liability. In the late 1950s, when many African countries regained their independence, the geographical map of Africa had been irredeemably fragmented, as a result of the years of ignorant, selfish, and greedy acquisitiveness demonstrated in Europe's insatiable search for minerals and markets.

There are several different divisions of Africa, which reflect different interests, but here I will look at it from the colonial angle, because my focus is precisely on how colonialism had shaped the continent, superimposing a colonial mindset, which continues to assail the pastoral, social, and political life in Africa.

The colonial angle has to do with, and is linked to, the European conquest of Africa. It is the unfortunate, end-result of the gradual encroachment, economic penetration, and religious mission of the major European powers who participated in the scramble for Africa.[2] When the European powers discovered Africa, the latter automatically was "opened" to the rest of world, and many of these European countries swiftly deployed their explorers, traders, and missionaries in a bid to establish contacts with the local populace. The initial aim of this rush was to establish new markets for their products and to get raw materials for their home countries. While trade with African countries seemed to be a major factor, it is very tempting, given some statistics, to say that trade was just a disguise. Philip Curtis notes:

> Great Britain had more trade with Africa than any other European country, yet export to Africa in the early Times to Independence, rarely amounted to more than 5 or 6 percent of all British exports, and British import from Africa were less than 5 percent of all imports. Nor were the 1880s an important decade for British African trade.[3]

---

1 Michael Crowder, *The Story of Nigeria* (London: Faber and Faber, 1962), 111.
2 Curtin et al., 398.
3 Ibid., 404.

Curtis believes very strongly that trade was not the main factor in the relationship between Britain and Africa. In fact, he notes that the fear that other European powers might annex a section of Africa and cut off their access to the market was the main anchor of the relationship. As Africa suffered the infringement into its territory due to the scramble, there arose a need to call a conference in Berlin to assure the peace of Europe. The Berlin Conference of 1884 that was called to settle these differences brought about the partition of Africa, which was completed by 1914 at the conclusion of World War I, in dividing the "spoils," and produced the present-day boundaries of Africa.

By 1914, with the exception of Liberia and Ethiopia, which had remained independent states, 90% of Africa had been divided among seven European countries. It is worthwhile to note that for the purpose of this study, the scramble, partition, and presence of Europeans in Africa changed the continent in innumerable ways; new borders were established, and European culture and rule was imposed, replacing the local African culture. Many of these imposed boundaries, which wiped out the natural landmarks or historic ethnic or political boundaries established by the Africans themselves, still endure today and have generated numerous conflicts – much suffering and loss of lives. Postcolonial borders left Africans bunched into countries that oftentimes did not represent their heritage, a problem that still troubles and haunts the second largest continent until the present. A case in point is the Cameroon and Nigeria dispute over Bakassi.

The presence of these European powers created an atmosphere of discomfort and resistance during the early years of European rule. The colonial masters saw their imperial penetration as a mission to bring civilization to savage Africans in order to upgrade them to the fullness of humanity.[4] Some of these resistances took the form of pragmatic violence. Other resistances were more subtle, focusing more on issues of political and economic autonomy. Some communities formed local movements to put up their resistance. At this point, the local villagers did not only have to resist the European colonial policies, but they also had to tackle the African leaders who served as "yes men" to the colonial administration. A case in point was the 1929 Aba Women's Revolt, or Igbo Women's War, in southeastern Nigeria. It is worth underlining the role the women played. The leadership was composed entirely of rural women. What is unique about this movement is the fact that the only mass protest to take place in Nigeria prior to the years leading to independence in 1960 was

---

4   George Ayittey, *Betrayed* (New York City, NY: St. Martin's Press, 1992), 87.

led by women. Feeling that their autonomy was threatened by an impending tax imposed by the local colonial administration, they confronted the then chief, Okugo, who oversaw the tax policies for the colonial administration, and demanded his resignation. Even though the protest led to the loss of about 55 lives, it galvanized the women, giving them more courage to know that they could make their voices heard, because they were a vital part of the culture and society where they counted as nothing. The Aba Women's Revolt was not a movement against the European colonial rule; rather, it aimed at challenging specific policies that the women perceived had originated with the British-imposed warrant chiefs.

One of the strategies that these foreign powers used was to acquire as much land as possible. They did this by signing treaties with the local chiefs, many of whom could not read or write, and so did not understand the implications of what they were agreeing to. There was, for instance, the case of King Lobengula of Matabeleland, leader of the Ndebele. The people, although not liking the fact that their land had been given out, were at the same time willing to accommodate the white settlers. The latter reacted with force and generated even more conflict.[5] It is unfortunate that in the face of all these resistances, the European colonizers typically refused to engage in diplomacy with African rulers, and relied primarily on their weaponry. After World War I, when European powers had been weakened, African nationalism began to arise. The Gold Coast (Ghana), having been proclaimed a British colony in 1874, struggled for and achieved its independence in 1957, but in some cases, violent resistance brought colonial rule to a close. In the case of the Mau-Mau and Maji-Maji uprising in Kenya and Tanzania, respectively, it was a guerrilla warfare that led to change. This was also the case in Rhodesian (Zimbawean) and the Portuguese colonies of Mozambique, Angola, Cape Verde, Guinea-Bissau, and Namibia wars for independence. Resistance was serious in the other places, such as in the Bornu Empire under the Sudanese warrior Rabeh Zubayr, in Opobo under King Jaja, the Itsekiri under Chief Nana Olomu, and in Benin under Ovoramwen Nogbaisi (1888–1897). The case of South Africa was different because, apart from a few mass uprisings and sporadic guerrilla attacks, which eventually brought down the apartheid regime in 1994, there was no military confrontation within South Africa during apartheid.

There is no doubt that the arrival of European powers caused Africa to undergo some shifts in culture. These shifts led to resistance, as many African

---

5 Glass Stafford, *The Matabele War* (London: Longmans, 1968), 269.

tribes, and many kingdoms did all they could to fight back. In his *West African Resistance: The Military Response to Colonial Occupation*, Michael Crowder argues that a good majority of West African states opposed European rule with military action, which included tactical guerrilla warfare[6] against those who argue that colonial occupation was through peaceful negotiation and that the Africans willingly gave up their land and sovereignty, Crowder notes:

> The greater part of this area was occupied by force of arms, and where occupation was peaceful it was usually because African leaders, having seen the success with which European-led forces overcame their neighbors, decided resistance would be futile. There were of course, numerous instances of occupation by peaceful negotiation... but few African leaders desired that political control of their countries should be alienated permanently to the newcomers.[7]

According to Crowder about two-thirds of West African countries resisted colonial penetration in armed conflict,[8] noting that even in situations where African resistance failed, it was because of the overwhelming technological superiority of the colonials.[9] Gann and Duignan, on the other hand, in their *The Rulers of British Africa*, touch on the response of Africans to the European invasion.

> Some societies accepted colonial rule, others resisted. Some chose to corporate with the new rulers in order to manipulate them to their purposes; others tried to opt out of the imperial system by force...[10]

In the face of these European invaders, Africans put up different types of resistance, ranging from primary resistance (bow and arrow), through to gun confrontation. In his article on "The Formulation of Cultural Policy in Colonial Nigeria," Dr. Kalu Ogbu points out:

> Africans did not fold their arms or meekly surrender their fatherland: At least in Ahiara (Mbiase, South Eastern Nigeria), the people dug trenches in which they mounted spikes and covered the top with leaves. The conquering troops after

---

6 Michael Crowder, *West Africa Resistance: The Military Response to Colonial Occupation* (Teaneck, NJ: Holmes & Meier Publishing, 1971), 1–2.
7 Ibid., 3.
8 Ibid.
9 Ibid., 4.
10 L. H Gann and P. Duignan, *The Rulers of British Africa, 1870-1914* (Standford, CA: Standford University press, 1978), 361–62.

the Aro expedition fell into those trenches... In retaliation, some villages were burnt.[11]

In some cases, sometimes after breaking down high walls of resistance, the African tribes, via their chiefs, signed peaceful negotiations with the colonial invaders. To an extent, these negotiations could also be viewed as a culmination of tactical manipulation and intimidation.[12]

With colonialism came not only evangelization into Christianity but also a destruction of the African Traditional or indigenous Religions. In fact, in superimposing their domain on the African continent, the European invaders had as their main objectives exploitation, under the guise of commerce, civilization, and Christianity, thus shaping not only the then politico-geographical map into a permanent liability but also destroying the African Traditional Religions that constituted the life of the people. African Traditional Religions (limited geographically to Africa South of the Sahara Desert; since the northern region was, and is predominantly Muslim) are the religious, cultural, or spiritual manifestations indigenous to the continent of Africa. It provided the structure around which all cultural, economic, political, and social organizations were built. African Traditional Religions believe in a Supreme Being or creator, with myths, folktales, songs and dances, liturgies, rituals, and proverbs, all transmitted orally from generation to generation.

Christianity, under the guise of colonialism, had to resort to denigration and destruction of the African Traditional Religions in order to survive and establish roots. It should be noted that the African traditional religious rulers did not just sit and watch their religions ebb away in favor of a foreign religion. They fought back vigorously. African traditional religious leaders and rulers were also mounting resistance against the colonial invaders. Good examples are the aforementioned Maji-Maji revolt and the Mau-Mau uprisings in Tanzania and Kenya respectively. According to Benjamin. C. Rays, the Maji-Maji revolt was orchestrated by a traditional diviner called Kinjikitile, who was possessed by powerful spirits. In this revolt, religion was used to fight against oppression, as people rushed to the region of Ngarambe to obtain the maji, or

---

11   Kalu Ogbu, "The Formulation of Cultural Policy in Colonial Nigeria," *African Humanities: Traditional and Modern Culture*, Vol. 33, no 2, Enugu: Fourth Dimension (1985): 129–30.
12   Paul Bohannan and Philip Curtin, *Africa and Africans* (Garden City, NY: Waveland Press inc, 1971), 322.

sacred water, which made them invulnerable to white man's bullets.[13] He notes that "Kinjikitile... utilized traditional religious ideas and institutions to mobilize action across ethnic boundaries in an area without political unity. He drew upon the widely-known water cult of Mokero, ancestor and possession cults, and hunting and warfare magic."[14]

African resistance to colonial rule and the importation of Christianity was resisted. It should be noted that Christianity, like colonialism, gradually took root and was implanted into the culture of the people. Missionaries came in their numbers and gained more converts. Even today, when we look at the life of the Church in Africa, it is hard to miss the colonial overtones of the missionary enterprise. In the words of John Mbiti, "... the image that Africans received, and to a great extent still hold, of Christianity, is much colored by colonial rule and all that was involved in it. We are still too close to that period to dissociate one from the other."[15] The colonial undertone of the missionary enterprise actually still affects the reception of the Gospel message by the African.

Some scholars argue that missionary activities had little or nothing to do with colonization, but when one looks at the timing, one is tempted to conclude, like Ayandele, that missionary activities were the "spiritual wing of secular imperialism."[16]

> His coming into interior about the same time as the trader and administrator was unfortunate for the missionary. Africans were often inclined to doubt the genuineness of his propaganda. They could not see their way to making any distinction between him and other white men.[17]

Walter Rodney in his *How Europe Underdeveloped Africa* contends that missionaries were agents of imperialism:

> The Christian missionaries were as much a part of the colonizing forces as were the explorers, traders and soldiers.... [M]issionaries were agents of colonialism in the practical sense, whether or not they saw themselves in that light.[18]

---

13 Benjamin Rays, *African Religions Symbol, Ritual, and Community* (Englewood Cliffs, NJ: Prentice-Hall, 1976), 14.
14 Ibid.
15 Mbiti, *African Religions and Philosophy*, 231.
16 Ayandele et al., *The Growth of African Civilization: The Making of Modern Africa*, 2:135.
17 Ibid.
18 Walter Rodney, *How Europe Underdeveloped Africa* (London: L'ouverture, 1972), 277.

Rodney expresses his dissatisfaction at the fact that while injustice and disrespect for human life were at its peak during concurrent colonization, the missionaries contented themselves in preaching humility, submission, and forgiveness. They made no effort in addressing the ills of the oppressed, but by their "blind eye" actively supported and preserved the status quo, encouraging the Africans to turn the other cheek while looking forward to an abundant, more fulfilling life to come in the next world.[19] He writes:

> The Church's role was primarily to preserve the social relations of colonialism.... the Christian Church stressed humility, docility and acceptance. Ever since the days of slavery in the West Indies, the Church had been brought in on condition that it should not excite the African slaves with doctrine of equality before God.[20]

Commenting on the collaboration of the missionaries and the colonial administrators, and traders and its detriment to Africa, N. S. S. Iwe notes that "missionary cooperation in cultural colonization was purely incidental, unofficial and unintentional."[21] Opposing Ayandele's view about the relationship of the missionaries and the colonial government, Kalu posits that there could not have been any complicity between the two, because, even though the missionaries heavily depended on the colonial government for aid and protection, "they were constantly embarrassed by the morals of the merchants and their brutal exploitation of African societies. . .." According to him, both the missionaries and the colonial invaders had different ideas, not only on how to civilize the black man but also on vital issues affecting their stay and success in the colonies. The colonial encroachers wanted to make use of some traditions as a foundation for their administration, while the missionaries, on the other hand, were bent on annihilating anything that had to do with the local culture and tradition.[22]

When one takes a close look at the Padroado agreement,[23] which gave absolute power and control on ecclesiastical matters to the Portuguese Crown,

---

19 Rodney, *How Europe Underdeveloped Africa*, 278.
20 Ibid.
21 Ibid., 230.
22 Kalu Ogbu, *The History of Christianity in West Africa* (Harlow: Longman, 1980), 7.
23 The Padroado (Patronage) agreement was an agreement between the Holy See and the sovereigns of Spain and Portugal (Papal bull of Pope Martin V and Romanus Pontifex [1455] of Pope Nicholas V), regarding the right to occupy the lands they discovered in exchange for the duty and privileges of supporting and administering Catholic missions in America, Africa, and Asia. On this agreement, Portugal was granted the right not only to administer local Catholic Churches but also of presenting candidates for episcopal and other offices. It was confirmed by Leo X in 1514.

it is very easy to agree with those who proposed the idea that missionary activity was the "spiritual wing of secular imperialism."[24]

As the Church grew in Africa, many Africans wholeheartedly embraced the religion of their colonial masters and, to an extent, it was seen as a source of pride to worship the God of Jesus Christ. Faced with the challenge of a new religion, Africans were therefore faced with either denying and abandoning the faith of their ancestors in favor of Christianity or stubbornly sticking to their own religion. Some outwardly gave in to Christianity, but also adhered to the African Traditional Religion, thus indulging in what, from the standpoint of Christianity, could be a questionable syncretism.

The missionaries did everything in their power to keep out traces of African cultures from Christianity. Africans had to have Christian names before baptism, the tradition of polygamy was frowned upon, and cultural instruments, such as the drums, were forbidden and condemned as demonic, among others. As many Churches started gaining some financial control, with a rise in theologians and philosophers, it was then a question of what the future face of the Church in Africa would look like. Should it just keep repeating the same old, colonial ways of doing things, or adopt an approach that would go beyond the colonial method of theology and ministry?

The colonial mindset placed Africans in a box where they were literally not only unable, incompetent, and immature to manage their own affairs but also to think and self-reflect on their own culture and experiences. It eroded self-confidence, washed out dignity, resourcefulness, and creativity. Iwe explains that colonial mentality is

> ...the belief that the white man or the West knows best and what is best for us in every instance and situation unreflecting tenacity in the maintenance of colonial structures even if these have become outdated, outmoded, dysfunctional and irrelevant to the present needs of Africa; the perpetuation on and addiction to those futile, unfair and unprogressive colonial methods, procedures, techniques... which have served only to uphold the arrogance and pretensions of the colonial masters and to hold down the African in perpetual tutelage and thralldom.[25]

24 Ayandele et al., *The Growth of African Civilization: The Making of Modern Africa*, 2:135.
25 Iwe N. S. S, *Christianity, Culture and Colonialism in Africa* (Port Harcourt: COE, 1985), 199. In his "Western Theology in Africa: Christian Mission in the Light of the Undermining of Scientific Hegemony," Jim Harries highlights the ways in which Western culture has affected the genuine growth of the Gospel in Africa. He advocates for a thorough study of the local African languages as a gateway to effective interaction between the gospel and African cultural realities. (Jim Harries, "Western Theology in Africa: Christian Mission in the Light of the Undermining of Scientific Hegemony," *International Review of*

Colonial mentality had so much affected the Africans that inculturation in some Churches was looked upon as unimportant, and considered as proof of a lack of holiness and orthodoxy. Unfortunately, some African prelates are still too ready to accept anything, if it has a Western label. Islamic historian and philosopher, Ibn Khaldun observed,

> The vanquished always seek to imitate their victors in their dress, insignia, belief, and other customs and usages. This is because men are always inclined to attribute perfection to those who have defeated and subjugated them. Men do this either because the reverence they feel for their conqueror makes them see perfection in them or because they refuse to admit that their defeat could have been brought about by ordinary causes, and hence they suppose that it is due to the perfection of the conquerors. Should this belief persist long, it will change into a profound conviction and will lead to the adoption of all the tenets of the victors and the imitation of all their characteristics.[26]

I posit that this cancerous theology of repetition has oftentimes been an unconscious phenomenon. Sometimes, it has been conscious as some prelates, challenged by the culture of their people, believed that the only way to pay homage to their Roman degree was to stick indiscriminately and unreflectively to Rome. It is not unknown to see prelates fuss about who did or did not study in Rome, or for clergy to make a mockery of liturgical vestments made with local Africa fabric. The missionary pole is still present in Africa. Contrarily, there are also those who seek a complete deconstruction of everything handed on from the Apostles, theologically and pastorally, in favor of a new method, which begins and ends with the local culture. I seek, in this research to get a careful balance between these two poles.

When the missionaries came to Africa with the Gospel, the openness with which the Africans received the good news of Jesus Christ was also matched by many questions around the person of Christ. How could this God-man, Jesus, resonate with Africans? Who is he? Is he one of them, or just an abstract figure? The nationalist struggles and the drive toward independence that characterized Africa in the 1950s and 1960s also created an evangelization atmosphere where Africans started asking the questions that a Euro-centric theology does not ask.

Mission 2, Vol. 106, (2017), 259.) The way of engaging, using locally available languages and resources, is referred to as "vulnerable mission" (p. 260).

26 Ibn Khaldun, *An Arab Philosopher of History* (London: John Murray, 1950), 50–51.

Historical Unfoldment of Modern Evangelization Periods in Africa

Adrian Hastings presents the modern evangelization of Africa in his *Church and Mission in Modern Day Africa*. He distinguishes four periods of evangelization. Each of these periods has specific characteristics, methods of evangelization, and sociopolitical situations. The first period is the "Christian village," or the "chrétienté." It is the longest period of the four, beginning from the time of the arrival of the missionaries around 1840 to around 1890 or 1900.[27] According to Hastings, there was a huge shortage of missionaries during this period and the few who were available focused more on opposing and ending slavery and the slave trade. The slaves who succeeded in escaping, those who were bought out of slavery by the missionaries and those who were cast out of the local society were all brought together in a village setting. The atmosphere in these villages was very favorable to Christian ideals, because it was removed from "pagan" influence.[28] Elizabeth Isichei, commenting on these Christian villages, notes that "the establishment of Christian villages often reflected the belief that Africans could not practice a Christian life in a traditional environment, and that it was necessary to make a clean break."[29] With all the merits of this method, one must note its inwardness. In the words of Hastings, the Christian village put in place a cul-de-sac to evangelization.[30]

The second period falls during the European rule in Africa. Unlike the first period of the Christian village, which favored an inward movement, this period is marked by an outward orientation. Describing this period, Hastings notes that "[t]he missionary was turning his interest outward from the Christian village to a network of catechist' schools established roughly but vigorously over wide areas."[31] Isichei further explains, "After 1914, the ideal Christian village was gradually abandoned, as it was realized that it was essentially a ghetto, and unlikely to transform society as a whole. Increasingly, the emphasis was on the 'bush outstation,' led by a catechist, and the village school."[32] This period opened the way for a more pronounced role of the catechist. The catechists

---

27 Adrian Hastings, *Church and Mission in Modern Day Africa* (London: Burns & Oates, 1967), 80.
28 Ibid.
29 Elizabeth Isichei, *A History of Christianity in Africa: From Antiquity to the Present* (Grand Rapids, MI: Eerdmans, 1995), 135.
30 Hastings, *Church and Mission in Modern Day Africa*, 81.
31 Ibid., 81.
32 Isichei, *A History of Christianity in Africa: From Antiquity to the Present*, 169.

were the ones on the ground. They were the ones who had a great mastery of the terrain, and it made absolute sense to use their knowledge, exposure, and expertise to spread the Gospel. Even though the catechists were empowered and given a central role, the missionaries were still the ones in the lead.[33]

The second period closed just following the end of World War I ushering in the third period. It was the catechists who were at the forefront championing the creation of schools. Gradually, the government started providing funding to these schools, thus giving this period a robust emphasis on building the educational system with up-to-date standards from primary to university level.[34]

The fourth and last period is the independence period. In the words of Hastings, it was characterized by the "growing expense of educational institutions, staffed and equipped for the needs of the times."[35] This period saw a gradual decline in the influence of the Church on education. As the government stepped in with their robust funding in the education sectors, power and control gradually shifted into the hands of the government, leaving the Church's endeavors in this issue very vulnerable. Catechists were replaced by new graduates from government teachers' training schools. This shift of power from the "catechists to the government" actually challenged the Church to discover more effective ways to build up the Christian life.[36]

Church Identity in Africa: Exploring a Major African Ecclesiological Model

In his *Models of the Church*, Avery Dulles proposes six models to explain the meaning of the Church. These models include: the Church as Institution, the Church as Sacrament, the Church as Herald, the Church as Mystical Communion, the Church as Servant, and the Church as Community of Disciples. For Dulles, the models do not exist independent of each other, but together they provide the uniqueness of the Church as a whole. In the same way, as no one Christological title/model can exhaust the person and mystery of Christ (as shall be seen in Chapter 4), so too does Dulles hold that no one model fully captures what the Church in its entirety constitutes.

33 Hastings, 82.
34 Ibid.
35 Ibid.
36 Ibid., 185.

Without prejudice to traditional and biblical images of the Church, such as community of faith, spouse of Christ, and Church as Sacrament, these models challenge us to read the signs of the times and assess, within our present-day sociocultural and political realities, how to answer the fundamental question of *what do Africans say the Church is?*[37] We remind ourselves that to succeed in our missiological endeavor, the Church as a whole, and the African Church in particular, consistent with Vatican II's pastoral constitution *Gaudium et Spes*, needs to constantly update its perception of the world by exploring new and appropriate styles of being Church, based on sociocultural and political realities.

During the first Synod of bishops in Rome in 1995, the African Bishops expressed their intention to reorient the indigenous Church in accordance with the African view of the family. For them, *Ecclesia in Africa Familia Dei in Africa Est*. (The Church in Africa is the family of God in Africa). This is because the African model of the family "emphasizes care for others, solidarity, warmth in human relationships, acceptance, dialogue and trust."[38] The New Evangelization in Africa therefore has as its most important aim, "building up the Church as Family, avoiding all ethnocentrism and excessive particularism, trying instead to encourage reconciliation and true communion between different ethnic groups, favouring solidarity and the sharing of personnel and resources among the particular Churches, without undue ethnic considerations." (EA, 63). Once the Church is lived as family, the mystery of the Church would have been brought to people's concrete realities. In fact, according to *Ecclesia in Africa*,

---

37 A group of African theologian came together to answer questions of ecclesiological concerns and propose insights on the Church in Africa and published their research in *The Church We Want: African Catholics Look to Vatican III*, ed. by Agbonkhianmeghe E. Orobator. In the Introduction titled, *Reading the Signs of the Future*, Agbonkhianmeghe E. Orobator notes that because our environment provides sources and shapes theological discourse, it is indeed a high risk to ignore it. "To ignore it [the environment] is to risk producing a sanitized theology that neither stimulates action nor breathes the gospel of life into the broken conditions of human existence in the world." *The Church We Want: African Catholics Look to Vatican III* ed. by Agbonkhianmeghe E. Orobator, (Maryknoll, NY: Orbis Book, 2016), xv. This calls for a renewed reflection on what the Church is in Africa.

38 John Paul II, *Ecclesia in Africa*, Post-Synodal Apostolic Exhortation to the Bishops Priests and Deacons, Men and Women Religious and all the Lay Faithful on the Church In Africa and Its Evangelizing Mission Towards the Year 2000 (Nairobi, Kenya: Pauline Publications, 1995), #63.

> It is in the heart of the family that parents are by word and example ... the first heralds of the faith with regard to their children.... It is here that the father of the family, the mother, children, and all members of the family exercise the *priesthood of the baptized* in a privileged way 'by the reception of the sacraments, prayer and thanksgiving, the witness of a holy life and self-denial and active charity.' Thus the home is the first school of Christian life and "a school for human enrichment." (EA, 92).

The family is the most basic unit of human society and of the Church. In Africa in particular, it is the foundation on which the social edifice is built (EA, 79). It is also considered the Church in itself.[39] In this regard, the Second Vatican Council terms the family *ecclesia domestica*.[40] Pope John Paul II interprets the Church as a family in terms of the "community of love and life"[41] (John Paul II, Apostolic Exhortation, *Familiaris Concortio*). For Benedict XVI,

> The family is the "sanctuary of life" and a vital cell of society and of the Church. It is here that "the features of a people take shape; it is here that its members acquire basic teachings. They learn to love inasmuch as they are unconditionally loved, they learn respect for others inasmuch as they are respected, they learn to know the face of God inasmuch as they receive a first revelation of it from a father and a mother full of attention in their regard."[42]

Building on *Ecclesia in Africa*'s theme of "Church as Family of God," Benedict XVI further describes the family as a place of belonging, dialogue, solidarity, human respect, and dignity – a place that propagates the culture of forgiveness, peace, and reconciliation.

39 Karl Rahner, *Studies in Modern Theology* (London: Herder, 1965), 293–294. Rahner makes a subtle nuance about attribution the concept of family to Church. He says, "We are not saying that the family is 'like' the Church, or that is 'part' of the Church. The family 'is' the Church in that it is a genuinely ecclesial expression of God's presence among specific communities of people. The family is, in fact, a local Church, and local Churches, are not merely members of the total Church. They are actual realizations of what the Church is as a whole."
40 *Lumen Gentium*. Dogmatic Constitution on the Church (21 November 1964). Accessed on January 2018 at http://www.vatican.va/archive/hist_councils/ii_vatican_council/documents/vat-ii_const_19641121_lumen-gentium_en.html. #11
41 John Paul II, *Familiaris Consortio*, Apostolic Exhortation on the Role of the Christian Family in the Modern World (Homebush, New South Wales: St Paul's Publications, 1982), 8–10.
42 Benedict XVI, *Africae Munus*, Post-Synodal Apostolic Exhortation to the Bishops, Clergy, Consecrated Persons and the Lay Faithfulon the Church in Africa in Service to Reconciliation, Justice and Peace (Nairobi, Kenya: Paulines Publications, 1995), 42.

> The family is the best setting for learning and applying the culture of forgiveness, peace and reconciliation. "In a healthy family life we experience some of the fundamental elements of peace: justice and love between brothers and sisters, the role of authority expressed by parents, loving concern for the members who are weaker because of youth, sickness or old age, mutual help in the necessities of life, readiness to accept others and, if necessary, to forgive them. For this reason, the family is the first and indispensable teacher of peace."(*Africae Munus*, 42)

The Church therefore has a major part to play in reconciliation and in the strengthening of justice and human dignity in society. The family is a domestic Church, a place where seeds of reconciliation are born.

To say that the family is the basis of the Church is to hold, like Hilary O. Okeke, that "the Church begins in the home, not in the parish."[43] According to Okeke, anchoring the Church on the basics of the family is a type of "ecclesiological Copernican revolution" because it is not the Church that provides the image of the family but the family that is the "paradigm of the Church."[44]

In order to avoid subtle misunderstandings, we have to note emphatically at this juncture that the idea of Church as family in Africa does not in any way mean that the African cultural experience would *uncritically* set the terms for the construction of this "new family of God."[45] As a Church family, we are brothers and sisters of the same father and mother. Stripped of all patriarchal dominance common in most African families, the Church family of God in Africa is based not only on the way Jesus lived family life but also on the African concept of *ubuntu*, as discussed in Chapter 2. It is based on a new kind of relationship, which, while not excluding periodic division among its members on certain issues (Lk 12:52ff), certainly prioritizes an openness that knows no limits (Mk 3:31–35).[46] Because the Church as family goes beyond clan and ethnic divide, it has the potential to heal not only the wounds of division within the Christian communities but also between Christian communities and those of other faiths (EA, 65).

Calling the Church a family automatically makes it a place of nurturing and education. As the African family has the responsibility to look after its

---

43 Hilary O. Okeke, "From 'Domestic Church' to 'Family of God': The African Christian Family in the African Synod," *Nouvelle Revue de Science Missionnaire*, no. 52 (1996): 193.
44 Ibid.
45 Eluchukwu Uzukwu, *A Listening Church: Autonomy and Communion in African Churches* (Maryknoll, NY: Orbis, 1996), 66.
46 Ibid.

members, especially the old and sick, grandparents, parents, and widows without children, so too does the Church. It is a place of mutual respect, where parents love and assist the children who in turn obey, honor, and care for their parents, as exemplified in biblical families (Ex 20:12; Dt 5:16; Prv 19:26; 30:11; Sir 3:1–16). The Church as family manifests to the world the work of the Spirit of God, who desires unity among His children. This makes the Church a living, active family, rooted in African culture consisting of children of the same father, ancestor. This image opens and broadens our understanding of what the Church consists of, while emphasizing co-responsibility in the work of mission.

The concept of family points to an ecclesiology of being and cherishing beyond differences. The focus on an ecclesiology hinged on the notion of family serves as an organizing principle to regulate our relationship not only with Christ's humanity and divinity but also with one another and with all other sociocultural, political, and economic concerns within the Church. Using the model of the Church as family as it emerged from the 1994 African Synod of Bishops, Orobator noted:

> [W]e recall that when the synod opted for the model of Church-as-family, it noted the compatibility of this model with some fundamental cultural and anthropological disposition of Africans. Naturally, therefore, elements of cultural anthropology intermingle with theological considerations in the discussion of this topic.[47]

Developing an ecclesiology based on the African understanding of family indeed comes with far-reaching implications. Orobator holds that it "undercuts the basis of monopolistic clericalism and episcopalism, rendering them counter-productive and inimical to the social mission of the Church."[48] In addition, calling the Church family means recognizing the legitimate vocation of the larger body of the Church, that is, the lay Christian members, to participate creatively and actively. In other words, the Church as a family enjoys the empowerment of its members, recognizes the *sensus fidei* from which it derives its strength, meaning, and ultimate expression. Moreover, the Church as family model "eliminates any attempt to preach pietistic quietism as a virtue in Africa." This makes the image of the "Church as a flock of sheep, led by a shepherd" to be very dangerous and foreign to African traditional sensibility, because it feeds on a top-down approach that stifles not only personal initiative

---

47 Agbonkhianmeghe E. Orobator, *The Church as Family: African Ecclesiology in Its Social Context* (Nairobi: Pauline Publications, 2000), 138.
48 Ibid., 143.

and growth but also the work of the Holy Spirit received at baptism. The synod fathers noted that "a certain idea of the Church produced a type of lay person who was too passive" and called upon every member of the Church family to "concentrate resolutely on the grace of your Baptism and Confirmation and utilize every initiative which the Holy Spirit will give you, so that our Church may rise to the challenge of her Mission."[49]

In 2008, Orobator wrote a book titled *Theology Brewed in an African Pot*, in which he discusses theology from the point of view of Africa's unique socio-cultural perspective. Klaus Fielder also edited a book in 2000 called *Theology Cooked in an African Pot*. Both of these books touch on the specific nature of African theology and underline the need to do, even in theological matters what Moses did in the burning bush when approaching cultures, "Take off your shoes for where you are standing is holy ground." (Ex 3:5). Cultures must be respected because culture is holy and carries meanings that go beyond their physical expressions. Cultures must be respected because they provide context.

The concept of the African pot used in these two titles is closely related to the African proverb *"The cooking pot sits on three stones."* Traditional African cooking is done by placing the pot on a wood-burning fireplace made up of three stones arranged in a tripod shape, with fire lighted in the space created by the stones beneath the pot, using wood. These three stones provide support, sustainability, and stability to the pot. The stones also provide space for the firewood to penetrate, touch each other, and unite in the middle, directly under the pot, creating space for the fire to be strong enough to provide the heat needed for preparing the meal. It is with this background that Orobator, drawing from the riches of the three stones, notes that, metaphorically speaking, the Church as family, at the service of the society, sits on three stones – life, solidarity, and service.[50]

The first stone is life. The Igbo name: *Nduka*, meaning life is supreme, expresses the African regard for the sanctity of life. The fundamental purpose of human existence is the protection, preservation, and attainment of the fullness of life.[51] Amadi Elechi recounts, "In many (African) tribes, the

---

49 *Special Message of the Synod for Africa* 1994 at https://www.vatican.va/roman_curia/synod/documents/rc_synod_doc_20090319_instrlabor-africa_en.html, accessed on January 2018, #57. In this light, Orobator says, "An authentic contemporary African ecclesiology can hardly prescribe pietism or passivism as a virtue in Africa." Orobator, *The Church as Family*, 143.
50 Orobator, 164.
51 Ibid.

killing of a kinsman, the antithesis of caring for him, was not only a crime but also an abomination. After the murderer had been executed, his family would have to perform sacrifices and rites to remove the stain of evil and ward off the anger of the gods."[52] God is the originator, creator, and sustainer of creation and life. Life is a communal affair which involves a relationship and communion between God and human beings.[53] Chapter 3 will dwell elaborately on the concept of life in African culture, illustrating the unique sociocultural dimensions of life.

The second stone is Solidarity.[54] This stone is informed by the fact that community is key. Community is used here in the same sense as Oliver Onwubiko, who, talking about the important place of community in African culture, distinguishes between intercommunity and intracommunity. According to Onwubiko, "Intercommunity relationship realised in the interaction between individuals of different communities is different from the intra-community relationship based on inter-personal relationship realized in a definite community, among its members, to express the practical traditional African concept of humane living."[55] Solidarity informs life both within the community and between communities. It informs how members interact with leaders and those responsible for the resources of the community. Orobator remarks:

> The community stands together in good times and in bad times for life.... It is not enough to define the Church-as-family negatively, that is, by concentrating only on what it opposes. More importantly, this Church is defined positively, that is, essentially by what it *pro*-poses. Church-as-family stands for "more human life...in striving for life, the Church does not avoid striving against structures of sin, death and destruction."[56]

The third stone is service or servanthood.[57] For the Church to be family, it must stand for the poor. Pope Francis never ceases to insist on the Church's concern for the poor and vulnerable. For him,

---

52 Elechi Amadi, *Ethics in Nigerian Culture* (Ibadan: Heinemann Educational Books, 1982), 58.
53 Francis O. C Njoku, *Essays in African Philosophy, Thought & Theology* (Owerri: Claretian Institute of Philosophy & Clacom Communication, 2002), 169.
54 Orobator, 165.
55 Oliver Onwubiko, *African Thought, Religion and Culture* (Enugu: Snaap Press, 1991), 19.
56 Orobator, 165.
57 Ibid.

God shows the poor "his first mercy." This divine preference has consequences for the faith life of all Christians, since we are called to have "this mind... which was in Jesus Christ" (*Philippians* 2:5). Inspired by this, the Church has made an option for the poor which is understood as a "special form of primacy in the exercise of Christian charity, to which the whole tradition of the Church bears witness".... This is why I want a Church which is poor and for the poor. They have much to teach us. Not only do they share in the *sensusfidei*, but in their difficulties they know the suffering Christ. We need to let ourselves be evangelized by them.[58]

Commenting on Pope Francis' vision for the Church, which of course, squarely connects with this third ecclesiological stone that sustains the Church, Dr. Bienvenu Mayemba writes:

> Pope Francis would like the Church to recognize the special place of the poor in the midst of God's people and kingdom (EG, nos. 197–201), to develop a greater care and concern for the vulnerable (EG, nos. 209–16), and to promote social justice as an aspect of distributive justice that includes the just distribution of goods, resources, and income (EG, nos. 202–208). For him, if the Church wants to stay credible or become more credible, it should face the challenges of today's world (EG, nos. 52–75) and say no to what is bad, wrong and evil...to the new adulatory of money (EG, nos. 55–56) and to a financial system that rules rather than serve.[59]

Like the three stones that support and provide space for the African pot to receive the fire which cooks a good meal, these three ecclesiological stones all go together to sustain and nourish the Church as family. None of them works and stands in isolation. A popular African proverb comes to mind here to express the complementarity of the three stones: "One stone no dey cook pot." (One stone cannot cook a meal.) Just as the three stones beneath the pot unite to embrace the flames and bring forth a wholesome feast, these three ecclesiological pillars stand as one to nurture and fortify the Church family. In unity, they flourish; in isolation, they falter.

---

58 Pope Francis, *Evangelii Gaudium*, Apostolic Exhortationto the Bishops, Clergy, Consecrated Persons and the Lay Faithfulon the Proclamation of the Gospelin today's world, at https://www.vati can.va/cont ent/france sco/en/apo st_e xhor tati ons/docume nts/papa-francesco_esortazione-ap_20131124_evangelii-gaudium.html , accessed on January 2018, 1998, #198.

59 Bienvenu Mayemba SJ., "Reviving a Church of the Poor and for the Poor, AndReclaiming Faith Doing Justice and Seeking Liberation Convergence between Pope Francis and Jean-Marc Ela," in *The Church We Want: African Catholics Look to Vatican III*, ed. by Agbonkhianmeghe E. Orobator (Maryknoll, NY: Orbis, 2016), 51.

Key Issues Framing the Discourse in the African Church

In this section, I will look at three major issues that the Church as a family faces in Africa. These include problems like anthropological poverty and human immunodeficiency virus/acquired immune deficiency syndrome (HIV/AIDS). I will also examine the existence of political, social, and psychological vulnerability that affects the people who daily seek the face of Christ in the Church. These problems negatively affect the spiritual life of Christians.

Anthropological Poverty

The term "anthropological poverty" was coined by the Cameroonian Jesuit, Engelbert Mveng. He used it as a metaphor to refer to the situation of the political, economic, religious vulnerability, alienation, and poverty of the African continent. According to him, anthropological poverty is the direct effect of the long years of slavery and colonialism that have beset the African continent.[60] Colonization played a vital role in dispossessing Africans who were considered and treated like sub-human beings with no history or culture.[61] It has affected the dignity of Africans, paving the way for the present-day fragility, dependence, and alienations, which in turn opened avenues for the normalization of the "Stockholm syndrome" tendency in the continent. Ngussan Sess Julien says that because of anthropological poverty

> Africans are poorer than during the colonial time and worse than during the pre-colonial period. This poverty appears in their inability to envision a brighter future for themselves. People seem to be condemned to perpetuate their own suffering and remain entrapped in their predicament of domination, dependence, poverty, fragility and alienation.[62]

---

60 Engelbert Mveng, "Impoverishment and Liberation: A Theological Approach for Africa and the Third World," in *Paths of African Theology*, Edited by Rosino Gibellini (Maryknoll, NY: Orbis, 1994), 156.
61 Engelbert Mveng and Benjamin Lipawing, *Theologie, Liberation et Culture Africaine. Dialogue Sur l'anthropologie Negro Africaine* (Yaounde: Presence Africaine, 1996), 95.
62 Julien Ngussan, "Conversion to Jesus Christ in the Context of Anthropological Poverty of Africa: A Case Study of Cote D'Ivoire," Doctor in Sacred Theology Dissertation, Jesuit School of Theology of Santa Clara University, 2015, 31.

Seen as the lack and privation of the basic necessities of life,[63] poverty also extends to the domain of the spiritual, the moral, the cultural, and the sociological. In the words of Mveng, it is "a kind of poverty which no longer concerns only exterior or interior goods or possessions but strikes at the very being, essence, and dignity of the human person."[64]

For Mveng, anthropological poverty can be either active or passive. It is active when the cause of the poverty is from an external agent who dispossesses the people and deprives them of their identity and ability to succeed in effecting their own wellbeing. On the other hand, it can be passive when people become poor by losing what they have and their ability to know and effect their interest.[65] A combination of both the passive and the active constitute the situation in present-day Africa in which poverty, depersonalization, and a Stockholm-syndrome-like assimilation pushes people to think-like, and conform to, and be like the master.[66]

The Church in Africa, faced with this situation is aware of the vicious circle within which the Christian family is confronted every day, as people daily try to seek recourse to the very mechanism and institutions that have caused them to be in poverty and misery in the first place. This constitutes an added challenge to the Church, which finds itself in a sociopolitical context where the good news and ultimate fullness of life are preached within a sea of bad news.[67]

HIV/AIDS

When the HIV/AIDS epidemic broke out in Africa in the 1980s, many Africans reacted with deep skepticism and denial. In fact, in some popular anglophone circles, many considered it as an "American invention to discourage sex."[68] In some francophone settings, SIDA (French acronym for AIDS) was

---

63 Engelbert Mveng, "Impoverishment and Liberation," 155–56.
64 Ibid., 156.
65 Yvon Christian Elenga, "Engelbert Mveng (1930–1995), l'invention d'un Discour Theologique," in *Recoil d'homages* (Kinshasa: Editions Loyola-Canisius, 2005), 133.
66 Yves Kizito Menanga, SJ., "Meriter Notre Bonheur: Deux Meditation Philosophiques Sur La Pensee Du Pere Engelbert Mveng," in *Recuil d'Hommages* (Kinshasa: Editions Loyola-Canisius, 2005), 96.
67 Julien Ngussan, "Conversion to Jesus Christ in the Context of Anthropological Poverty of Africa," 3.
68 Brooke Grundfest Schoepf, "AIDS," in *A Companion to the Anthropology of Politics*, ed. D. Nugent and J. Vincent (Malden: Blackwell Publishers, 2004), 46.

referred to as "*syndrome imaginaire pour decouragerlesamoureux*" (imaginary syndrome to discourage lovers).[69] Today, the denial of the existence of AIDS among the people has greatly diminished but not completely disappeared. Pope John Paul II stressed the seriousness of this disease that affects the whole of humanity.

> AIDS threatens not just some nations or societies but the whole of humanity. It knows no frontiers of geography, race, or age or social condition. The threat is so great that indifference on the part of public authorities, condemnatory or discriminatory practices toward those affected by the virus or self-interested rivalries in the search for a medical answer should be considered forms of collaboration in this terrible evil which has come upon humanity.[70]

Worrying details of HIV/AIDS abound in Africa in general and in sub-Saharan Africa in particular.[71] Today in sub-Saharan Africa, HIV/AIDS breeds a certain degree of hopelessness among God's people, leading to the exclusion of the suffering from the table of life.[72] The Church's response, as a family of God, reflects, to a great extent, the African principles of humanism (*ubuntu*) manifested in solidarity, which calls for non-discrimination against people living with the virus. Far from being a punishment from God, the Church advocates on behalf of those living with the virus, encouraging people not to impose on them, the onus of "sinners."

---

69 Simon Watney, *Practices of Freedom: Selected Writings on HIV/AIDS* (Durham: Duke University Press, 1994), 103.
70 Quoted by Lisa Sowle Cahil, *Theological Bioethics: Participation, Justice, Change* (Washington D.C.: Georgetown University Press, 2005), 163.
71 According to the 2016 Joint United Nations Program on HIV/AIDS, of the 36.7 million people living with HIV in the world, 6.1 million were in western and central Africa; of the 1.8 million new HIV infections in the world, 370,000 were in western and central Africa; of the 1.0 million AIDS-related deaths in the world, 310,000 were in western and central Africa. We also note, as per the 2016 Joint United Nations Program on HIV/AIDS that of the about 5,000 new HIV infections (adults and children) a day in Africa as a whole, about 64% are in sub-Saharan Africa. UNAIDS 2017, Joint United Nations Program on HIV/AIDS, at http://www.unaids.org/sites/default/files/media_asset/20170720_Data_book_2017_en.pdf, Accessed on January 2018, 12
72 George William Byarugaba, 2009, "The Response of the Roman Catholic Church in South Africa to the Problems of HIV/AIDS in Light of the Modern Catholic Social Teaching," Jesuit School of Theology of Santa Clara University, 101.

Political, Social, and Psychological Vulnerability

Another problem that faces the people of God in Africa is their political, social, and psychological vulnerability. Sub-Saharan African countries enjoy a whole range of natural resources that can enrich their populations and serve as a source of political, social, and psychological empowerment. Unfortunately, because of corruption and mismanagement, many people are left to themselves, creating the serious situation of vulnerability.

Politically, many African states still owe strong allegiance to their former colonial masters. This makes it difficult to effect meaningful development that would strengthen the people. Many states do not have the power, sovereignty, and independence to implement their mission for the good of the people. Many African governments, as part of the terms and negotiation for independence from France, signed secret agreements not only granting the latter privileged access to its raw materials but also military protection of new regimes. A case in point is Ivory Coast where the French are in charge of the national territorial security.[73] This gives the former colonial powers the chance to change political regime as they see fit. This leads to a situation where the leaders, instilled by a spirit of selfishness and power, decide to focus on amassing wealth and keeping power by pleasing the former colonial masters. The people are therefore sacrificed, disenfranchised, and disempowered.

Socially and economically, poverty as a result of chronic corruption affects people very negatively, creating a situation where the rich become richer and the poor become poorer. The influence of Westernization on the continent also goes a long way to erode African values. Values such as hospitality and generosity now compete with egoism, nepotism, and tribalism, which are all faces of the individualism prevalent in the Western world. Psychological vulnerability, which could come about as a result of political and socio-economic problems leads to self-hate, self-negation, fear, and lack of confidence. Psychological fragility produces a "morbid imagination which inhibits the development of self-worth, the sense of dignity and responsibility, the source of creativity and progress."[74] It is so disempowering that it leads to fatalism – a state of defeat whereby one abandons one's lot to fate, feeding exclusively on the imaginary hope of a future change of life circumstance.[75]

---

73 Julien Ngussan, "Conversion to Jesus Christ in the Context of Anthropological Poverty of Africa," 73.
74 Ibid., 78.
75 Ibid.

Conclusion

Alioune Diop states that because of colonization and an ideology that encourages repetition, the "Western religion has succeeded in converting African Christians into a people without soul or visage, a pale shadow of the dominating pride of the Christian West."[76] The effect of colonialism on the African Church is very evident in its tendency to repeat colonial theological methodologies, with little recourse to the local context. Looking at the local cultural context in Africa, and without prejudice to other traditional images and models of the Church, the Church as family connects very well with the people. It is very interesting to note that the phrase "family of God" appears 19 times in the second Vatican Council: six in *Lumen Gentium*, nine in *Gaudium et Spes*, and one each in the encyclicals *Christus Dominus*, *Unitatis Redintegratio*, *Ad Gentes*, and *Presbyterorum Ordinis*.[77]

The African family is a "heuristic paradigm" that gives insights into a renewed vision of Church. Given the social context of Africa, the "Church-as-family at the service of society embodies a community of solidarity at the service of life."[78] We note with Orobator that African ecclesiology assumes two essential factors. First, "only a Church that remains in constant touch with the real-life situation of Africans can become the Church-as-family at the service of society."[79] Second, "ordinarily, the family creates the place par excellence for attaining, protecting, and propagating the fullness of life."[80]

Also, worthy of attention is the analogical and reciprocal resemblance between the triune God and our human family. The former serves as a model for the latter, bringing out far-reaching theological implications. In fact,

> If the Triune God serves as a model for the Church as family, then the narrow bond of kindship and consanguinity no longer constitute a hindrance to our entrance into a membership of this Church.... Because filial adoption and the grace of Baptism become the most important qualifications, entrance into the Church-as-God's family

---

[76] Alioune Diop quoted by John Parratt, *Reinventing Christianity: African Theology Today* (Grand Rapids, MI: Eerdmans Publishing Company/Trenton Africa World Press, 1995), 7.

[77] Kusiele J.M Dabire, "Eglise-Famille de Dieu," *Revue de l'Institut Catholique de l'Afrique de l'Ouest*, Vol. 25. no. 14–15 (1996): 81.

[78] Orobator, *The Church as Family*, 138.

[79] Ibid., 74.

[80] Bruce L. Shelley, *Church History in Plain Language*, 50.

implies a rupture of those restrictive and particularistic ties of consanguinity or kinship... *the waters of baptism is thicker than blood.?*[81]

Anchoring the Church in Africa on the image of family does not in any way mean that other models of the Church do not apply to Africa. Neither does it mean that this model owes its origin to the African Church. In fact, Scripture[82] and Patristic writings[83] use family terminologies to refer to the Church. It simply means that this model appeals to African sensibility more than any other model. It is precisely because it is more appealing to African sociocultural and anthropological sensibilities that *Ecclesia in Africa* hopes that it will deepen and strengthen the Gospel in Africa, help solve some societal issues, and bring about a more significant contribution to the ecclesiology of the universal Church. In the next chapter, I will study five major African Christological models. This will enable us to grasp how African Christology is firmly grounded in the principles of African anthropology.

---

81 Bruce L. Shelley, *Church History in Plain Language*, 148.
82 We note that Scriptures attest to and uses images of the Church in relation to family terminology. Jesus asked us to call God "Father." God is addressed using the very intimate, family term "*Abba*, Father" (Gal 4:6). Vincent Branick, *The House Church in the Writings of Paul* (Wilmington, De: Michael Glazier, 1989), 16; Also see Robert Banks, *Paul's Idea of Community* (Peabody, MA: Hendrickson Publishers, Inc., 1998), 56. and Philip F. Esler, "Family Imagery and Christian Identity in Gal 5:13 to 6:10," in *Halvor Moxnes: Constructing Early Christian Families* (London: Routledge, 1997), 134–44.
83 Ignatius of Antioch (died c. 115) calls the Church "household of the master" (Ignatius of Antioch, *Epistula ad Ephesios* 6; PG 6, 650). In his commentary on Mt 24:45, Hilary of Poitiers (315–367) uses the word "family" to refer to the Church. Hilary of Poitiers, *In Matthaeum* 27; PL 9, 1058. Also, in *The City of God*, the bishop of Hippo, Augustine (354–430), referring to the Church, says, "The whole family of God, most high and most true, has therefore a consolation of its own – a consolation which cannot deceive." Augustine, *The City of God*, I, 35 (New York: The Modern Library, 1950), 34; 38; cf. Tertullian, *De Patientia* 2; PL 1, 1252. The "Church as mother" is another Patristic family terminology or metaphor used to refer not only to the selfless motherly love of the Church toward all people but also to the understanding of the Church's role in generating new children through baptism. (Henri de Lubac, *The Motherhood of the Church* (San Francisco: Ignatius Press, 1982), 47–58.)

· 4 ·

WHO DO YOU SAY THAT I AM?' IN AFRICA: AN EXPLORATION OF CHRISTOLOGICAL MODELS

Introduction

In his classic novel, *Things Fall Apart*, the African novelist, Chinua Achebe, describes the advent of Christianity in an Ibo village in the southeastern part of Nigeria called "Umuofia." The Christian missionaries assembled the local inhabitants, speaking to them about the One, true God, the creator of all things. When the mention of Jesus, the Son of God came up, the people began to retort with so many questions: "You told us with your own mouth that there is only one God, now you talk about his son. He must have a wife, then."[1] This brings to light the African Christological problematic and the response to the question of who Jesus is for the African people.

To answer the "Who do you say that I am?" in the context of African Christianity, I will examine some major African Christological titles in order to see how African anthropology informs African Christology in a unique way, similar to how the various anthropological outlooks of the school of Alexandria and Antioch influenced Patristic Christology which consequently became normative, thanks to the early ecumenical councils, which culminated at Chalcedon.

---

1 Chinua Achebe, *Things Fall Apart* (Ibadan: Anchor, 1956), 103.

Articulating an African Christology and highlighting its anthropological background is indeed relevant, given the fact that for many centuries, in spite of Africa's cultural specificity,

> Christ has been presented as the answer to the questions a white man would ask, the solution to the needs that western man would feel, the Savior of the world of the European world-view, the object of the adoration and prayer of historic Christendom. But if Christ were to appear as the answer to the questions that Africans are asking, what would he look like? If he came into the world of African cosmology to redeem man as Africans understand him, would he be recognizable to the rest of the Church Universal? And if Africa offered him the praises and petitions of her total, uninhibited humanity, would they be acceptable?[2]

This shows that the problems faced by the Church in Africa are different from those faced by the Church elsewhere; these are problems to which European theology can provide no relevant ready-made answers. For this reason, I will examine five major African Christological titles.

Christ as Master of Initiation

In Africa, initiation has to do with undergoing certain rites in order to start a new phase in life. Every initiation facilitates transformation and transition. Initiation rites – such as the rite of adulthood, the rite of eldership, and the rite of ancestorship – foster transformation on the part of the beneficiary. For the Bakoko people in Cameroon, the transition or passage into adulthood, called *ligwee*, is an indispensable stage for every male child. Similar to the Bakoko of Cameroon, the Edda community in Igboland, belonging to the former Afikpo Division in the southeastern part of Nigeria, also has an initiation into manhood or puberty for adolescent boys. Theirs is both extensive and expensive. It marks the end of emulating other adults and introduces the young adult into a life that other youngsters would be called to emulate. Simon Ottenberg describes its major characteristic functions as follows: "The initiations bring them more fully into adult life in their compounds and agnatic groupings, establish a life-long pattern of a loving but separate adult relationship with their mothers, are an early prelude to marriage, and a prerequisite to full

---

2 John V. Taylor, *The Primal Vision: Christian Presence Amid African Religion* (London: SCM Press, 1963), 7.

relationships with the boys' matrilineal kin."[3] It is the time in which circumcision takes place, making it possible for the child to become a mature individual.

The impact of circumcision on the society is significant, and indeed very determinant, for the success and life of the adult male. According to Mbiti, "What affects the initiate affects corporately the parents, the relatives, the neighbours and the living dead."[4] It cultivates solidarity among the youth and gives the initiate the right to share full privileges, duties, and responsibilities of the adult world. For the Bakoko people, the time of convalescence after circumcision is a very crucial time, for during that time, the initiate is secluded and schooled on a variety of life issues. In general, "initiation rites have a greater educational purpose. The occasion often marks the beginning of acquiring knowledge which otherwise would not be accessible to those who have not been initiated."[5] For the Eda people in Igboland, it provides sources of informal education and military training. The rigorous spiritual and ritual activities that qualify one for this lasts as long as eight or nine years.[6] It is a type of schooling and military training in Edda culture, equivalent to the eight-year academic school year.

> The strenuous training exposes the candidates to the art of traditional warfare, and use of herbs. The hard drilling steels them against hazardous task of defense. War veterans are invited continually to give the neophytes lectures, which dispose to acquire these skills.[7]

This training makes the boys become viable soldiers with the reliable capability to defend the land in case of military aggression. It imbues into the initiates courage, patience, endurance, and the ability to withstand hunger, as they endure hardship and austere conditions during the process of initiation.

In understanding Jesus' life as related by the gospels and the New Testament, and analyzing them in relation to African traditional initiation rites, it is safe to say that, in the African context, Jesus is indeed a Master of Initiation[8]

---

3 Simon Ottenberg, *Boyhood Rituals in an African Society: An Interpretation*, (Seattle, WA: University of Washington Press: 1989) 135. It therefore serves as a prelude to marriage.
4 Mbiti, *African Religions and Philosophy*, 121.
5 Ibid., 122.
6 Christopher Agwu, *Ipu Ogo: Traditional Rites of Initiation into Manhood in Edda* (Owerri: Nnamdi Printing Press, 1994), 6.
7 Agwu, *Ipu Ogo*, 6.
8 Anselme T. Sanon, *Enraciner l'évangile: Initiations africaines et pédagogie de la foi* (Paris, Cerf, 1982).

because after being initiated into the Jewish tradition by being named, circumcised, and presented in the temple (Lk 2:21; 2:22–40), and baptized by John in the Jordan (Mk 1:9), He himself perfected the concept of initiation by his works, life, and resurrection. His herald, John the Baptist, acclaimed, "I baptize you with water for repentance, but after me will come One more powerful than I, whose sandals I am not worthy to carry. He will baptize you with the Holy Spirit and with fire" (Mt 3:11). This makes Jesus' initiation unlike that of others before him. In fact, "the initiatory rhythm that he inaugurates is that of his entire life – [To] be born, to grow, to suffer, to die, and to be buried with the desires of an endless happiness."[9]

We see how Jesus' oblation and total giving of self on the cross is the definitive act of initiation of himself, as it is written, "For by one sacrifice he has made perfect forever those who are being made holy." (Heb 10:14). In this passage, we see not only a vocabulary of initiation but also the stages of the initiation experience, into which Jesus enters on his own freewill.[10] Jesus' uniqueness in matters of initiation and the response he got makes Anselme Sanon to note that "in the footsteps on this initiation master, so full of constancy and perseverance, the disciples race to the fore, catching what he says word for word, desirous of beholding what he delineates in draft, hoping to arrive where he leads."[11] In him and by him, Jesus is the definitive model of initiation.[12]

Like a typical African master of initiation, Jesus' initiation is community-oriented and directed toward the welfare of the people. He promoted the best of Israel consciousness as God's covenant people by castigating all forms of legalism, ritualism, and religiosity against the wish of the scribes and Pharisees, who, under the pressure of Roman imperial rule, had undermined the fact that they were brothers and sisters, made in the image of God, equal in dignity and called to be stewards of God's creation. Calling the people in his time to a brotherhood and sisterhood of equals puts him at loggerhead with the religious leaders, who later decided to kill him by crucifixion. Jesus' rising from the dead made him the source of eternal salvation for those who believe in him. By sending the Holy Spirit to teach and strengthen humanity, Jesus singles himself as an ideal Master of Initiation, helping to bring the new people of God to a sustainable growth, visible maturity, and *ubuntu* community life, based on

---

9 Anselme T. Sanon, "Jesus Master of Initiation," in *Faces of Jesus in Africa*, ed. by Robert J. Schreiter (Maryknoll, NY: Orbis, 1991), 94.
10 Sanon, "Jesus Master of Initiation," 95.
11 Ibid.
12 Ibid.

the love of God and others. Via the Church, and led by the Holy Spirit, Jesus Christ is the true master of initiation who initiates God's people to the mystery of the Trinitarian God of Christian tradition. In the words of Sanon:

> Jesus is the initiation elder. . . ..what he has done more than anything else is to posit the act of redemption as the initiatory "great deed": for us, the mystery of his death and resurrection is easily deciphered in an initiatory context. He becomes the eldest child, the eldest sibling, the master in initiation, at once in solidarity with, and mediator of, his sisters and brothers. . .he is the initiation chief because he alone has carried to its term the hidden project at the heart of any initiatory tradition: that of leading a human candidacy to the full authentic dignity and worth of children and siblings in the community of human beings. If until now, the various initiatory undertakings, in their manifold rituals, have adopted so many initiation masters, we, for our part, know but one, and in his discipleship we are all siblings. (Mt 23:8)[13]

Like any good African master of initiation who uses symbols as vehicles of the highest value of community, Jesus used symbols to transmit his love and life to humans, especially by means of the sacraments. For Sanon, Christ's death, burial, and resurrection (Rm 6:1–11) are the symbols of the paschal, baptismal experience, as well for the initiation of each baptized person.[14] All the various rituals and traditions of initiation reach their ultimate perfection and fulfilment in the life of Christ's community, making it possible for people to transition easily from their complex traditional rituals to the one mystery of God incarnate, from all their secret words to the one Word of God, from all the trees of initiation, to the one tree of the cross, and from all the diverse traditions to the one tradition in Jesus.[15]

Jesus is indeed an ideal master of initiation. Unlike the traditional African master of initiations, whose rituals and symbols are external to themselves, Jesus fulfills everything he says by the example of his own person. He delivers not words alone but his own life, thereby accomplishing the will of the father in assuming his solidarity with his fellow human beings. In the words of Sanon, "[I]n him, we have the definitive model of initiation, in fidelity to our fragile human rhythm and our desire to attain the invisible infinite."[16]

We note, however, that this model of Jesus as Master of Initiation is weak because of the fact that many Africans today no longer live in situations where

---

13 Sanon, "Jesus Master of Initiation," 96.
14 Ibid.
15 Sanon, *Enraciner l'évangile*, 183.
16 Sanon, "Jesus Master of Initiation," 99.

initiation rites are commonplace. This is because the influence of Westernization has infiltrated some African cultures.

Christ as Healer

Another major African Christological model is that of Jesus as Healer. It very much meets the Chalcedonian Jesus paradigm from the fact that it articulates both the human and divine attributes of Jesus. As the kingdom of God is at the center of Jesus' preaching, so too are healing and exorcism parts of his activities. The gospel of Mark presents Jesus as an exemplary healer who heals both the inside and the outside of the person. "Go in peace and be healed of your afflictions" (Mk 5:34b). The clause "go in peace" more naturally suggests interior wellbeing.[17] In the words of Roger Haigh, Jesus possesses

> the ability to heal, but without being a professional physician. His healing power is connected with being able to mediate God's authority and power over sickness. He is an exorcist, able to drive out spirits, and this is closely connected with healing. Such a religious figure can drive out demons also forgive sins. . ..Jesus' roles as healer of the physically ill, exorciser of the oppressed, and dispenser of forgiveness to sinners, must be seen in the context in which they belong, namely charismatic Judaism.[18]

The image of Jesus Christ as healer resonates very much with the Scriptures because Jesus went around the cities healing people of all their sins, sicknesses, and evil. The evangelist Matthew notes that Jesus traveled all of Galilee, teaching in the synagogues, proclaiming the good news of the kingdom of God, and healing every illness among the people (Mt 4:23). This healing ministry or role of Jesus is consistent with his mission of bringing life to the full to all of humanity (cf. Jn10:10).

African traditional healers have supernatural powers and knowledge. They have the capacity to "dialogue" with the divine, who reveals to them the origin and cure for any difficulty or sickness. Traditional healers have divine powers to reward and punish, to cure and inflict curses. This is because, being a partaker in both the divine and human world, the traditional healer has ready access to the spiritual realm, which in fact does contain many mysterious elements that can either enhance life or make it extremely difficult and miserable. The

---

17 Joel B. Green and Mar Turner, *Jesus of Nazareth: Lord and Christ* (Grand Rapids, MI: Eerdmans Publishing Co, 1994), 76.
18 Roger Haight, *Symbol of God* (Maryknoll, NY: Orbis, 1999), 72.

traditional African worldview holds that sickness and other afflictions can be caused not only by evil spirits but also by human beings who collaborate with them, such as sorcerers and witches.

Looking at the heavy demands and the desire for healing in Africa today, it is very easy to agree with Emmanuel Milingo, who notes that "everywhere in Africa, healing has been a function of religion. This may be because disease is so prevalent, so much part of everyday life, and people have been so powerless to deal with it."[19] Many priests and bishops see the need for a healing ministry because of the numerous demands from Christians who suffer from all forms of diseases, ranging from misfortunes to infertility. Many desire security, not just from cultic friends and family but also from robbers, witchcraft, and sorcery.[20]

> The intentionality of Christian life in Nigeria in so far as it is integral wellbeing can be called the autobiography of the ancestors, which has become a Testament for posterity. In other words, despite the fact that the ancestors did not know Jesus the Christ, nor felt any need for his saving (healing) work, their experience and interpretation of life as an integral whole have directed their offspring to invite/accept Jesus into their life as healer, as mediator of well-being.[21]

The Bassa people of Cameroon refer to Jesus as the healer of all sickness. For them, Jesus the healer is the most important title of Jesus, because it caters to their immediate needs and makes him relatable. It is also interesting to note that the Jesus as healer image challenges not just the Bassa tribe of Cameroon, or the Cameroonian society as a whole, but Africa in general, as it strives toward complete liberation, especially from anthropological poverty, oppressive governments, outdated cultural norms, and other forms of spiritual and social ills.

In Cameroon, people believe that everyone should be free because Jesus the healer has set everyone free. The pivotal place of Christianity in Cameroon, with its emphasis on healing, has contributed enormously to the growth of the state. This is because healing is always done in the context of and for the community. Each person is an integral part of the community, from which he/she derives meaning and wholeness. The Jesus as healer image reminds people of the community, of belonging and wholeness. This is because in the gospel, Jesus' healings all took place in the social environment of the

---

19 Emmanuel Milingo, *The World in Between* (Maryknoll, NY: Orbis, 1984), 4.
20 Eugene E. Ezukwu, "Towards an African Christology," *Foundation of African Theology* 3, no. 2 (1992): 7.
21 Ibid., 8–9.

patient. He integrated the leper and the hemorrhagic woman into the milieu of their origins after their communities and religion had excluded and kept them in marginalized positions, due to their sickness. By healing them, Jesus re-socialized them.[22]

This image is also very relevant today in Africa, and Cameroon in particular, because of the political atmosphere that is embedded with unjust structures and policies that impoverish the people and keep them perpetually sick.[23] Today, many Cameroonians, especially Anglophone Cameroonians, cannot boast of a good healthcare system. This prompted the Cameroonian Jesuit, Jean-Marc Ela, as far back as 1988, to observe that healthcare is in danger of becoming a thing reserved only for the rich few because peasants and manual laborers in remote areas cannot access it.[24] Poor allocation of resources endangers good, healthy living and is indeed the enemy of health, and one of the situations or structures of oppression and evil that the people need to be delivered from.

This image of Jesus as healer is especially appealing not only to women who have been oppressed and placed on the margins of society but also to the people who are plagued by sickness and misfortune, and it is in this wise that Jesus supplies physical, spiritual, social, political, and economic help to the people.

Many of the Africans who accept Jesus as a healer do so on the basis of contemporary experience, and on the Bible stories where Jesus heals many people, and thereby shows his divinity. The African paradigm of Jesus as healer, similar to the belief of the Jews, comes from the biblical belief that only God can heal.

> He is healer because he is God, and God says, "I am Jehovah Rapha, I am the Lord your God that heals you." And lots of times in the gospels, we see Jesus as healer. The summary that Peter gives of him in Acts 10:38 says that "God anointed Jesus of Nazareth with the Holy Spirit and power and because of that he went about doing

---

22 Cece Kolie, "Jesus as Healer" in *Faces of Jesus in Africa*, ed. Robert J. Schreiter (Maryknoll, NY: Orbis, 1991), 130.
23 An example is the political tension that exists in the Anglophone part of Cameroon, where in 2017 English-speaking Cameroonians decided to seek liberation from the predominantly francophone government which crafts policies to the former's disfavor. Frequently, leaders of the liberation movement ask the population to add fasting and prayers to the day-to-day physical struggles of sit-down strikes and negotiations.
24 Jean-Marc Ela, *My Faith as an African* (Maryknoll, NY: Orbis, 1988), 69.

good and healing." Mathew 8:17: "He himself bore our sins, in his own body, bore our infirmities." The prophecy of Isaiah 53: "He himself, in his own body, was wounded for our transgressions, bruised for our iniquity." And so by the stripes we are healed. So you cannot separate God from that. And you can't separate Jesus from that.[25]

The fact that Jesus went to the towns and places of those asking to be healed is an indication that he intended to be accepted as a healer. Thus, whether Jesus is healing humanity from sickness or from sin, many Africans relate to him as a traditional healer.

One has to always keep in mind that the African universe of sickness is inseparable from the spirit world, and that consequently, healing must be addressed within this symbolic universe. This ongoing propensity for Christians to seek out traditional priests is a serious challenge to the Church of Africa. Jean-Marc Ela strongly emphasizes the importance of such healing ministries, and again calls for the Bible to be reread in a way that permits the Africans to relate to the invisible world. This emphasis assumes the symbolic universe of sickness and healing in order to bring about the salvific power inherent in the gospel.

> In a context where the African is confronted with invisible forces at work in the universe, the Church had to find an adequate manner of proclaiming the primacy of Christ (Col 1:15–20), remembering that Saint Paul did not condemn the powers and the principalities to which the new converts from the Greek still accorded great importance. For he emptied himself above all to specifying the paramount position of Christ from whom comes all salvation.[26]

Oduyoye, remarking on Christianity in Africa, notes:

> It is therefore not strange that if belief from evil influence, from the spiritual oppressor, is not felt by members in Christian Churches, they move from Church to Church, as well as to-and-fro between the Church and the *odunsini*, the traditional healer of body and soul. Nevertheless, Jesus, the great physician, is the anchor of their faith, for he is preached as the healer par excellence.[27]

---

25 Dianne B. Stinton, *Jesus of Africa: Voices of Contemporary African Christology* (Nairobi, Pauline Publications Africa, 2004), 68.
26 Jean-Marc Ela, "De l'assistance á la Liberation: Les Taches Actuelles de l'église en Milieu Africain," *Foi et Dévelopement* (1981): 83.
27 Oduyoye Mercy Amba E, *Hearing and Knowing: Theological Reflections on Christianity in Africa* (Maryknoll, NY: Orbis, 1985), 44.

The consideration of Jesus as healer reveals both human and divine powers in place. A traditional healer, though human, enjoys supernatural powers that only divine beings and their proxies enjoy.

Like the image of Jesus as ancestor, the image of Jesus as healer has not been without controversy. One such conflict is the issue of mingling traditional African healing beliefs with the beliefs in Jesus. Ela describes the problem in this manner,

> Christians, you unfortunate people! In the morning at mass, in the evening at the diviner's! Amulet in your pocket, scapular around your neck!' This Zaïroise song reveals the tragedy of the majority of black African Christians.[28]

The problem of mingling traditional healing and Jesus as healer makes one question whether Jesus as healer is an accepted parallel, or whether this is simply a manner of clinging to the continuing aspects of African traditional religion considered pagan.

A second possible conflict, evident in the works of Teresa M. Hinga, is that Jesus as healer runs the risk of being considered by some as an over-privatized version of Jesus. According to her, accepting Jesus as a personal healer and friend is a modern portrayal of Pharisaism. Hinga, however, prefers to view Jesus as a friend.

> The image of Jesus as a personal friend has been one of the most popular among women…the image of Christ who helps them to bear their griefs, loneliness, and sufferings is a welcome one indeed.[29]

In line with the caution about referring to Jesus as a traditional healer, the Ghanian Catholic priest, Joseph Aggrey, also suggests some dangers.

> So sometimes, what Jesus is to somebody can be seen by what that person is going through. There are some people who see Jesus only as healer, because they are sick. There are some people who, because they are poor wants Jesus to change stones into bread for them. So, if you don't take care, you will be kind of parochial in your thinking about Jesus Christ. But Jesus Christ embodies everything. So, there is no danger, of losing sight of who Jesus is. You are only thinking of who Jesus is in reference to your problem, the situation in which you find yourself.[30]

---

28 Ela, *My Faith as an African*, 73.
29 Teresa Hinga, "Jesus Christ and the Liberation of Women in Africa." In *The Will to Arise: Women, Tradition, and the Church in Africa* (Maryknoll, NY: Orbis, 1997), 190–91.
30 Stinton, *Jesus of Africa*, 76.

Another problem, related to the above, in presenting Jesus in the image of a traditional healer, is the confusion surrounding the figure in terms of the definition and role of African traditional healers. In Africa, witch doctors are sometimes referred to as traditional healers. Because of this confusion in terminology, the two roles are, or can be, confused. It tarnishes the name of the person of Jesus Christ, as there would be a tendency to ascribe to Christ the limitations and shortcomings of witch doctors. John Gatu expresses the danger of referring to Jesus as *nganga* – a term used for traditional healers

> The only problem is that in our own concepts today, *Nganga* is seen as a person who practices superstition. We don't see him as a healer in the sense that you're talking about Jesus now. And so, if you say to someone, "*Christo Yesu ni Nganga*" the immediate concept – because of the distortion that has been made in some of our concepts – you are talking about that fellow who plays juju.[31]

Furthermore, some theologians have argued that this image places Jesus on a par with evil, or with the devil, rather than adequately acknowledging his omnipotence over all the forces of evil. While conceding some instructive value to Jesus as the *Nganga* or traditional healer, Stinton warns that the mentality may overshadow the real meaning. *Nganga* constantly fights against other forces to secure healing and protection for their patients or members. They, in fact, are constantly at loggerheads with other forces. To say that Jesus is a *nganga* can lead some to think that the main task of Jesus is to fight other forces. Jesus may be portrayed only in the light of the biblical story of Moses who confronts the wise men of Pharoah in that contest of power.[32] With the image of Jesus as *nganga*, the emphasis is on the power, whereas, in the case of Jesus, the emphasis is not on the power but on the person, on his presence, and on his ultimate power over all evil, because he stands against all evil.[33] The image of Jesus as a traditional healer also works to downplay his divinity. Jesus, unlike the traditional healer, does not just receive powers from somewhere but his position as God gives him that power. He is divine by his very nature.

One point of note about traditional healers is that they have not been entirely successful in freeing humankind from the things that affect them. Yet, on the cross, Christ was able to successfully do this, once and for all. This puts him in a position of superior healer, who heals all diseases, without exceptions. The point of convergence is on Christ's victory over the forces of evil. As the

---

31 Stinton, *Jesus of Africa*, 87.
32 Ibid.
33 Ibid.

healer, he conquers evil in both its individual and structural manifestations. Thus, Christ the traditional healer paradigm portrays Jesus as someone who loves, cherishes, and gives life.

Both the Alexandrian and Antiochene school of thoughts, which culminated at the Council of Chalcedon of 451, determined that Christ was both divine and human. In this same reasoning, whatever is true of God would also be true of Christ, for they share in the same adoration and the same glory. If God and Christ are one, and God is Creator, then it follows that Jesus would also be an active participant in the act of creating. As a creator gives life, so does Jesus give life, and healing is just one way of giving life.

Christ as Liberator

In viewing Christ as Liberator, it is important to underline the crucial and indispensable need for liberation in Africa. This leads to the question: To what extent can the title of "liberator" be applicable to Christ in the African contemporary context? What is the ground on which Christ the Liberator Christology stands?

Many in Africa today are oppressed by diseases, poverty, civil wars, and many other ills. There are also many spiritual and cultural oppressions which range from oppressive and vengeful attacks of angry ancestors in search of appeasement or vengeance; to spirit-possession, which leads to witchcraft; and evil spells and curses cast on innocent and vulnerable individuals and families. In the face of all these actualities, there is the need for a deep and meaningful liberation from these structures of oppression.[34] Christ "must be presented, first and foremost as the Victor and Liberator par excellence, who forever lives to destroy the demonic forces wherever found."[35] According to Mercy Amba Oduyoye, because Christ extends to and touches human needs at every level, and Africans are but ordinary members of the human race, feeling the need for salvation is an absolute endeavor.[36]

Liberation in our context presupposes the existence of an unjustifiable situation that has to be eliminated. Anything that limits the fullness of life that

---

34 Taiye Adamolekun, "Christ as a Social Liberator: A Challenge for African Christianity," in *Christology in African Context*, ed. S. Abogunrin, (Ibadan: University of Ibadan Publishers, 2003), 389.
35 Osadolor Imasogie, "The Church and Theological Ferment in Africa," *Review and Expositor* 82, no. Spring (1985): 225.
36 Oduyoye Mercy Amba E, *Hearing and Knowing*, 99.

Jesus talks about in John 10:10 ought to be completely eradicated. In the words of Nasimiyu Wasike

> Jesus is calling all the people of Africa, women and men and children, not to accept their hardship and pain fatalistically but to work at eliminating the suffering and creating a better Africa for all. They have to focus on Jesus, the one who enables and empowers and who wants to liberate them from all that denies them life: political oppression, economic oppression, social, cultural and religious oppression.[37]

This gives Christ his rightful place of the liberation from burden and all forms of oppression, as he transcends and transforms all cultures. Biblical texts certainly draw out various facets of how African Christians understand Jesus as Liberator, but personal experience does a good job in shaping and buttressing such an interpretation.

The Christ as Liberator image resonates very much with the African culture and experience because the struggle for a better life, a better country, and a better world, and even the effort to be a better person never ends. Basing his analysis on the experience of the general mass of African people, the analysis of various social sciences on that experience, and a theological examination of the socio-economic and political life in Africa, Laurenti Magesa outlines the ethical and moral questions in need of liberation:

> [Q]uestions of excessive wealth in the midst of dehumanizing poverty and vice versa; questions of exploitations of the majority of the African peoples by internal and external forces; questions of political dominations by domestic and international power brokers; questions of suppression of the African cultures by dominant conceptions of life by means of refutations and ridicule; questions of monopolies of power by ecclesiastical oligarchies at the expense of the liberty of the people of God; questions, in short, of instrumentalization and exploitation of the life of the African person.[38]

With this in mind, it is fair to say that liberation in Africa requires a certain, deep understanding by Christian believers of the political and socio-economic level of their faith. This understanding is solely and simply to sort out what belongs to whom and whom to return it to. The words of the Protestant New Testament scholar Walter Brueggemann very aptly describe the dynamic process of liberation:

---

37 Anne Nasimiyu Wasike, "Witnesses to Jesus Christ in the African Context," *Propositum*, 1, no. 3 (June 1998): 25.
38 Laurenti Magesa, "Christ the Liberator and Africa Today," in *Faces of Jesus in Africa* (Maryknoll, NY: Orbis, 1991), 154.

> There are certain entitlements which cannot be mocked. Yet through the uneven workings of the historical process, some come to have access to or control of what belongs to others. If we control what belongs to others long enough, we come to think of it as rightly ours, and to forget it rightly belongs to someone else. So the work of liberation, redemption, salvation, is the work of *giving things back*. The Bible knows that when things are alienated from those to whom they belong, there can only be trouble, disorder, and death. So, God's justice at the outset has a dynamic transformative quality. It causes things to change, and it expects that things must change if there is to be an abundant life.[39]

Liberation, therefore, involves genuine, active commitment because "Christians are not simply those who profess Christ with their lips, but ones who...live the structure and comportment that Christ lived; love, forgiveness, complete openness to God..."[40] This active commitment, necessary for liberation, extends to all facets of life. According to Jean-Marc Ela, "The Bible, which speaks of God and human beings in the same breath, always includes in the deliverance of God's people their political, economic, and social liberation – without, however, it being reduced to these."[41] For him, "The faith cannot be lived a-temporally: It must be inscribed in a historical context, and be expressed in a praxis, for it must manifest, in comprehensible signs, the Christian message of liberation in Jesus Christ."[42] In the words of Magesa:

> When we speak of Jesus as liberator, then we refer to his assurance of solidarity with us, particularly but not exclusively as Church, in the struggle – his struggle- to diminish poverty among the masses of the people. It is a struggle to prevent the untimely death of millions of children due to malnutrition, poor hygiene, and lack of medical care. We refer to Jesus' life example in cultivating a better person and a better world. We refer to his commitment to forming the rule of God by refusing to accept as right sinful structures of religious or civil domination, corruption, and tribalism.[43]

Christ is Liberator because on him lies not only the foundation, inspiration, and basic reason for the struggle but most especially because his presence constitutes the ultimate guarantee of success in any liberation struggle.[44] Because

---

39 Walter Brueggemann, *To Act Justly, Love Tenderly, Walk Humbly* (Eugene, OR: Wipf & Stock Publishers, 1986), 5–6.
40 Leonardo Boff, *Jesus Christ Liberator: A Critical Christology for Our Time* (Maryknoll, NY: Orbis, 1995), 247.
41 Jean-Marc Ela, *African Cry* (Maryknoll, NY: Orbis, 1986), 90.
42 Ibid., 87.
43 Magesa, "Christ the Liberator and Africa Today," 158.
44 Ibid.

of God's solidarity with us, through the Church, Magesa considers the Church to be the main medium of a liberation struggle. By positing the Church as the medium of the struggle for liberation, Magesa unavoidably connects African Christology to Ecclesiology.[45] For him, the sum of the content of a liberation Christology lies in the fact that "the Church as ideally the agent and articulator of Christ's liberation in the world."[46]

We have to note that Jesus did not limit his liberation mission to the poor. He gave special attention to women, thereby challenging the many cultural inclinations of his day – inclinations that touch everyone including women. Because of many male-centered cultural realities in Africa today, many women are relegated to second-class citizens, and their rights and human dignity trampled upon by the men who build and encourage oppressive sociocultural structures. They too, like men, are in need of the liberation that Christ brings. By becoming human, God self-emptied himself (Phil. 2:6–8) making us share in his being and his mission to renew the face of the earth. This self-emptying through the incarnation is the theological justification for the struggle for Africa's liberation. Christ's sharing in our humanity gives us reasons to ensure that everyone is treated with dignity and respect.

Like all the other portraits of Jesus, that of Jesus as the liberator is not without problems. There is the challenge of how to reconcile liberation with peace. Seeing Jesus as a liberator may drive home the impression that Jesus was a political messiah and a revolutionary. It may largely cloud the fact that Jesus' liberation is a peaceful liberation from all the things that separate people from the source of life – God. Christ as a liberator need not be considered in political terms, as many may tend to believe.

In Africa, a "growing awareness of the socio-economic and political dimensions of liberation is also manifest, together with caution against portrayals of Jesus in narrowly conceived political terms."[47] The term "liberation" is not limited to politics. It is and could be used in a non-political way so that Christ can be understood as a liberator in terms of social ills or even in terms of economic and cultural liberation.

As this image of Jesus is being understood in its proper sense, and gaining ground in Africa, its significance becomes more and more evident. First of all, Jesus as Liberator conveys his solidarity in suffering, as discovered by encountering Christ in the concrete, everyday reality of the struggle for life. Secondly,

---

45 Magesa, "Christ the Liberator and Africa Today," 158.
46 Ibid.
47 Ibid., 213.

there is a deep relevance to Jesus' life, death, and resurrection in the contemporary African context, most especially with regard to women who seek freedom from some cultural bondage. Thirdly, this image testifies to a need for a holistic image of Jesus as Liberator, which, of course, as noted above, is not limited to political oppression but to anything that serves as a dehumanizing tool in society.

Christ as Chief

These titles stem not only from the gospel or an encounter with the African heritage but also with African contemporary realities. In this section, I will discuss how, or to what extent, Jesus can be said to fit into the human role of Chief/King.

The title of Jesus as Chief has its New Testament equivalent in the way in which Jesus is addressed as Lord (*Kyrios*). In his *The Many Faces of Jesus Christ*, Volker Kuster explains the traditional notion of chieftaincy in Africa.

> The term chief is extremely diverse. The colonial rulers were already called *Mukalenge*, chief, in the general sense, but so too were the missionaries and later the representatives of the indigenous clergy. Titles like *Ntita* for chiefs who had the right to initiate and invest other chiefs and *Luaba* for those claiming to be chiefs are different; they imply an elevation for those so designated and remain reserved to few.[48]

Among Kuster's three names for chief, the closest one that fits Jesus is *Ntita*. Christ is the *ntita*, with the power to invest in other chiefs. The cultural significance of the title *Ntita*, applied to Christ, is very significant. Not all chiefs are equal in status, rank, and authority.[49]

---

48 Volker Kuster, *The Many Faces of Jesus Christ: Intercultural Christology* (Maryknoll, NY: Orbis, 1999), 59. It is worthy to note the fact that Luaba is a royal title destined for those who, while still striving to gain power, do not yet have power. Referring to Jesus as *Luaba* and *Ntita* at the time is in keeping with eschatological tension between the "already" and the "not yet" a way of saying Jesus' chiefdom is in effect but at the same time, its plenitude has not yet been made manifest.
49 The Bassa-Mpoo (Bassa and Elog Mpoo) of Cameroon have two kinds of traditional leaders. There are *Traditional chiefs* who serve as "administrative auxiliaries" with the task of ensuring the smooth running of administrative affairs, such as collecting taxes, taking the census, registering births, and organizing elections of local neighborhood leaders called "quarter heads" and *Patriarchs* who have overall traditional authority and power over other tribe members. Patriarchs are chiefs who can install other chiefs. In the same light, the *Ntita* is no ordinary chief. He has the task of enthroning other chiefs and on him they depend. Translated in Christian context, Christ as *Ntita* is very much expressed on the

The Congolese theologian François Kabasele, one of the most outspoken figures of the Jesus the Chief model, notes that "Jesus Christ is called "Chief" (mukalenge) by virtue of the primary denotation of this general word which designates someone who holds some authority and who governs a part of the people."[50] Even the colonialist and others such as parish priests and civic leaders were called mukalenge because of the leadership role and authority they held among the people. We have to note emphatically with John S. Pobee that "[t]he institution of chieftaincy is the focal point of culture and a model for leadership patterns in Africa."[51] All villages have chiefs and consider them as being persons of reverence and respect. With this in mind, we note the important role that Africans place on chieftaincy and on their chiefs. According to Prof. Thomas W. Bennett:

> A chief is a traditional leader of a specific traditional community who exercises authority over a number of headmen in accordance with customary law, or within whose area of jurisdiction a number of headmen exercise authority.[52]

Given the Scriptural revelations, the Patristic Traditional witnesses and the daily Christian experiences of the person and works of Jesus, Jesus, to a large extent, very much fits into the African Traditional category of chief. How or why is Jesus a Chief?

According to Kabasele, Jesus is the chief because he is a hero, by virtue of the fact that he defeated Satan. His defeat of Satan makes him a great defender of the community – a duty reserved for chiefs. The Luba Christians of Congo ascribe to Jesus titles like "Ciloba," that is, the hero whose courage and resilience in the face of the enemy is compared to no other. The Luba offertory prayer reads: "Jesus the Annoited, Ciloba, who never flees the enemy,

---

feast of Christ the King and Epiphany, during which we celebrate Jesus' kingship over and above other kings. The entrance prayer of the missal of the diocese of Mbuji-Mayi for the feast of Epiphany reads "Chief of chiefs, *Ntita*, hierarch of hierarchs, with the chiefs of the East we have come to prostrate ourselves before you and worship you for your glory is supereminent, you the living God...Amen." (Missal of the Diocese of Mbuji-Mayi, published by Cimanga-Dipa-Dia-Nzambi under the title, *Didia dia Mfumu* (The Lord's Supper)), Kinshasha, 1980, Year A, p.232.

50 François Kabasele, "Christ As Chief," in *Faces of Jesus in Africa*, ed. Robert J. Schreiter, (Maryknoll, NY: Orbis, 1991), 104.
51 John. S. Pobee, *Christ Would Be an African Too* (Geneva: WCC Publications, 1996), 24.
52 Thomas W. Bennett, *Customary Law in South Africa* (Cape Town: Juta Legal and Academic Publishers, 2004), 104.

accept the offering of our faith, and send it to the father, you who have life and power...Amen."[53]

According to Kabasele:

> He is acclaimed as the *Kanda Kazadi*, that is, the one who wins victories, whom no one dares to confront.... He is the *Mpanga-wa-mananga*, that is, the ram of the mighty sinews and majestic carriage. He is the "*mukokodu-wa-ku-muele*," the one who never strifles with his hatchet, the one whose hatchet never fails to strike home. He is the "rainbow that ends the rain" (*muanzanko golo-lukanda-mvula*).[54]

In the perspective of Christ as hero, he is also seen as the pillar – a title given to people who hold important, indispensable positions in specific cases. Culturally, the support pillar is very significant in the sense that it is the main pillar that holds up the house and is the most resistant and resilient of all pillars.[55]

Secondly, Jesus is the chief because he is the son and emissary of the chief (God). "That Christ is the son of God, the Bantus have learned only through Christian revelation. But that God is the chief of the universe, the ultimate recourse, they know by their ancestral faith."[56] Among the Luba of Katanga, the emissaries of the chiefs are called the Mulopo. Jesus is God's *Mulopo*, the presentative of God who reveals the thoughts, being, works, and nature of God. It is in the same light that Paul refers to Jesus as the "image of the invisible God" (Col 1:15).

Thirdly, Jesus is the chief because he is strong. For the Bantu people, the chief is like a link between the earthly and the heavenly. This mediating role necessitates not only a great deal of strength but also "a life force that protects and strengthens the life of a group and its individuals, while employing a certain violence that constrains, punishes, and even destroys."[57] A Bantu chief is constantly in the region of the "strong"[58] – sphere of intercession between the earthly and the beyond. The region of the strong "includes fortune-tellers, "mother of a *Mulopo*," healers, initiators of various orders and social groups,

---

53 *Didia dia Mfumu* (The Lord's Supper), Missal of the Diocese of Mbuji-Mayi, published by Cimanga-Dipa-Dia-Nzambi (The Lord's Supper) Kinshasha: 1980, Year A) p. 160.
54 Kabasele, "Christ As Chief," 106.
55 Ibid., 108. The Luba Christians use the word *cipanda-wa nshimdamenu* to denote this support pillar. Supporting pillars are supposed to be very smooth because after a meal, it could be used to wipe hands (paper towel).
56 Ibid.
57 Ibid., 109.
58 Ibid.

manipulators of natural forces."⁵⁹ The world is a vast field of circuits of interdependence and mutual influences among beings, and chiefs have that power and ability, not only to locate these circuits but also the power to direct them to a particular end. He therefore can see what others cannot see.

> A chief belongs to the category of the "strong," by the fact that he is the guarantor of growth of life in the social group, and the fact that, in virtue of his function as chief, he shares in the charge entrusted to those-beyond (to the ancestors). The Bantu chief does not "exercise" power – he hold it in his hands.⁶⁰

It should be noted that among the different reasons why Jesus fits into the category of an African chief is that the aspect of "strength" is one of the major supports of the attribution of this title to Christ, because,

> His activity, his thoughts, his mission have appeared to the Bantu, such as to place him in the category of the "strong." The Gospel surely presents him as the one who comes from on high (as in the annunciation and the infancy narratives). Jesus says this of himself explicitly: he comes from the Father, and is seen by him (John 8:42). Again, in Jesus the invisible is rendered visible: God has shown himself.⁶¹

Also, the fact that the Scripture and tradition attest to Jesus as the word made flesh, which connects him all the more to his chiefdom because "for a Muntu, a flesh of this sort, a mirror of the beyond, can only belong to the order of the strong."⁶² His numerous miracles as attested by Scripture, his indirect way of talking, and his rather sphinx-like utterances fit squarely into the model of chief.⁶³

Fourthly, Jesus Christ is a chief because he is generous and wise. By virtue of his role, a chief works for the interest of the people. He holds the people and their wellbeing in top priority. He is there to offer guidance and counseling, tapping inspiration and wisdom from the world beyond, which he represents with all faithfulness. Generosity, wisdom, and the spirit of conciliation among human beings are an indispensable hallmark of a Bantu chief.⁶⁴ Moreover, presence among the people is key to being a chief – being the Emmanuel (God with us) as attested by Scripture, and being the generous distributor of good

---

59 Kabasele, 109.
60 Ibid., 109–10.
61 Ibid., 110.
62 Ibid.
63 Ibid., 110–111.
64 Ibid., 111.

things, even of his own life (Jn 10:18). In the same way as Chiefs act and conform themselves to the will of the ancestors, so too did Christ follow the will of the Father (Jn 5:19).[65]

Lastly, Jesus Christ is Chief because of his ability to reconcile.[66] When a Bantu opens the Gospel and notices that Jesus opposes the spirit of vengeance (Mt 5:38), that he preaches forgiveness of offenses (Mt 18:21), and that his last injunction before his death is love and union, they readily bestow on him the traditional title of "Cinkunku-who-gathers-the hunters" or of "mortar-who-gathers-the-grinders."[67]

The person of Jesus Christ, as well as his works, makes us support and acknowledge Jesus as the chief, but ascribing to Jesus Christ the title of chief is not without limitations and problems. The chief analogy is more like a *theologia gloriae* as referred to by Martin Luther, without a *theologia cruces*. In other words, it gives the impression of a power and authority attained through means other than suffering. Biblical accounts show Jesus as entering his kingly glory only through humility, suffering, and martyrdom, as evident in the symbolism of the cross.[68]

Contrary to traditional chiefs, who were very generous with the people, and who put their time and talent at the disposal of the people, the lifestyle of contemporary African chiefs, and the way they rule the people, impede the reference to Jesus as *nana*/chief. Many are very dictatorial, authoritative, selfish, and often use the people for their personal gain. Many exploit the obedience that people owe them and do not serve as good examples. Many chiefs live very opulent lifestyles and have many wives, which do not fit with the image that we have of Jesus.

It is worthwhile to note at this point that kingship or chieftaincy in Africa is vested not only with secular power but also with profound religious power and function. Civil authority in the African setting is always from God (Rom 13:1).

In the past, chiefs were usually resident in their palaces where they served their people, but today, many chiefs live away from their palaces and villages and return home only when there is an important festival or occasion. This is the notion of the "absentee chief," a concept that one should avoid attributing to Jesus Emmanuel unless one wants to highlight the contrast with Jesus, who is always present. In addition, Jesus' divinity and sinlessness are in contrast with

---

65   Kabasele, 111.
66   Ibid., 112.
67   Ibid.
68   Stinton, *Jesus of Africa*, 188.

chiefs bedecked with human frailty, which oftentimes led to their dethronement. Jesus' reign is eternal and universal.

> He is greater than every chief! Chief, *Nana*, they are human beings! And like the radiance that fills the heavens, a little atom of his dignity, he gives to the *Nana*. And we have no words, we have no mentality to picture his greatness, the awesomeness of his power, and the radiance of his glory. So if we compare him to Nana, we are belittling him. We dare not![69]

Also, African feminist theologians regard with extreme repugnance or aversion the use of this Christological model on the grounds that behind the notion of chief is a very patriarchal mindset that leaves no room for participation and inclusiveness of those whose humanity is trampled upon.

It is worthwhile to note that even though the image of Jesus Christ as chief does not exhaust the mystery of the incarnation, it does shed more light on the person of Jesus. Jesus is not an ordinary chief, but the chief of chiefs. The Igbo people of southeastern Nigerian refer to Jesus as the *Ezendieze*, meaning King/Chief of Kings/Chief (Rv 19:16). He embodies all the positive characteristics for which the chief is known. As *Ezendieze*, Jesus is one in a preeminent way. He is a servant par excellence, a model for the other "little" chiefs to emulate. With Stinton, it can be affirmed that "if the intention is to communicate the identity and significance of Jesus Christ ... then some people would believe that the African kingship/chieftaincy image hampers that goal. In contrast, the majority is evidently convinced that it enhances their understanding of Jesus."[70]

Note that the concept of Jesus as chief has also led to examining what chieftaincy is for the African people. The words of Bishop Peter Sarpong summarily touch the notion of Jesus' leadership role:

> The Asante Christology, therefore, is a Christology that is based upon their conception of leadership in the traditional political set-up – chieftaincy.... Jesus came not to destroy the tradition given to us, but to uphold it for us. He is our leader in the war against the domination of anything that is inhuman or dehumanizing. Jesus is our military leader. But as he himself said, the war he fights is not for earthly hegemony, but to liberate us from the shackles of all that makes it impossible for us to be true sons and daughters of God.[71]

---

69 Stinton, *Jesus of Africa*, 188.
70 Ibid.
71 Peter K. Sarpong, "Asante Christology," *Studia Missionalia*. 45,no. 45 (1996): 194.

Here we see that Jesus represents both the fulfillment of chieftaincy expectations in traditional African thoughts and of current yearnings for liberation and guidance in all dimensions of life.

Christ the Ancestor

One prominent model of African Christology is that of Christ as Ancestor. This model, rooted in local culture is very much propagated by African theologians like John S. Pobee, Bénézet Bujo, François Kabasele, and Charles Nyamiti. In his journal article "African Ancestral Veneration and its Relevance to the African Churches," Charles Nyamiti notes his aim in developing a Christology anchored on the concept of ancestors, "...what I propose to do is to offer a brief presentation as to how the Christian mysteries could be interpreted from the African ancestral view point for the purpose of African systematic theology."[72] Commenting on Nyamiti's Christology Gwinyi Muzorewa notes:

> Ancestrology is the frame of his Christology. For instance, as our African ancestors heals, serve as prophets and pastoral advisors, and as priests so does Christ except he excels them. Nyamiti takes advantage of the similarities between the African ancestral functions and Christ's pastoral and redemptive functions to draw conclusions that demonstrate how much more the latter can do .... Then he also uses the dissimilarities and divergencies between the two to prove how superior the redeemer shines forth as THE brother-Ancestor par excellence, of whom the African ancestors are but faint and poor images.[73]

Who is an ancestor? Given the limitations of "confining" Christ to one title, in what sense could Christ be considered an ancestor? An ancestor is "a blood relative of a living community; this relationship could be of common parentage or shared ancestry."[74] Ancestors share a close relationship with God, and because of this closeness, they enjoy the ability or power to exist everywhere, even though they have loci of preference (places charged or filled with ancestral spirits), like shrines or sanctuaries, particular trees, tombs, and large bodies of water. The formal place of encounter with ancestors remains specific,

---

72 Charles Nyamiti, "African Ancestral Veneration and Its Relevance to the African Churches," *The Journal of African Christian Studies*. 9, no. 3 (1993): 17–18.
73 Gwiny Muzorewa, "Christ as Our Ancestor: Christology from an Africa Perspective by Charles Nyamiti: A Review Essay," *Africa Theological Journal*. 17, no. 3 (1988): 258.
74 Agbonkhianmeghe E. Orobator, *Theology Brewed in an African Pot* (Nairobi: Paulist Publications, 2008), 107.

sacred areas where sacrifices and incantations take place. Although ancestors are physically dead, they "enjoy a sacred super human status with special magico-religious powers that can be beneficial or even harmful to the earthly kin."[75]

The Bakoko parents of South Cameroon often exhort their children never to forget their ancestors. This emphasizes the place that ancestors should have in the life of the people. If families or the community neglect their ancestors, great bodily or spiritual calamities can befall them. In fact, because of the great and decisive influence of ancestors, the living community cannot hope to survive unless they render due honor to their dead and continue faithfully along the track laid down by them.[76] The Bamileke tribes of the western region of Cameroon have a tradition of burying their deceased loved ones beside the kitchen. This is to assure nearness to the family members, especially during meals and conversations. This subject opens up the African conception of death. In Cameroon, for instance, the words of the Senegalese poet, Birago Diop, is often heard on the lips of many *"les morts ne sont pas morts."* meaning the dead are not dead.[77] This is because Africans do not believe that death is the end of life. Death is part of life, for one does not cease to exist at death but is ushered into a different way of life. According to Mbiti, death is a person's transition from the *"Sasa"* period to the *"Zamani"* time-period. *The Sasa* period is that of physical existence on earth, as well as the period after death within which the departed is remembered by relatives and friends who knew him. When the last of these survivors die off, the departed now enters the "Zamani," which is complete death.[78] In the words of Hebga, in Africa,

> Death is a process at the end of which the elements that constitute a person are separated for ever. . … but we can also say that the entire body is consumed, while keeping all the functions of life.[79]

---

75 Charles Nyamiti, "Jesus Christ, the Ancestor of Mankind, Methodological and Trinitarian Foundations," *Studies in African Christian Theology* Vol. I (2005): 66.
76 Bénézet Bujo, *African Theology in Its Social Context*, trans. John O'Donohue (Eugene, OR: Wipf & Stock Publishers, 2006), 23.
77 S. Azombo-Menda, *Precis de Philosophie Pour l'Afrique (Nathan Afrique)* (Paris: F. Nathan, 1981), 145.
78 Mbiti, *African Religions and Philosophy*, 25.
79 Hebga, *La Rationalite d'un Discours Africain Sur les Phenomenes Paranormaux*, 138. "la mort est un procès au terme duquel les constituants de la personne se séparent définitivement (...) mais on pourrait dire aussi que le corps tout entier est consommé, gardant toutes les fonctions de la vie." This is my translation of the text

Death is just a change of state. Such a worldview found among some Bamileke groups of Cameroon is in perfect resonance with the Christian belief. Because the African family is not limited only to the living but to the dead relatives as well, it is normal for ancestors to be in constant communication with their loved ones in this world. Ancestors in African traditions are considered to have a share in both the world of humans and in the world of the divine. In many African milieus, Jesus is considered to be a great ancestor. According to the Cameroonian-born Catholic priest, Marc Ntetem, Christ is not only a great ancestor but he is "the ancestor *par excellence*."[80]

Because ancestors are the true masters of initiation, it should be clear that Jesus Christ is the ancestor *par excellence*, because he initiates or introduces us to the Father (Col 1:15). Jesus is an ancestor because of his work of mediation and because he "passed over" to the Father. In the words of Jean-Marc Ela, "the cult of the ancestor is so widespread throughout Africa that it is impossible to avoid the question this practice raises for Christian life and reflection."[81] Human beings, created in the *Imago Dei*, have the responsibility to provide for creation. Ancestral veneration links the creature to the creator. When ancestral veneration is done with an eschatological character, it brings with it all its benefits. John Paul II, in his *Ecclesia in Africa*, notes that ancestral veneration in Africa is intrinsically linked with "a profound religious sense, for Africans have a profound sense of the sacred, of the existence of God the Creator and of a spiritual world.[82] The Africans believe in ancestral mediation and in God as the great Ancestor of a spiritual world" (EA, 42). The disdain with which the early missionaries approached African cultural realities proclaimed the cult of ancestors devilish. It was considered diabolic, idolatrous, a sin against the first commandment "thou shall have no God except me" (Dt 5:7).

It is true that ancestral veneration may consciously or unconsciously lead to tribalism or nepotism as members of the same family or clan unite by the blood-line to venerate the same ancestor, but the reality is that, with the purification that comes with the inculturation of the Gospel, these limitations can give way to an authentic God-experience. It can, as well, instill a solid sense of solidarity not only with God at the vertical level but also with other human

---

80 Marc Ntetem, *Initiation: Traditional and Christian: A Reader in African Christian Theology* (London: SPCK Publisher, 1997), 102.
81 Ela, *My Faith as an African*, 14.
82 John Paul II, "Ecclesia in Africa: Post Synodal Apostolic Exhortation," September 1995, 42, http://w2.vatican.va/content/john-paul-ii/en/apost_exhortations/documents/hf_jp-ii_exh_14091995_ecclesia-in-africa.html.

beings at the horizontal level. Solidarity is the backbone of African communal life. "I am because we are, and we are because I am" is the maxim. This reiterates the African philosophy of *ubuntu*,[83] which holds that a person is a person only through, with, and for the community. The identity of a person or human being (*umuntu*) is defined by his or her relationship to the community. However, even though participation is given high place, *ubuntu* may create a danger of "parasitism" as some members of the community may just tend to profit from their kin.

The ancestors were regarded as transmitters of life, with God as the ultimate source. Being in the world beyond, they have access to God, and have the capacity to communicate God's will to the people. In his oneness with God, Christ is not only the fountain of life through creation but also through his work of salvation. It should be noted that whatever the ancestors were understood to be performing in the lives of their descendants can be posited as reaching its perfection in Christ. As the prime ancestor, Christ has fulfilled the leadership roles that passed from the ancestors to their delegates and representatives in society. There is a strong correlation between saints and ancestors, for both have lived exemplary lives and both form part of a communion. The Christian saints form part of the communion of saints – a single "mystical body," with Christ as the head, and in which each member contributes to the good of all, sharing in the welfare of all. This encompasses all those on earth, those in heaven, and those in purgatory, while the ancestors form part of the community that stretches from the land of the living to the land of the dead.

Based on the concept of ancestor and anchored in both Christ's humanity and divinity, Charles Nyamiti develops a Christology which is both from above and from below.[84] From above, he argues that Christ's role as "... brother-ancestor requires, in the first place, a Christology from above ... This implies that such a Christology will be bound to start its reflection from the mysteries of the Trinity, Incarnation and Redemption."[85] His Christology from below, based on the humanity of Christ, is anchored on the veneration of ancestors, because he believes that "it is fitting to start from the concrete humanity of Jesus and His terrestrial activities and to show how the divinity was manifested

---

83 At the very heart of the Zulu maxim, *umuntu ngumuntu ngabantu*, ("a person is a person through (other) persons") is the word *ubuntu* that can be rendered "humanity," "humanness," or even "humaneness."
84 Charles Nyamiti, *Christ as Our Ancestor* (Zimbabwe: Mambo Press, 1984), 25.
85 Nyamiti, *Christ as Our Ancestor*, 80.

through His humanity and activities."[86] Integrating the ancestral Christology from below with that of above leads Nyamiti to affirm that "radically speaking Jesus became our Ancestor through the Incarnation at the moment of his conception in the womb of the Blessed Virgin."[87] For Nyamiti, Christ's close relationship with us is understood from his "Adamite origin."[88] All of humanity is from Adam.

> Considered as *man* Jesus is our natural Brother in Adam, like anyone of us is. It is obvious that when seen from this purely human perspective Christ was like all men a descendant of Adam, and had natural family, clanic and tribal relationships. After His death He became – again like all men – a Brother-Ancestor in Adam. This Brother-Ancestorship is purely natural, it is Christian in origin of all men in Adam. In this case, however, Jesus became the natural Brother-Ancestor only of those who lived on earth after His death.[89]

Nyamiti's use of the term *brother-ancestor* stems from the fact that because all humanity, including Christ, is a descendant of Adam, we are all brothers. We share a common lineage. Christ is our ancestor by virtue of our common lineage. By this reasoning, all Christians are therefore of a common ancestor, Jesus Christ.[90] Moreover, through the act of worshiping Christ, humanity shares in the adoption of the Father thus making Christ our brother-ancestor.[91]

> [B]rother-ancestor indicates common sonship to a progenitor of the ancestor and his brother-descendant. In connection with our common filiation with Christ, this is only possible through habitual grace whereby we become adopted sons of the Father and brothers of the Logos. Without this adoption Christ is our Brother-Ancestor only "in principle" but not "in fact." Through His Incarnation, death and resurrection, He saved us in principle and became thereby our true Brother-Ancestor. This is not only because his Incarnation and paschal mystery enabled us to be God's adoptive sons in Him, but also because through Him, as *natural Son of the Father even as man*, humanity was reconciled to God. On the other hand, by our acquiring of habitual grace Christ's brother-Ancestorship no longer remains *principal* (= in principle) but becomes *factual* (= in fact). This is confirmed by the fact that what happens to His members affects Him also as Head.[92]

---

86 Nyamiti, 80.
87 Ibid., 24.
88 Ibid. 19.
89 Ibid. 28.
90 Ibid., 27–28.
91 Ibid., 30.
92 Ibid.

It is also worthwhile to remember that not all cultures have the same belief when it comes to who an ancestor is. The Bassa people of South Cameroon, for instance, have three main functions of ancestors, which resonates with the Patristic representation of Christ. First, ancestors are the guardians of the social and moral order. Anyone considered an ancestor is undoubtedly someone who lived a well-cherished moral life in the society. Second, ancestors give and sustain life, and thirdly, they serve as mediators between God and humans.

Some theologians argue very strongly that the diverse cultural nature of black Africa makes it impossible to come up with a set of characteristics of who merits the name of ancestor. Despite the cultural differences in black Africa, there are five common elements that are considered for someone to be an ancestor.

First, there is always a natural relationship between the ancestor and his earthly relatives. This relationship can be based on either a parental relationship, a fraternal relationship, or on membership in a sacred society.[93] Orobator defines an ancestor as a blood relative of a living community, including the fact that this relationship can be of common parentage or shared ancestry.[94] Hence, rituals are directed to particular ancestors; otherwise, they are valueless. Kinship is also fundamental to ancestral relationship. One is only an ancestor for a particular kinship. This is why consanguinity is of vital importance in the ancestral kinship.

Secondly, they must have some supernatural status that comes with death and understood in terms of super-human powers and nearness to God.[95] One thing to bear in mind about ancestors is that they have the capacity to intervene in human affairs, either to bring about punishment for an offense or to bless the people and the community.

The manner of death is a very important factor. All ancestors must die of natural causes. Tragic deaths such as suicide or of unclean diseases can disqualify someone from being on the list. Because of the powers that they have, it is not unknown to see people who fear ancestors and who try to appease them with prayers and various forms of rituals.

Thirdly, all ancestors enjoy the role of mediator, thanks to their nearness to God, the Supreme Being,[96] the ineffable, the almighty that sustains cosmic life, whose majesty is so great. This nearness to God qualifies them to "enjoy

---

93   Stinton, *Jesus of Africa*, 113.
94   Orobator, *Theology Brewed in an African Pot*, 107.
95   Stinton, *Jesus of Africa*, 113.
96   Nyamiti, 30.

a sacred super-human status, with special magico-religious powers that can be beneficial or even harmful to their earthly kin."[97] In cases where the living members neglect them or forget about them, they are said to "manifest their anger by sending to their descendants bodily or spiritual calamities."[98] One must also pass through the intermediary of one's ancestors.

Fourthly, ancestors serve not only as mediators but also long to maintain contact with their earthly relatives. So, it is not only the people or the community that long to communicate with the ancestors, but the ancestors, on their part, who look forward to that contact with their people. And lastly, in all of black Africa, all ancestors must have lived a life of high moral standards in the society with a family and children.[99]

The familiarity of the concept of ancestor enabled Christ to be easily accepted and understood when Christianity was introduced to Africa. This is because there seemingly existed many parallels between African ancestorship and Christ's relationship to humanity. Christ's supernatural status, his role as model of virtue exhibited throughout his life, his supernatural communication beyond the grave, and his ability to visit humanity via other beings after death all qualify Christ to be an ancestor. Like the Chalcedonian Jesus after his resurrection, ancestors are believed to be alive; "living dead" as they are often called. The ability to connect with the dead ancestors clearly aligns with Christian prayer and meditation and is believed to be a connection with the Patristic Jesus paradigm that could intercede and hear the prayer requests of his people.

When one looks very critically at the image of Christ as an ancestor, one is tempted to exercise some "cautious reservations" because, to an extent, it would be difficult to completely apply all the qualities of an ancestor to the Patristic traditional Christ. One real difficulty of accepting Christ as an ancestor is the emphasis on a complete separation with the past. When the missionaries came to Africa, they looked upon the attitudes toward the ancestors with some reservations, partly because of ignorance. The image of ancestor was important in bringing people to resonate and connect with Christ, but at the same time, the missionaries had a very negative attitude toward the ritual of libation. How could they be deprived of taking part in libation to their ancestors through whom family ties are symbolized, and at the same time consider or accept Jesus

---

97 Charles Nyamiti, "Jesus Christ, the Ancestor of Mankind, Methodological and Trinitarian Foundations," 66.
98 Ibid.
99 Stinton, *Jesus of Africa*, 113.

as a great ancestor? This approach, taken by the early missionaries, created a shadow of doubt in the minds of the people.

Second, there is a linguistic concern to considering Jesus as an ancestor. According to John Mbiti, the very word "ancestor" is one of the many attempts to translate African cultural terms. The difficulty in translating the English word "ancestor" back into any African language makes Mbiti to prefer the words "spirits" or the "living dead."[100] Richard Gehman, on his part, does not agree with Mbiti's choice of words, because for him, the notion of "spirit" is very incompatible with the Christian faith:

> In biblical perspective, these are none other than the unclean spirits, the fallen angels who serve their master, even Satan. Nothing could be plainer in the bible than the divine abhorrence and active opposition to any contact, communication or relationship with the ancestral spirits, divinities or other spirits.[101]

Despite the shadow of doubt cast by many theologians on the use of the word "ancestor" or "spirit" to fit the Chalcedonian fully human and fully Divine Jesus, we note that the image of Jesus as Ancestor continues to gain ground in African thoughts.

Also, no ancestors in Africa were ever celibate in their earthly life. Marriage is considered to be a transition to adulthood and maturity. An unmarried man is considered immature and incapable of leading and making any meaningful contribution. Childbearing is unavoidably tied to marital union, and the marital union provides the place for childbearing – a very important contribution to society. This is because African culture emphasizes fertility and reproduction to the extent that anyone who does not reproduce is considered to be an immature and useless person.

In addition, ancestors do not die unexpectedly nor do they die in a catastrophic manner. They die of natural causes. They live in dignity and die in dignity. The very fact that Jesus died a shameful death on the cross makes one clearly see the danger of calling Jesus an ancestor. Furthermore, all African ancestors maintain a familial relationship with those on earth for whom they mediate and utilize their powers, whereas, for Jesus there is indeed no consanguineous connection between humanity and himself. The very fact that Jesus was Jewish makes it difficult for African to relate to him within the boundaries of ethnicity. Quoting a Ghanian Catholic bishop, Stinton explains:

---

100 Mbiti, *African Religions and Philosophy*, 19–20.
101 Richard J. Gehman, *African Traditional Religion in Biblical Perspective* (Kijabe: Kesho Publications, 1989), 184.

You don't have the ancestors of the Asantes, you have the ancestors for the clan. My Father is my ancestor. And so before you adopt Jesus as your ancestor, you must be able to first of all convince the world that Christians are one family.[102]

Commenting on our ties to Jesus, Uchenna A. Ezeh, in *Jesus Christ the Ancestor*, argues very strongly that Jesus' ancestral relationship to Africans is based on an analogous African brother-ancestorship.[103] Based on our common descent from Adam, we share a consanguineous tie with Jesus. This consanguinity is also based on his supernatural status that he acquired through his death and resurrection. He became after his death our brother-ancestor in Adam, and we have regular communications with him through the sacraments, most especially in the Eucharist, through which he is present in his members. Jesus' "ancestor par excellence" nature must be maintained so as to satisfy the Chalcedonian "fully God" paradigm, and therefore affirm his divinity. For some people, even distinguishing him as an ancestor par excellence compromises his divinity. "He is higher than an ancestor and on that human basis, we could say he is an ancestor, but then coming back to his divine nature, that is where the difference lies."[104] For Stinton, the fact that Jesus is the Son of God and is worshiped, and the ancestors are not, affects one of the non-negotiables of the Chalcedonian Jesus – his divinity.[105]

Also, Jesus, unlike the ancestors, did not gain his authority from his manner of living among the people. He gained his authority by the fact that he was God from all eternity, proven by his resurrection. The ancestors were never regarded as God, but only as instruments in the divine-human relationship. So, if Christ had been presented as an ancestor, it would be only from the works he performed in human life. One is therefore recognized as an ancestor only due to one's works. From that point of view, the ancestor Christology tends to return to the division between Christology and soteriology, in which soteriology is either subordinated to Christology or reduced to it. Care must be taken not to separate the person of Christ from his works of redemption, for it is noted in the Nicaea-Constantinopolitan creed that he became man "for us and for our salvation." The authentic salvation of the words can be by the works of the Son, Jesus, who, in obedience to the Father's will, performs the

102 Gehman, *African Traditional Religion in Biblical Perspective*, 138.
103 Uchenna A. Ezeh, *Christ the Ancestor, An African Contextual Christology in the Light of the Major Dogmatic Christological Definitions of the Church from the Council of Nicaea (325) to Chalcedon (451)*, 201.
104 Stinton, *Jesus of Africa*, 134.
105 Ibid.

works of salvation with the help of the Holy Spirit. His works demonstrate that the Father who dwells in him is the one doing his work (Jn.14:10) and that one cannot separate the works from the one doing the work.

Even though the salvation done by Jesus on Calvary was done once and for all, we also know that the work of salvation is still in progress. This opens the way for new terminologies to explain the profound mysteries of the faith. Suffice it to note that as human expressions, these terminologies contain the limitations of our language, and so there is the need to develop more expressions as was the case during the early centuries of the Church when concepts such as nature *phusis*, *hypostasis*, procession, and generation were applied to the three divine persons. The different terminologies gave rise to the debates that proceeded to clarify the definition of Christological principles and titles.

Even though Jesus may have gone to the realm of the ancestors, we can argue that he did not go there as an equal, but as Lord, which makes him not merely an ancestor but a great and unique ancestor who rose from the dead. It should be noted again that, in the African context, the ancestor image looms very large. The ancestor in Christology became the attempt from the anthropo-cultural resources to develop an analogous concept of the Christ. The incarnation made God to dwell amongst us, to be one with us, our brother. He is in a transcendent status that enables him to mediate between God and human beings as ancestor, not just because of his redemptive death but also because of the special relationship that he enjoys with God the Father, as God-man. Jesus' consubstantial nature with the Father makes him an ancestor with a difference, or of a special class, a sort of exemplar, thanks to his preeminent role as mediator. He is like and unlike his brother ancestors, an ancestor "par excellence."

One has to keep in mind that the apparently profound disparities that exist between the natural ancestors and Christ do not in any way annul the consideration of Jesus as an ancestor. On the other hand, it greatly enhances it, and shows the unique place that Christ occupies among the ancestors. This unique place puts Christ on a very high ancestral pedestal on which he becomes the ancestor *par excellence,* of whom all the African ancestors are but faint and poor images. In this light, one can safely say that considering Jesus' ancestorship *par excellence* is a true *"preparatio evangelica"* of the Christian doctrines on Christ as the unique Ancestor of mankind. As the Great Ancestor, Jesus' authority over both the natural and the supernatural worlds encompasses all cosmic powers and all the other ancestors. Natural ancestors are mortals and subject to death. This limitation makes it impossible for them to save and protect other humans from death – the greatest enemy of mankind.

Furthermore, our natural ancestors only operated within tribal clans and family lines, but Jesus is the Savior of the whole world and thus encompasses all the different clans of the universe. This makes Jesus the great and supreme Ancestor, the Ancestor of all mankind who offers what our lineage ancestors cannot offer.

Bujo and Nyamiti are two African theologians who have written extensively on ancestral Christology. Nyamiti uses the term "brother-ancestor" because, for him, Christ is not only the perfect mediator between us and God, as written in the letter to the Heb 9:15–20, but Christ is also the foundation of moral conduct of Christians. For Nyamiti, Christ fulfills all the conditions required of an ancestor, whom he defines as "a relative of a person with whom he has a common parent, and of whom he is mediator to God, an archetype of behavior, and with whom, thanks to the supernatural status acquired through death, he is entitled to have regular sacred communication."[106] According to Orobator, Nyamiti's definition of ancestor meets all the five characteristics of African ancestorship, which are

> a natural consanguineous or non-consanguineous relationship with the living members of his/her family, clan or community, which is undiminished in death; a metaphysical proximity to God following death which facilitates, thirdly, his\her mediatory role on behalf of the living family or clan members and allows, fourthly, an entitlement to mandatory and regular communication and consultation (invocation, libation, ritual offerings, etc) with the living. Finally, based on the ancestor's exemplary life on earth he/she becomes a model of good living for the entire family and community of the living.[107]

For Nyamiti, Christ meets all the prerequisite conditions for being an ancestor and, therefore, qualifies to be a brother-ancestor in the African conception of the term. In his own words, "Christ realized in Himself – at least in principle – all that this definition (of brother-ancestor) entails,"[108] which would make him no longer an ancestor among many others, but the universal brother-ancestor *par excellence* "of whom the African ancestors are but poor and faint images."[109]

---

106 Nyamiti, *Christ as Our Ancestor*, 66.
107 Agbonkhianmeghe E. Orobator, "The Quest for an African Christ: An Essay on Contemporary African Christology," *Hekima Review*, no. 11 (September 1994): 82–83.
108 Nyamiti, *Christ as Our Ancestor*, 35.
109 Ibid., 23.

As our "brother-ancestor," Christ is the model of Christian behavior.[110] Ancestors are role models and Christ, consistent with biblical narratives, lived an exemplary life that all Christians should try to imitate. He was a man of compassion (Luke 7:13, Matthew 15:32). According to him:

> In fact, Christ's exemplarity includes also His quality as our Prototype of divine nature. The reason is because His exemplarity of conduct is based on the fact that we are through Him adopted sons of the Father. As noted earlier our Lord makes us His brother-descendants by communicating His divine life and nature to us and incorporating us into His own Body. This participated divine nature in us intrinsically requires that we live and behave according to His model. We can therefore, say that our Saviour is the Prototype of our Christian behaviour because He is the source of our participated divine nature. ... Consequently, in virtue of His Brother-Ancestorship Christ is our model of behaviour and nature as well.[111]

Commenting also on this notion of brother-ancestor, Orobator affirms that Christ's "ancestorship subsumes and eminently transcends the limited notion of ancestorship. Jesus Christ completes and perfects what Africans believe to be brother-ancestor. Christ is no longer one among many ancestors, but the universal Brother–Ancestor *par excellence*."[112]

Bujo, in another vein, speaks of a "proto-ancestor" or "Proto-Life Force." According to Bujo, the practice of ancestrology in Africa is a ritual enactment of the ingrained belief in the enduring nature of life force, guaranteed by the bond, which unites the dead and the living.[113] Ancestral cult is anchored in the belief that life is sacred and permanent. Viewed as such, life is a continuum. The cult of the ancestor creates an opening for the living to enter into communion with those who have gone to the world beyond. This communion is at once narrative, soteriological, and eschatological. The communion draws its life from the ancestors themselves who are the source of life to the living. The Chalcedonian Jesus, being divine and sharing in the same being with the Father, is believed to be not only the fullness but also the source and summit of Christian life as well. By his incarnation, Christ assumed what he intended to save, thus enabling the humanity to share in divine perfection. By his wounds, humans are healed, reconciled to God, and made to share in life after death by the resurrection.

---

110 Nyamiti, *Christ as Our Ancestor*, 31.
111 Ibid.
112 Orobator, *Theology Brewed in an African Pot*, 75.
113 Orobator, "The Quest for an African Christ: An Essay on Contemporary African Christology," 83.

Christ as the proto-ancestor not only reveals the supremacy and importance of the ancestors but also transcends and refines them in the light of biblical revelation. By this, Bujo implies that the Africans, having perceived the Divine in the concept of the ancestors, finds the typical expression of the divinity in the person of the Christ.

> If we look back on the historical Jesus of Nazareth, we can see in him, not only one who lived in the African ancestor-ideal in the highest degree, but one who brought that ideal to an altogether new fulfillment. Jesus worked miracles, healing the sick, opening the eyes of the blind, and raising the dead to life. In short, he brought life, and life-force, in its fullness. He lived his mission for his fellow-humans in an altogether matchless way, and furthermore, left to his disciples, as his final commandment, the law of love.[114]

Nyamiti and Bujo share many similarities in their approaches. Both authors agree on the link of African ancestors vis-à-vis Christ. As noted above, for Nyamiti, all the other African ancestors add up to no more than "poor and faint images" of the brother-ancestor, – Jesus Christ. For Bujo, the African ancestors are forerunners of the proto-ancestor. For both of them, Christ is that unique ancestor who perfects all there is in the traditional African conception of ancestorship. Nevertheless, while their starting points are the same, their aims are markedly different, because Nyamiti adopts an approach, which culminates in the formulation of an ancestral Christology, while Bujo, taking ancestral Christology as a starting point, elaborates a morality of the ancestors, which, eventually culminates in a "Proto-Ancestor Ecclesiology."[115]

Whether it is the Ghanaian John S. Pobee's portrayals of Jesus as the Nana, "the Greatest Ancestor," or the Congolese, Bénézet Bujo's, proto-ancestor, the Tanzanian theologian Charles Nyamiti's brother-ancestor, or the Congolese theologian, François Kabasele's, elder brother-ancestor, a common trait exists in this model. They all consider Jesus to be the ancestor unlike and above all other ancestors, or a unique ancestor before whom all others are but faint images.

---

114 Bujo, *African Theology in Its Social Context*, 79.
115 Benezet Bujo, "Pour Une Ethique Africano-Christocentrique," *Bulletin de la Theologie Africaine* 3, no. 5, January–June (1981): 42.

Conclusion

The Incarnation made it possible for God to physically dwell in a human community and share in human affairs. Jesus' life, work, and nature, as testified in Scripture, Tradition, and daily religious experience in Africa, earned him a series of leadership titles in African milieu, such as Chief or King, Liberator, Master of Initiation, Healer, and Ancestor. These titles testify to how African anthropology informs African Christology in a unique way, similar to how the various anthropological outlooks of the school of Alexandria and Antioch influenced ptristic Christology that became normative, thanks to the early ecumenical councils, which culminated at Chalcedon. Given that Christology in Africa is not a theoretical concept but a lived reality, in the next chapter, I will show how African Christology, anchored in an African understanding of anthropology, is lived out daily in the Church through songs.

· 5 ·

AFRICAN RELIGIOUS CHANTS: UNVEILING A LIVED CHRISTOLOGY THROUGH MELODIES – A THEOLOGICAL AND PASTORAL PERSPECTIVE

Introduction

After investigating various major African Christological models in their theological, cultural, and anthropological contexts, and moving effectively from anthropology to Christology, it is important to note that these models do not exist just in the abstract. They are very much present in the day-to-day life of the African Christian. These Christological models, rooted in the local culture, and consistent with Scripture and Christian Tradition, find deep expressions in popular religious songs. In these songs are identified not only expressions of a lived Christology but also a lens to the problems faced by the local Christian – problems to which Christianity has tried in its own unique way to propose and articulate solutions.

In this chapter, I will analyze popular African religious songs, bringing out Christological articulations to be found within the African context, in order to show how Christology is lived within concrete life situations. This lived Christology also expresses concrete responses to the problems of anthropological poverty that assails the continent. I will examine both West African and East African songs from different Christian denominations, highlighting how their Christology finds deep historico-cultural relevance in the sub-Saharan cultural ecclesial context.

Melodic Expressions of Christ: West African Popular Gospel Songs

In this section, I look at four West African songs, analyzing them as a means to bringing out how Christology is expressed in the daily lives of the people. All of these songs are unique in themselves, bringing out some aspects of Christology that are enriching.

"Only You Jesus" by Ada Ehi of Nigeria: A Window into a Christology of Supreme Strength and Unparalleled Power

Born on September 18, 1987, in Lagos, Nigeria to Victor and Mabel Ndukauba, who were both members of the local Church's choir, Ada Ehi is an award-winning gospel singer who became known for her albums *Undenied* and *Lifted*. In the words of her director and spokesperson, Ada is:

> A Lady made extra ordinary by the steadfast love of Christ Jesus. Ada Ehi popularly known as Ada, is a Nigerian/International Gospel Music Minister, Singer, Songwriter, Recording and Performing Musician who by the influence of the Holy Spirit Authored songs like, *Only You Jesus, I Testify, Jesus (You Are Able), Bobo Me, Cheta*, just to mention a few. Ada is gearing up for her 3rd studio album which is due out by the second half of 2017 to be released by Free Nation INC Record Label.[1]

Only You Jesus is a single that was produced on April 20, 2016, under the mandate of the Holy Spirit.[2] In an email response to me, Ada notes the following as the reasons and circumstances that led her to sing this song, "I was going through a very rough time in my life; it was a seemingly impossible situation, and the spirit of God prayed that song through me. My conclusion was and still is, He Is Capable!"[3]

---

1 Email response to the request of "Give me some background information about yourself" sent on July 15, 2017. This email was signed by Ada's director Steve Phronesis.
2 *Only You Jesus* By Ada Ehi can be found online at https://www.youtube.com/watch?v=MdQI NUBlPno
3 Email response to my request of "Give me some background information about yourself" sent on July 15, 2017. This email was sent by Ada's director Steve Phronesis.

***Only You Jesus* by** Ada Ehi– *Lyrics*

Eh eh eh eh
Only You, only You Jesus
Only You can do what no man can do
Only You can say what no man can say
Only You can change any situation at all
Only You able, Daddy soso You are capable Jehovah

Only You can do, what no man can do
Only You can say, what no man can say
Only You can do, what no man can do
Only You can change, any situation at all
Only You can do, what no man can do
Only You are able, Daddy only you are capable Jehovah meh
Only You can do, what no man can do
Jehovah meh eh, Jehovah oh
Only You, only You
Is only You, is only You, is only You

Just like You walked the streets of Galilee
You are doing the same today
And like You healed the sick and You raised the dead
You are doing the same today
Like You said Lazarus come forth, come forth
You are doing the same today (4X)

Ha oh God my promoter
You are doing the same today
Jesus my promoter, opening every door now
You are doing the same today
Fighting all my battle, healing the broken hearted
You are doing the same again

Only You can do, what no man can do
Only You can do, what no man can do
Only You are able, ha only You are capable
Only You can do, what no man can do

> Only You can change, any situation at all
> Only You can do, what no man can do
>
> Unfailing, unchanging, unfailing, resurrected Jesus
> Only You can do, what no man can do
> Jesus, Jesus, Jesus
> The Son of God
> The Word of Life
> The same today
>
> Say He is capable (Jesus)
> The resurrection (Jesus)
> And the Light (Jesus)
> Jesus, Jesus, Jesus
> Jesus, Jesus, Jesus
> .
> The Son of God (Jesus)
> The Word of God (Jesus)
> Jesus only You can make the blind to see (Jesus)
> Jesus only You can make the lame to walk again (Jesus)
> Jesus only You can make the dead to rise (Jesus)
> Jesus my promoter (Jesus)
> Jesus...
> Call His name, call His name, call His name
> He is capable...

Christological Analysis

In the midst of the religious plurality prevalent in present-day Africa, the place and work of Jesus in the life of the African people is very evident. In *Only You Jesus*, Ada Ehi brilliantly paints a picture of Christ-centered expressions that stem from the lived experiences of African people – A Window into a Christology of Supreme Strength and Unparalleled Power. Ada espouses how Jesus is viewed in the African milieu, bringing out a lived Christology that is consistent with tradition, biblically based and addressing the needs and aspirations of the people. Specifically, Jesus is seen as the one girded with the strongest power, the one who can do what no other person can do. "Only You can do, what no man can do." This puts Him in a position of God, above all other gods. Jesus' humanity brings us closer to Him in many respects, but the fact that he can do what no other person can do makes Him a reliable person of reference. It also drives home the fact that Jesus is the answer to the questions that assail the people on a daily basis, problems to which no one is able to provide solutions. Embedded in this is a lived hope in Jesus' ability to do what all others (individuals and governments) have failed to do, or are incapable of doing.

This Christological song does not limit itself only to "acts" of God. It is not limited to "doing." It extends to verbal power, and to the power to effect change. In other words, not only does Jesus have the power to do what no one can do but He also has the power to "say what no one can say," and to "change what no one can change."

Experiencing Jesus as the one who can say what no one can say is very significant, especially in the African context where freedom of expression is very often stifled.[4] It entails much courage and strength to speak up and do things considered to be against the authorities and powers. African Christians are therefore empowered, knowing and trusting that their Divine Master gives them power to follow in His footsteps, thereby sharing in His prophetic mission to speak the truth, especially truth to the powers that be.

The significance of Jesus as the one who can "change what no man can change" is also very evident in many sociocultural and political situations where people stick to old ways under the pretext of tradition. This is sometimes inspired by the traditional idea of, "the older the better," and that the more traditional something is, the more reason for it to endure and be respected. The idea of Jesus as one who can "change what no man can change," challenges a "theology of repetition," thus giving way to new areas of growth and progress. A Christology that puts Jesus as the one who can change situations and institutions alike, especially those that no one dares to change, resonates with the African people. This Christological model is very empowering and encourages

---

4 Jimmy Ocitti in his "Media and Democracy in Africa: Mutual Political bedfellows or Implacable Arch-foes" writes elaborately on the role of freedom of expression in African nation building. Despite the rhetoric concerning growing freedom of expression in Africa today, Ocitti highlights the deplorable condition under which many Africans live as a result of the fact that their government stifles freedom of speech and expression by setting up underlying currents of impediments to expression of self. (Jimmy Ocitti, Ph.D., "Media and Democracy in Africa: Mutual Political bedfellows or Implacable Arch-foes," Fellows Program, Weatherhead Center for International Affairs Harvard UniversityJuly 1999. Accessed on July 02, 2017 https://scho lars prog ram.wcfia.harv ard.edu/sites/proje cts.iq.harv ard.edu/files/fell ows/files/ocitti.pdf)

a culture of relevance and efficiency. Christians who find themselves in public administration can contribute to breaking down irrelevant structures and to lending their time, talent, and treasures to effecting meaningful societal change. Jesus Christ, while viewed and lived as a unique changer, is Himself consistent with Tradition, considered to be the unchangeable changer (Mal 3:6).

A strong expression of the unique functional and verbal attributes of Jesus is seen in this song. It is in this same light that, after rebuking the wind and silencing the storm, the disciples note the power of Jesus, "Who is this man that even the sea and the wind obey?" (Mt 8:27). Scripturally, Jesus' verbal authority is evident when He curses the fig tree (Mk 11:12–25, Mt 21:18–22) and casts out demons, simply by his words (Mt 8:28–34; Lk 13:32; Mk 5:8).

Ada's repeated, emphatic use of the phrase "Only you" underlines the uniqueness of Jesus; his proven ability to do, say, and change what no one is able or capable of.

> Only You Only Jesus Only You can do. . .
> Only You can say! What no man can say
> Only You can Change Every Situation at all
> Only You able Daddy Only You Capable.

The author uses the Old Testament title of Jehovah; a title which first appears in Genesis 2:4, to refer to Jesus, emphasizing his personal care for, and relationship with humanity "Only You are able, Daddy only You are capable *Jehovah meh*."[5]

The Jesus who can do what no one can do, say what no man can say, and change what no man can change, is the Old Testament Jehovah, the same person who walked through the streets of Galilee, the same one who healed the sick and raised the dead, as He did to Lazarus (Jn 11:38–53). These actions continue everyday today. It drives home the fact that, like an ideal ancestor and healer, Jesus is alive in the life of the African people, making His presence felt by the wonders of His acts of miracles and healing. Jesus is the one who promotes, and opens all doors, the strongest, the courageous; the one who fights our personal and community battles, who heals every broken heart, and empowers those who want to follow in his footsteps.

---

5 The "Meh" in *Jehovah meh* is an Igbo word that denotes the possessive word "my" (My Jehovah, God).

The song ends with affirmations of Christological titles. Jesus is referred to as the unfailing, unchanging, resurrected one, the Son of God, the Word of God, who is the same yesterday, today, and forever.

"Jesus Dey for Your Corner" by Glory Drops from Cameroon: Christology of Proximity in Focus

Referring to the song *Jesus dey for your corner*,[6] one of the composers and singers of *Glory Drops*[7], Aloysius Fonkeng the author of the song, noted:

> The main motivation for the writing of this song was the accelerated proliferation of Pentecostal movements and assemblies, with "Men of God" who opened "Churches" in almost every corner in Tiko town, promising people miracles, healing, jobs, promotions, marriages, success life, good health and a life void of suffering. Many Christians began moving from one pastor to another in search of these promises. Since satisfaction was hardly found in one, they would move to the other, and then to another. We felt people had lost the point. They were missing the focus. Therefore, there was urgency for a resounding of the twin messages: Whatsoever you do to the least of one of these, you do unto me, and that we should "pass through the narrow gate." We had to remind Christians that the Christ they sought from afar, had always been, and was still very close to them.

---

6 *Jesus dey for your corner* means "Jesus is by your side." It is in Cameroonian pidgin English, a West African language spoken along the coast from Ghana to Cameroon. It is a very active vehicular language in Cameroon. *Jesus dey for your corner* can be found online at https://www.youtube.com/watch?v=SH-KwFyuiYg

7 Glory Drops was born of Christ the King Choir Tiko, when five of its members, Polycarp Gumuh, Augustine Anuchem, Clive Nkeh, Julius Enow, Walta Nji, and Aloysius Fonkeng, embarked on spreading the Gospel of Jesus Christ in music through songs that would turn peoples' hearts toward God. The group adopted the name GLORY DROPS and inn 1999, released their first album titled *Redemption Man*. In 2002, they released their second album *Thank You Jesus*. *Jesus dey for your corner* is one of the tracks of the second album. The group still performs at shows and is currently working on another album.

Christology of Proximity in Focus – *Jesus Dey for Your Corner*

Original Lyrics	Translation
Refrain: *Jesus dey for your corner – o* (X2) *Why you de find He for far away* *Whe He dey for here - o* *For your corner, for place whey you dey?*	Refrain: Jesus is by your side Why are you searching for Him far away When He is here By your side, where you are?
You savy say that your neighbour, *You and he no de talk, wuna no de greet.* *When you see he, you de carry your nose,* *You talk say who be he? He no be something.* *You de forget say God He make he for He image*	Your neighbor, You do not speak to nor greet each other. When you see him, you ignore him You ask who he is; you say he is worthless Forgetting that God created him in His Image
You get to forgive'am when he do bad for you. *If you de make so, God He no fit hear your prayer,* *Why you de find God whe you leave He for road. (Ref)*	You must forgive him when he offends you. If you act/behave as such, God cannot hear your prayer Why are you searching for God, when you've left behind on the road? (Ref)
Oh! Everywhere you go for this world, *People them get plenty problem.* *You de see some pikin them for road,*	Oh! Everywhere you go in the world, People have many problems. You come across children on the streets,
Them de waka, them no get mama or papa *Everyday them just de beg for thing for chop-o*	Walking around, they are orphans Every day, they beg for food to eat

Original Lyrics	Translation
And sometime you de pass like say you no de see'em-o.	Yet sometimes, you walk by as if you do not see them
Jesus He done talk say make we do good for everybody	Jesus has commanded that we do good to everyone
Because if you do'em so: Na for Jesus you de do.	Because in doing good to them, you do it for Jesus
If you give sick man medicine, na for Jesus you de do.	If you give medicines to the sick, you do it to Jesus
You give some man water for drink, na for Jesus...	You give water to the thirsty, it's for Jesus
Man de hungry you give'em chop, na for Jesus...	You feed the hungry, it's for Jesus
He waka naked you give'em cloths-o, na for Jesus...	You clothe the naked, it's for Jesus
He dey for hospital you visit em, na for Jesus...	You visit the sick in the hospital, it's for Jesus
He problem plenty you make'em smile, na for Jesus...	You put a smile on the face of the troubled, it's for Jesus
Anything whe you do for some man, na for Jesus.... (x2)	Anything you do to someone else, it's for Jesus (2X)
Again make e no be say you de make some family suffer,	Never cause suffering on another family,
Even small whe them get, you de want for take'em.	Even the little they have, you want to take it away
If you de make so, God He no fit hear your prayer,	If you act/behave as such, God cannot hear your prayer
Why you de find God whe you leave He for road? (Ref)	Why are you searching for God, when you've left behind on the road? (Ref)
Whattin you de find, whattin you de find,	What are you searching for, what are you searching for
Before you de waka waka with confusion for your life?	Going about with so much confusion in your life?
Today you dey for here, you say Jesus dey for here,	Today, you are here, saying Jesus is here,

Original Lyrics	Translation
When trouble begin come, you say Jesus no dey for here.	When troubles come, you say Jesus is not here.
You go for other place, you say Jesus dey for there,	You go elsewhere; you say Jesus is there,
When trouble begin come, you say Jesus no dey for there.	When troubles come, you say Jesus is not there.
That your own Jesus na Jesus for happiness,	Your Jesus is a Jesus of happiness only
The Jesus whe I know them been nail He for cross.	The Jesus I know was nailed to a cross.
The problem whe you get be say you done confuse,	Your problem is that you are confused.
You de waka find God like say He done loss.	You are going around searching for God as if God is missing.
If you de make so, God He no fit hear your prayer,	If you act/behave as such, God cannot hear your prayer
Why you de find God, whe you leave He for road? (Ref)	Why are you searching for God, when you've left behind on the road? (Ref)

Christological Analysis

The song *Jesus dey for your corner* basically focuses on the Christology of Proximity of Christ, while washing away the mentality that we have to go far away to seek Jesus and the blessings that He gives. The refrain is put in the form of an emphatic, rhetorical question:

Jesus dey for your corner - o.
Why you de find He for far away
Whe He dey for here - o
For your corner, for place whey you dey?

Jesus is by your side
Why are you searching for Him far away
When He is here
By your side, where you are?

It is a very refreshing, reassuring, and consoling Christology, for it makes the incarnation more real and present. "The Word became flesh and dwelled among us."[8]

Emphasizing a Christology of proximity makes perfect sense from an African Christian perspective, because near and far are key cultural and biblical categories that describe relationship with the divine and with one another. Africans generally believe that the divine can make his/her habitat in certain specific places with their sphere of influence linked to the territory of their human populations. Their presence could be made "nearer" with invocations. Scripture also lends itself to this thought on the proximity and distance of the divine:

> The man of God came up and told the king of Israel, "This is what the LORD says: 'Because the Arameans think the LORD is a god of the hills and not a god of the valleys, I will deliver this vast army into your hands, and you will know that I am the LORD.'"[9]

Even though God's immediate presence is known to reside in the tabernacle and in the Holy of Holies – the innermost sacred area where the Ark of the Covenant was kept, God shows that He is not limited to those areas.[10] He is also found in the valleys, the places where people dwell.

The Christology of Proximity takes away fear and worry, especially if the person beside you is good and powerful. It instills trust. It is liberating. The song acknowledges the fact that human life is filled with moments of anguish, difficulties, and pain, and that the quest for liberation is rife. It encourages a renewed focus in the search for peace and consolation. Because Christ is near, He can hear those who call upon him. This song expresses the presence of an era where God has come right to our doorsteps so that we don't have to go searching for Him as if He were afar and lost. Looking to Christ is looking at our neighbor who reveals Himself in people who have many problems, in the orphans, and in the hungry.

Searching for Jesus in every place is akin to escapism, a situation where one seeks to be in constant flight from one situation to the other, without

---

8 John 1:14. The translation of the Message Bible is even more interesting "The Word became flesh and blood, and moved into the neighborhood."
9 1 Kings 20:28
10 In Catholic Sacramental theology, it is articulated by the expression that "God is bound to the Sacraments but not bound by the sacraments."

paying attention to the present and what is near, no matter how difficult it may be. The Jesus we know and preach is the crucified Jesus. Credit can be given to the authors of this song because it serves as a reminder against a growing sociocultural and political tendency that distracts Africans from making use of their present, available resources, skills, blessings, and opportunities, thereby giving way to societal ills, including corruption and looking up to non-African entities for ready-made solutions.

This song brings out the emotional element of the Christology of proximity lived by Africans and resonates very well with the cry of the prophet Isaiah: "These people come near to me with their mouth and honor me with their lips, but their hearts are far from me."[11] Since Jesus is beside us and has made Himself available, it implies that a relationship in which closeness is expressed only with words is not truly close; it would be empty, without the corresponding attitude of the heart. That is why the song repeats not only with the admonition to *"forgive'am when he do bad for you"*[12] but also with the question:

You de waka find God like say He done loss. . .
Why you de find God, whe you leave He for road?

Why do you go around searching for God as if He is missing. . .
Why are you searching for God, whom you left behind on the road?

A way to Christ is through reconciliation with those nearest to us – you can't leave your neighbor who is in need and go searching for Christ far away – why are you searching for God, when you left Him at home?

It should be noted that the Christology of Proximity does not in any way jeopardize the metaphysical relevance of Christological dogma, which, of course, is the foundation on which lies the supernatural nature of that proximity. In fact, it is thanks to Jesus' place in the divine Trinity that He is capable of being closest to everyone at the same time. This clarification is necessary because today, many tend to erroneously oppose tradition to innovation and continuity to development. *Jesus dey for your corner* testifies to what the eastern Patristic scholar, Clement of Alexandria meant when he said "If you have really found your brother, then you will have found your *God* as well."[13]

---

11 Isaiah 29:13.
12 Forgive him when he offends you.
13 Clement of Alexandria, *The Stromata* 1,19.

A Golgotha by Le Rossignol De New-Deido – Cameroon: Unveiling the Redeeming Christ in a Christology of Sacrificial Innocence

Golgotha[14] was composed by the New-Deido – Douala-based choir called *Rossignol*. In 1998, they produced a very popular heart-touching album that has inspired many other choirs across West Africa, and, *A Golgotha* is one of their songs with Christological overtones. It unveils the Redeeming Christ in a Christology of Sacrificial innocence.

A Golgotha

Original Lyrics	Translation
Refrain 1: A Golgotha, A Golgotha, il a souffert (x2)	Refrain 1: In Golgotha, In Golgotha, He suffered (x2)
1- Il fut amené dans le prétoire sans avoir rien fait	1 - He was taken to the Pretorium even though he was innocent
2 - On l'a trahi, on l'a saisi, on l'a jugé Jusqu'a la croix, il fut conduit à Golgotha	2 - He was betrayed, He was dragged, He was judged up to the cross, He was led to Golgotha
3 - Etant sur la croix, on l'insultait: "libère-toi" On a craché sur lui, on l'a frappé, on l'a torturé.	3 - While on the cross, He was insulted thus: "free yourself" They spat on Him, they beat Him, they tortured Him.
Refrain 2: A Golgotha, Golgotha, Golgotha (x2)	Refrain 2 - In Golgotha, In Golgotha, He suffered (x2)
Ils sont venus vers lui: a Gethsémané Ils l'ont capturé: a Gethsémané Ils l'ont frappé avec les bâtons, avec les épées malgré son innocence, a Golgotha ee	They came toward Him: in Gethsemane They captured Him: in Gethsemane They beat Him with sticks, with swords in spite of His innocence, in Golgotha.

14   *Golgotha* can be found online at https://www.youtube.com/watch?v=DcHYzDhw598

Original Lyrics	Translation
Dans sa souffrance: a Golgotha *Point de secours: a Golgotha* *Quel abandon, quelle trahison malgré son innocence, a Golgotha ee*	In His suffering: in Golgotha Moment of need: in Golgotha What an abandonment, what a betrayal, in spite His innocence, in Golgotha eel
Refrain 3: S'il a souffert, c'est pour nous sauver de nos pèches	Refrain 3 – If He suffered, it was to save us from our sins
Par son sang: *il nous a purifiés* *il nous a sauvé* *il nous a délivrés* *il nous a libérés*	By His blood: He has purified us He has saved us He has delivered us He has liberated/freed us

Christological Analysis

A *Golgotha* expresses a scripturally based Christology of the suffering of Christ at Golgotha.[15] In Luke 23:33, Judges. 9:53, and 2Kings 9:35, Golgotha denotes the site in Jerusalem where Christ and the others were crucified. The term "Golgotha" appears in the Old Testament twice, in Judges. 9:53 and 2Kings 9:35. In the New Testament, the term appears at the crucifixion in Matthew. 27:33, Mark. 15:22, and John 19:17. It emphasizes the fact that Christ our Savior was an innocent victim who willingly accepted suffering for the salvation of humanity. The very first line of the first verse highlights Jesus' innocence *"Il fut amené dans le Prétoire sans avoir rien fait"* (He was innocently taken to the Pretorium.). Jesus' trial before the Jewish Sanhedrin and the Roman governor Pilate (Mt 26:57–27:25, Mk 14:46–15:14, Lk 22:54–23:24, Jn 18:12–19:16) was a planned attempt by the authorities to make Him suffer innocently at Golgotha, where He was crucified (Mt 27:35, Mk 15:24, Lk 23:33, Jn 19:17–18). The gospels narratives recount what happened during the hours the Savior hung on the cross, until the end, when He died (Mt 27:39–50, Mk 15:29–37, Lk 23:34–46, Jn 19:25–30).

---

15 Golgotha is the Hebrew word for the Latin, *Calvaria* (Calvary). See Lk 23:33; Jgs 9:53; 2Kgs 9:35. It denotes the site in Jerusalem where Christ and the others were crucified. The term "Golgotha" appears in the Old Testament twice; (see Jgs 9:53 and 2Kgs 9:35). In the New Testament, the term appears at the crucifixion (Mt 27:33; Mk 15:22; Jn 19:17).

Christ, the innocent victim, is absolutely significant and meaningful for it really expresses a lived Christology, in a sociopolitical atmosphere, where the innocent continue to suffer at the hands of the powerful in society. Jesus is presented as the suffering one, the one who suffered in spite of His innocence. Jesus was betrayed, dragged, judged, and taken up to Golgotha, carrying his own cross. His suffering makes Him relatable to many who carry the weight and effects of anthropological poverty every day. Also, given that fact that He was also innocent makes this Christology even more relevant. It is not Jesus who volunteers Himself to suffer. He simply accepts it as the will of the Father.[16] Because Jesus endured suffering, He is in a position to fully understand the suffering of the African people.

A *Golgotha* does not limit itself just to presenting Jesus' suffering and innocence but also goes as far as giving the reason why he suffered. "*S'il a souffert, c'est pour nous sauver de nos pèches.*" (If He suffered, it was to save us from our sins.). It highlights the fact that Jesus' suffering was not in vain, and the shedding of His blood did not go to waste. It was to save us from our sins. It also emphasizes a very common dimension of Christian spirituality in Africa – the Blood of Jesus. African Christians believe so strongly in the power in the blood of Jesus. The blood of Jesus purifies, saves, delivers, and liberates, which present Jesus' death as a sacrifice. Many African Christians relate to, and identify with, Jesus at the level of his blood. In many Christian circles, invoking the blood of Jesus during prayer is commonplace. According to Dr. Daniel Olukoya, the blood of Jesus gives physical, emotional, mental, and financial healing. It has life-giving power, creative and re-creative power, bondage-destroying power, and renewing power.[17]

Par son sang: (by his blood)
il nous a purifiés (he has purified us)
il nous a sauvé (he has saved us)
il nous a delivrés (he has delivered us)
il nous a liberés (he has liberate/free us)

---

16 He cried out, "O my Father, if it be possible, let this cup pass from me: nevertheless not as I will, but as thou wilt" (Mt 26:39; see also Mk 14:36; Lk 22:42).
17 Many African Christians relate to and identify with Jesus at the level of his blood. In many Christian circles, invoking the blood of Jesus during prayer is common place. In his book, *The Blood of Jesus*, the Nigerian pastor and general overseer of Mountain of Fire Ministries, Dr. Daniel Olukoya, presents and sums up the belief that many African believe in the power behind the blood of Jesus.

In his *Introduction to African Religion*, John S. Mbiti argues that "in African societies sacrifice was very common and that most involved shedding of blood of a human being or an animal."[18] He continues by noting that because in African societies, life is closely associated with blood, every time blood is shed in a sacrificial context, it implies that human or animal life is being given back to God, who is, in fact, the ultimate source of all life. Jesus's suffering and eventual death at Golgotha, as an innocent victim (as affirmed by Holy Scripture), therefore highlights a lived Christology in Africa that is consoling and empowering. It is consoling, because God himself underwent the same experience and can therefore feel or relate to the human pain, especially in the face of anthropological poverty, HIV/AIDS, political, social, and psychological vulnerability. It is empowering not only because His death liberates and saves but also because it avails us of the power in the blood of Jesus.

Victory by Eben of Nigeria: Presenting Divine Triumph in a Christology of Ultimate Victory

Emmanuel Benjamin, popularly known as Eben, is a Nigerian Christian gospel musician, who released his debut album in November 2006, entitled "On The Rock" with hit songs like *"imaranma,"* *"God dey,"* and *"i don hammer."* In 2010 he released a follow-up album, entitled "Phenomenon," with hit songs like *"Imela Papa,"* *"siya Nma Nma,"* *"Super Man,"* just to mention a few. In 2013 he released a worship album called "Justified," with hit songs like "You alone are Worthy," "Jesus How I love you," *"Onye Nwem,"* "Forever," and *"All the Way."* His latest album is "Magnified," in which he uses very down-to-earth, daily terms to refer to Jesus. *"Victory"* by Eben[19] is a song of joy and victory for the marvels done by Jesus proclaiming the awesome deed of Jesus,

---

18 John Mbiti, *African Religions and Philosophy* (London: Heinemann, 1969), 63.
19 Eben is married to Jahdiel, a gospel music minister with whom they have two sons. Victory can be found online at https://www.youtube.com/watch?v=6_eJs-LSCgg

Yeeeeh!
He has given me victory!
Almighty God has given me victory!
He has given me victory!
Ooooh!!!

Verse 1
All the days of my life I praise You
Everything that I have na You gave to me Baba
Lord I say for Your love I'm grateful
Yes You love me plenty You came to die for me
Jehovah Alpha, Jehovah Nissi, I am that I am My great provider
I searched around
There's no one else like You
Lion of Judah
You're the Mighty Man in battle
CHORUS
Ah iyeeee!
God has given me victory! (He has given me victory!)
Ah iyeeeee!
He has given me victory! (God has given me victory!)
Ah iyeeee!
God has given me victory! (He has given me victory!)
Ah iyeeeee!
He has given me victory!
Hallelu...halleluyah eh... Halle!
Halleluyah eh... Halle!
Halleluyah eh... Halle!
Halleluyah eh... Halle! (x2)
VERSE 2
Come and see what the Lord has done for me
He has taken away my sorrows and now I'm free
Agama e buru halleluyah buru
Aga nma para halleluyah para
Because of Jesus everyday na shakara I dey do
Double double heavenly blessings na im I dey receive
Ah ah ah eh eh eh

> God Your grace and mercies always dey follow me
> Repeat Chorus Bridge
> If Jesus has given you victory
> Come let's dance, let's give Him praises now
> If Jesus has given you victory
> Come let's dance, let's give Him praises now
> Because of Jesus everyday *na shakara I dey do*
> *Double double heavenly blessings na im I dey receive*
> Ah ah ah eh eh eh
> God Your grace and mercies always dey follow me
> Repeat Chorus
> Because of Jesus everyday *na shakara I dey do*
> Double double heavenly blessings na im I dey receive
> Ah ah ah eh eh eh
> God Your grace and mercies always dey follow me

Christological Analysis

The song *Victory* expresses a Christology that is based on the things that Jesus did in his life. It is a kind of functional Christology, based on Scripture and experience, that attributes to Jesus the victories and successes of life. He uses the word *alleluia*[20] to describe joy in the face of that victory. There is a popular African gospel song that says, "Alleluia is a heavenly language for special people" to denote the traditional concept that Alleluia is the main language of praise of the choirs of angels, as they worship around the throne of God in Heaven. Jesus is the Lord who is worthy of all praise. He deserves all the praise because "Everything that I have na You give to me Baba" (Everything that I have it is you who gives it, Daddy.) The song uses the word "baba"[21] to refer to Jesus, a term similar to the biblical word "abba" that the gospel writer uses in Mark 14:36.

---

20 "Alleluia" the Greek and Latin form of the Hebrew word Hallelujah means "praise Yahweh" or "praise the Lord." It is a term of great joy. The primary Hebrew root word for *Alleluia* is *Hellel* which means praise. It appears many times in the Scripture such as in Judges 16:24; 2 Samuel 14:25; 2 Chronicles 7:6; Ezra 3:10–11; Nehemiah 5:13; Psalms 18:3, 56:4, 63:5, 150:2–4; Isaiah 62:9; Jeremiah 20:13; Joel 2:26.
21 Baba is a pidgin English word which can be translated as daddy, father, or elder.

Jesus is presented as the one whose love for humankind led to His death. In fact, the song goes as far as giving the reason for the incarnation. *"Yes You love me plenty You came to die for me"* (Yes, you loved me so much that you came to die for me.). Jesus came to earth to die for us. Using biblical images, Jesus is described as the *Jehovah Rapha*,[22] *Jehovah Nissi*,[23] *the I am that I am*,[24] *My great provider*.[25] Consistent with 1Chronicles 17:20, "There is none like you, O LORD, and there is no God besides you, according to all that we have heard with our ears,"[26] Jesus is addressed as the one who cannot be replaced by or with anyone else – "there's no one else like you." Jesus is the "Lion of Judah."[27] The image of Jesus as the "lion of the tribe of Judah" is very relevant for the African people, given the important place the lion occupies in the animal kingdom. In Africa, the lion signifies immeasurable strength, both in personality and physicality. It is a symbol of courage, valor, and pride, all put together. Even in the Scripture, the lion occupies a very important place because of its strength. In Judges 14:14, the riddle asks, "What is stronger than a lion?" or in Proverbs 30:30, "The lion which is mighty among beasts and does not retreat before any." The strength of the lion is in its ability to easily stalk and kill

---

22 *Jehovah Rapha* is first used in Exodus 15:26, meaning – "I AM the Lord who heals you" or "I am the Lord your Physician."
23 *Jehovah Nissi* means the Lord is my banner. In Exodus 17:12-13, after Israel defeated the Amalekites in battle, Moses built an altar and named it *Jehovah Nissi*, "the Lord is my banner."
24 The Hebrew phrase אהיהאשראהיה (transliterated Ehyeh-Asher. Ehyeh meaning I am that I am) appears only in Exodus 3:14. "And God said unto Moses, I AM THAT I AM (אהיהאשראהיה): and he said, Thus shalt thou say unto the children of Israel, I AM (אהיה) hath sent me unto you." I am that I am could be translated as "He who is" or "He who will be" or even "The being/existing (one,)" which is to say one who is defined by or performs the act of being.
25 My great provider (Jehovah-Jireh) is one of the titles applied to God in Genesis 22:14, "The LORD Will Provide." It is the name memorialized by Abraham when God provided the ram to be sacrificed in place of Isaac.
26 We also see this image in Exodus 8:10. Then he said, "Tomorrow." So, he said, "May it be according to your word, that you may know that there is no one like the LORD our God" and Psalm 86:8 "Among the gods there is none like to you. . ."
27 While Jacob was blessing his 12 sons, when he gets to Judah, he said, "Judah, your brothers will praise you, your hand will be on the neck of your enemies; your father's sons will bow down to you..You are a lion's cub, Judah;you return from the prey, my son. Like a lion, he crouches and lies down, like a lioness – who dares to rouse him? The scepter will not depart from Judah, nor the ruler's staff from between his feet, until he to whom it belong shall come" (Gen 49:8–10).

its prey, no matter how large the prey is. It represents royal authority, power, courage, and fearlessness. Jesus as "the lion" image espouses a Christology that expresses the place that Jesus occupies in the victories and successes of the people in all aspects of their lives. The Cameroonian National soccer team, for instance, is named the "Indomitable Lions of Cameroon," which drives home not only the strength of its players but also their skills and ability to defeat their opponents in any game.

It is quite interesting how the author employs images and titles used in the Old Testament attributed to God the Father to refer to Jesus Christ, the second person of the Trinity. Here we see a visible, lived expression of the Early Church's concept of Trinity, played out in daily African Christology. What can be said of the Father can be said about the Son, a kind of communication of idioms.

Jesus is seen to as the one who gives freedom by taking away sorrows, and because of Jesus, there is joy, grace, and mercy. The author uses a very interesting image when he talks about the grace and mercy that Jesus brings. "*God, Your grace and mercies always dey follow me*" (God's grace and mercies always follow me.). This literally means that the grace and mercies of God always come after or chase after him – a beautiful image that tells of how readily available Jesus' mercies and graces are.

Melodic Expressions Christ: East African Popular Gospel Songs

I will give a Christological analysis of three popular songs that serve as a window to how Christ is lived in this part of sub-Saharan Africa. This live Christology is scriptural, consistent with tradition and stems from the unique daily experiences of the people.

Hoziana by the Ambassador Choir, Rwanda: Introducing the Significance of Regal Christology

The Ambassadors of Christ Choir (AOCC) is a Church choir affiliated with the Seventh-Day Adventist Church of Remera, Kigali in Rwanda. It began in 1995 with the aim of providing worship (by presenting music that exalts and praises God), service (by evangelizing and drawing people to Christ), fellowship (by uniting with Christ and the community), and growth (nurturing their members toward a holistic maturity). They consider themselves to be ambassadors, chosen to proclaim the grace of Him who has called us from darkness to His marvelous light. The song *Hoziana*,[28] composed and sung by the Ambassador Choir, is a song of jubilation and praise to Jesus. It is a window into regal Christology.

Hoziana

Original Lyrics	Translation
Refrain: *Hoziana* *Hozi... Hoziana ah* *Hoziana* *Hozi... Hoziana ah* *Hahirw'Umwami uje mw'izina ry'Uwiteka* *Amahoro n'icyubahiro bibe ahasumba hose* (X2)	Refrain: Hosana Hosana Hossna Hosana Blessed is the king who comes in the name of the lord Peace and glory to the highest (X2)
Umunsi umwe Yesu yinjiye mu murwa Yerusalemu *Mu cyubahiro cy'Umwami w'abami* *[Abaturage b'uwo murwa basasa imyambaro yabo* *Mu nzira hose Yesu yagiye anyura]* *Baririmba Hoziana*	One day Jesus entered the city of Jerusalem With the glory of king of kings The inhabitants of the city laid their clothes down And went singing Hosana
Bari bazi ko azanwe no kubakiza ingoma mbi zo mw'isi *Kuko yahanuwe ko ari we uzarengera ubwoko bw'Uwiteka* *Ibyishimo bitaha mu mitima yabo baririmba* *Banyeganyeza amashami y'ibiti* *Indirimbo zikwira i Yerusalemu*	They thought he had come to deliver them from the bondage of civil operation Because the prophesy said he was the one to deliver God's people Joy overflowed their hearts They say waving tree branches and the sound of music filled the streets of Jerusalem

28 The song *Hoziana* can be found online at https://www.youtube.com/watch?v=xMGez-OFKw8

Original Lyrics	Translation
Nyamara we yazanywe no gutegura imitima y'abantu	But he had come to prepare hearts
Ayigobotore mu ngoyi y'icyaha no mu rupfu rw'iteka	To deliver them from the bondage of sin and eternal death
Umunsi umwe bazatahe mu rugo iwabo	So that one day they will return home
Baririmba banyeganyeza imisingi y'ijuru Indirimbo zikwire i Yerusalemu	With great singing that will shake the very foundations of heaven and the sound of music will fill Jerusalem
Bridge:	**Bridge:**
Twegereje umunsi wo kuzimurirwa iwacu	The day is at hand when we will be translated to our home
Umukwe n'umugeni we binjira mu cyubahiro	The bridegroom and bride will enter with glory
Baririmba indirimbo y'akataraboneka Izaririmbwa n'abamalayika	They will sing the song of songs Sang by the angels
Izaba ari indirimbo yo kwakira umukweacyuye umugeni we	A song of the bridegroom welcoming his bride
Uwo munsi tuzasezera kw'iyi si y'ibyago	That day we will sing farewell to the painful world
Icyaha n'urupfu bizaba bikuweho by'iteka	Sin and death will forever be removed
Turirimba n'ijwi rirenga ry'icyubahiro	We will sing with a loud and glorious voice
Dufatanye n'abamalayika dusingiza Umwami w'abami Kandi Nyir'ubutware bwose.	Together with the angel Glorifying the king of kings and the lord of kingdoms
Turasabwa twese gutegura umwambaro w'ubukwe wera kuko ntanumwe uzinjira atawufite.. Ntawe umutima wawe niwo mwambaro Yesu akeneye	It behoves us all to prepare pure wedding garment For none shall enter without it, none Your heart is the garment that Jesus requires

Original Lyrics	Translation
kugira ngo akwandike ku rutonde rw'abazinjirana nawe ahera	inorder to write your name in the glory list
Ntagisigaye tugeze ku nkengero z'I Yerusalemu	In a moment we will reach the borders of Jerusalem
Suzuma intekerezo zawe mwene da nange nsuzume izanjye	Examine your thoughts and i will eamine mine
Nta kizira kizinjira aho hera kandi buri muntu ku giti cye	For nothing impure shall enter the holy city, Let every individual
Reka twese twiyambure ibizira byatubuza kugenda (X2)	and us all cast away our impunity (X2)
Bridge	**Bridge**
Uwo munsi tuzasezera kw'iyi si y'ibyago	That day we will sing farewell to the painful world
Icyaha n'urupfu bizaba bikuweho by'iteka	Sin and death will forever be removed
Turirimba n'ijwi rirenga ry'icyubahiro	We will sing with a loud and glorious voice
Dufatanye n'abamalayika dusingiza Umwami w'abami Kandi Nyir'ubutware bwose.	Together with the angels Glorifying the king of kings and the lord of kingdoms

Christological Analysis

Hoziana is based on Jesus' entry into Jerusalem as recounted by the gospels.[29] It puts forth a Christology which is, at the same time, biblical, actual, eschatological, and prescriptive. It is biblical in the sense that it relates and interprets Jesus' triumphant entry into Jerusalem; actual, because it puts Him, as manifested in this encounter, at the very heart of the lives and experiences of the people, and eschatological, in the sense that it presents Jesus as the hope of the future; that time when *"Icyaha n'urupfu bizaba bikuweho by'iteka"*(Sin and death will forever be removed).

Consistent with biblical narratives, Jesus is referred to, not as an ordinary "king" but as a king who comes in the name of the Lord. The name of the Lord

---

29 In Matthew 21:1–11, Mark 11:1–11, Luke 19:28–44, and John 12:12–19.

is what makes Jesus' kingship unique and powerful. It is worth mentioning the aspect of names and the authority they come with in African society. Names have very deep significance. When being sent, the name of the sender gives weight to the message being transmitted. That is why the triumphant entry carried particular power because it is "in the name of the Lord."

"*Hahirw'Umwami uje mw'izina ry'Uwiteka*" (Blessed is the king who comes in the name of the Lord) brings to mind many biblical passages where power and authority of the name determines the outcome of an encounter. The encounter between David and Goliath readily comes to mind. Even though David was no match against the experienced, giant Goliath, the fact that he came in the name of the Lord made all the difference.[30] The Lord's name is so powerful and brings with it strong authority. It is this authority that David used to overcome the most feared Goliath of the Philistines. As king, coming with His unique authority, Jesus is presented as coming with the glory of the King of kings. The respect due to the king justifies the laying down of cloaks for Jesus to walk on as they sing the Hosanna.

While this song also narrates the mission of the king, it also highlights the common misconception of His mission.

Original Lyrics	Translation
Bari bazi ko azanwe no kubakiza ingoma mbi zo mw'isi	They thought he had come to deliver them from the bondage of civil operation
Kuko yahanuwe ko ari we uzarengera ubwoko bw'Uwiteka	Because the prophecy said he was the one to deliver God's people
Ibyishimo bitaha mu mitima yabo baririmba	Joy overflowed their hearts
Banyeganyeza amashami y'ibiti Indirimbo zikwira i Yerusalemu	They say waving tree branches and the sound of music filled the streets of Jerusalem.

Jesus' entry was filled with contrasts, for unlike our earthly kings, Jesus did not fill Himself with the royalties of the king. He wore no royal robes, but the clothes of the poor and humble. He came to offer love, not the force that was required to effect a political liberation from the hands of the Romans. His is not a kingdom of armies, power, and splendor but of humble service that

---

30 1 Samuel 17: 45–47.

aim at conquering people's hearts and finding lasting solutions to the problem of peace.

The people were hoping for a king who, being a descendant of David,[31] would restore the kingdom of Israel under the Davidic dynasty. This of course fitted very well with the biblical narratives.

Original Lyrics	Translation
Nyamara we yazanywe no gutegura imitima y'abantu	But he had come to prepare hearts
Ayigobotore mu ngoyi y'icyaha no mu rupfu rw'iteka	To deliver them from the bondage of sin and eternal death
Umunsi umwe bazatahe mu rugo iwabo	So that one day they will return home
Baririmba banyeganyeza imisingi y'ijuru	With great singing that will shake the very foundations of heaven
Indirimbo zikwire i Yerusalemu	and the sound of music will fill Jerusalem

Far from being a political messiah, and consistent with biblical witnesses, Jesus, in this song, is portrayed as the one who came to prepare hearts for the kingdom of heaven and to deliver human beings from the bondage of sin and eternal death. Jesus is presented as the great deliverer from bondage – a theme that resonates very deeply in the experiences of the African people who daily strive to protect themselves from the forces of evil, such as witchcraft, in all its various manifestations.

The eschatological aspects of the Christology embedded in this song, based in the book of Apocalypse, are articulated with the singing of the song of songs by angels, as the bridegroom and bride enter with glory. This point will mark the end of all the pains of the world, the end of sickness, sin, and death.

---

31 Jesus was often referred to as the "Son of David." See the two blind men in Matthew 9:27, the woman of Canaan in Matthew 15:22 and the blind men at Jericho in Matthew 20:30. In Matthew 12:22–23, when Jesus healed a demon-possessed man who was both blind and mute, "all the multitudes were amazed and said, 'Could this be the Son of David?'."

Original Lyrics	Translation
Uwo munsi tuzasezera kw'iyi si y'ibyago	That day we will sing farewell to the painful world
Icyaha n'urupfu bizaba bikuweho by'iteka	Sin and death will forever be removed
Turirimba n'ijwi rirenga ry'icyubahiro	We will sing with a loud and glorious voice

This coming at the end times is indeed accompanied with intense preparations and daily prescriptions, because no one will enter the kingdom of God without the wedding garment. The garment represents the human heart which Jesus desires that it be made ready by a good examination of conscience, so as to cast away all forms of impurities.

Hoziana presents a high Christology which is biblical, eschatological, actual, and prescriptive. It is also a Christology of consolation, because after knowing the real mission of Jesus, one is left not only with a strong encouragement to self-identify with "the one who comes in the name of the Lord" but also with a desire to examine one's own thought, hearts, and conscience. Jesus is referred to as blessed, the King of kings, the one who comes in the name of the Lord, the one whose coming brings joy, the one whose coming prepares hearts, the one before whom angels will continually sing the song of songs.

Amenitendeya (He Has Done It for Me) by the Mwamba Children Choir, Uganda: Displaying Divine Abundance with Christ the Generous Giver

The Mwamba Children's Choir[32] was founded in 2008 to promote talent and to change lives through music. This multilingual choir, composed of children

---

32 In 1998, there was an outbreak of cholera that affected part of Kampala where the family of Ponsiano Lwakatale, a local pastor in Kampala, lived. During that time, an 8-year-old girl, Omega, the pastor's daughter would "steal" some rice and maize from the family kitchen to give to one of her friends whose father had died from the diseases. Pastor Lwakatale, noticing a shortage of food at home came to realize that it was the little Omega who was sneaking out with the food destined for the family. As he was about to punish her, she said, "If you beat me for giving to the needy can you still be a pastor?" These words opened his eyes, as he saw the greater needs beyond his family walls. This led him to open up an organization that helps orphans and widows in their Kampala community and the Mwamba Children's Choir that travels the world to raise funds and create awareness about the orphans and underprivileged children in Uganda.

from ages 6–13 focuses on Christian songs of inspiration and hope. *Mwamba*, means "rock" in Swahili.

Amenitendeya (He has done it for me)

Amenitendeya (amenitendeya) 4X
Emmanueli (Emmanueli amenitendeya)
Emmanueli (Emmanueli amenitendeya)
Amenitendeya (amenitendeya) 4x

Emmanueli (Emmanueli amenitendeya)
Emmanueli (Emmanueli amenitendeya)

He has done it for me (He has done it for me) 4x
Emmanueli (Emmanueli He has done it for me)
Emmanueli (Emmanueli He has done it for me)
Yesu akyikoze (Yesu akyikoze) 4x

Emmanueli (Emmanueli Yesu akyikoze)
Emmanueli (Emmanueli Yesu akyikoze)
Amenitendeya (amenitendeya)4x

Emmanueli (Emmanueli amenitendeya)
Emmanueli (Emmanueli amenitendeya)
Amenitendeya (amenitendeya)4x

Emmanueli (Emmanueli amenitendeya)
Emmanueli (Emmanueli amenitendeya)
Amenitendeya (amenitendeya) 4X

Emmanueli (Emmanueli amenitendeya)
Emmanueli (Emmanueli amenitendeya)

Christological Analysis

In *Amenitendeya (He has done it for me)*, the Mwamba Rock Choir expresses a Christology common among Africans – a Christology that portrays Jesus as the one who acts on behalf of His people. He is generous, and his generosity is related to his abundance. In the face of many social and political obstacles, the quest for solutions is rife, as people seek to make their way through life. Many people find themselves in helpless situations and, in turning to Jesus, they realize the answer to their cries. This song is an expression of joy in the face of Jesus' intervention.

It is not uncommon in Africa for people to ascribe to Jesus the answer to their prayers and aspirations. Jesus' ability to do things for those who call upon Him with faith is very common in Africa. He is the "go-to" person, the one people turn to when they cannot do it for themselves. It should be noted that the expression "He has done it for me" is associated with the name *Emmanueli* (Emmanuel),[33] a name which personifies God and shows Him to be among us. In African Christology, Jesus is lived and experienced as God among us, the one who does things, especially difficult and humanly impossible things, for us.

Unikumbuke (Remember Me) by Christina Shusho, Tanzania: In Sync with Human Plight with Christ as the Merciful Listener

Unikumbuke, by Christiana Shusho, a Tanzanian born-again Christian,[34] is a song that portrays Jesus as the unique, almighty, and merciful liberator. It brings out a Christology of liberation that draws from Jesus' might and mercy. *Unikumbuke* is an invocation for Jesus' intervention in human affairs and a plea to have Jesus remember His people as they face the difficult moments of their daily social and political life.

Original Lyrics	Translation
Unikumbuke Baba,	Father remember me
Unapowazuru wengine naomba unikumbuke	When you visit others I pray – remember me
Usinipite Yesu	Do not pass me by Jesus
Unapowazuru wengine naomba unikumbuke	When you visit others I pray – remember me

33 Emmanuel means "God with us."
34 Christina Shusho was once a Church cleaner, until when she discovered her talent in singing. She is married to John, a practicing preacher and they have three children. She has several albums. Unikumbuke can be found https://www.youtube.com/watch?v=82uwOrdj3xM

AFRICAN RELIGIOUS CHANTS: UNVEILING A LIVED CHRISTOLOGY 149

Original Lyrics	Translation
Unikumbuke x2	Remember me x2
Yesu naomba unikumbuke	Jesus I pray, remember me
(Repeat)	(Repeat)
Usinipite x2	Do not pass me by x2
Yesu naomba unikumbuke	Jesus I pray, remember me
(Repeat)	(Repeat)
Mnyonge mimi dhaifu mimi, unikumbuke	The weak and wretched me, remember me
Na mama utaka kunyonyesha, umkumbuke	The barren mother yearning for children, remember her
Ona huyo asiye na kazi, mkumbuke	The one without a job, remember him
Lazima na wajane wanalia, uwakumbuke	The grieving widows, remember them
Kijana huyo ataka mwenzi, umkumbuke	The youth who wants to marry, remember him
Na mwingine huyu ataka elimu, umkumbuke	And the one yearning for education, remember them
Umasikini sasa ndio wimbo, utukumbuke	Poverty now is so common, remember us
Nchi nzima vilio vimetanda, utukumbuk	Grief is over the country, remember us
Refrain	Refrain
Utukumbuke x2	Remember us x2
Yesu twaomba utukumbuke	Jesus I pray, remember us
(Repeat)	(Repeat)
Usitupite x2	Don't pass us by x2
Yesu twaomba utukumbuke	Jesus I pray, remember us
(Repeat)	(Repeat)
Prayer:	Prayer:
Ewe mwenyezi Mungu mwenye rehema; mwingi wa utukufu	Almighty and merciful God full of Glory
	Lord over all creations
Bwana wa viumbe vyote	The Creator of heaven and earth
Muumba wa mbingu na dunia	We humbly pray to grant us wisdom and knowledge
Twakuomba kwa unyenyekevu utupe hekima na busara	

Original Lyrics	Translation
Sisi waja wako tuliokusanyika hapa	Us your children who have gathered here
Uibariki Tanzania iwe nchi ya amani	Bless Tanzania to be a peaceful country
Na wote wanaoishi humo wawe na upendo halisi na umoja	And all that live in it to have real love and unity
Serikali yetu na viongozi, uwakumbuke	Our government and leaders, remember them
Waongoze nchi kwa hekima yako, uwakumbuke	To lead the country with your wisdom, remember them
Uchumi wa nchi yetu Baba, uukumbuke	Our country's economy Father, remember it
Bunge pia na mahakama, uikumbuke	The parliament and Courts, remember them
Sikia kilio cha watanzania, utukumbuke	Listen to the cries of Tanzanians, remember us
Majibu ya matatizo yakoke kwako, utukumbuke	The answer to our troubles to come from you, remember us
Tazama majanga yanayotukumba, utukumbuke	See the tragedies we go through, remember us
Ajali nyingi twazika wengi, utukumbuke	Many accidents – we bury many, remember us

Christological Analysis

As the title of the song itself reveals (Remember me), this song is a cry of desperation, a prayer, and therein, we see the place that Jesus occupies in the life of the people.

Original Text	Translation
Unikumbuke Baba,	Father remember me
Unapowazuru wengine naomba unikumbuke	When you visit others I pray – remember me
Usinipite Yesu	Do not pass me by Jesus
Unapowazuru wengine naomba unikumbuke	When you visit others I pray – remember me

It is filled with lines that are grounded in Sripture, such as *Unikumbuke* (Remember me) and *Usinipite* (Do not pass me by). *Unikumbuke* makes one recall the passion narratives as related in Luke 23:42. It alludes to the words of the thief who was crucified on the cross beside Jesus, "Remember me when you come into your kingdom" (Lk 23:42). The words of the thief on the cross hold particular significance in the African context, for they emphasize certain aspects of Jesus vis-à-vis His people, and reveal a Christology that makes Him all the more relatable and reachable. Jesus is the one who can intervene in, and liberate us from, all situations, even in the midst of what Paulo Freire refers to as "limit Situations," as those situations or conditions which impede or prevent one's drive to becoming more fully human as a result of one's "hosting" or "housing" the oppressor's mindset.[35] Calling on Jesus to "remember us" underlines a theology in which Jesus is considered as the God to whom heaven and earth belong, "Behold, to the Lord your God belong heaven and the highest heavens, the earth and all that is in it" (Dt 10:14).

Usinipite is a Swahili phrase that literally means "do not go away." It alludes to the passage in Mark 10:46–52 where Jesus was passing by, and a blind man named Bartimeus grasps the opportunity to call Jesus' attention to himself; "Jesus, Son of David, have mercy on me!" Many rebuked him, telling him to be quiet. It prompted him to shout all the more, "Son of David, have mercy on me!" (Mk 10:47–48) It presents Jesus as a compassionate healer who mends all forms of life situations.

Jesus is called upon to remember all people, including the weak and wretched,

(*Mnyonge mimi dhaifu mimi*), the barren mother yearning for children (*Na mama utaka kunyonyesha*), the jobless (*Ona huyo asiye na kazi*), the grieving widows (*Lazima na wajane wanalia*), the youth who wants to marry (*Kijana huyo ataka mwenzi*), and the one yearning for education (*Na mwingine huyu ataka elimu*), as well as our government and leaders (*Serikali yetu na viongozi*).

---

35 Paulo Freire defines a "limit-situation" as a situation or condition that impedes or prevents one's drive of becoming more fully human as a result of "hosting" or "housing" the oppressor's mindset. Paulo Freire, *Pedagogy of the Oppressed* (New York: Continuum, 2002), 49. In his *Pedagogy of the Oppressed*, Freire argues that a true human being is one who has a consciousness is their own, with a humanity and identity of their choosing. For him, "In order for the oppressed to be able to wage the struggle for their liberation, they must perceive the reality of oppression not as a closed world from which there is no exit, but as a limiting situation which they can transform. This perception is a necessary but not a sufficient condition for liberation; it must become the motivating force for liberating action." (Paulo Freire, *Pedagogy of the Oppressed* (New York: Continuum, 2002), 49).

Jesus is seen not only as the one who intervenes in the lives of people but also the one who intervenes in real situations, such as in leading the country with His wisdom, and in assisting the parliament and the courts. Jesus is portrayed as one who will supply the answer to all troubles, tragedies, and the many accidents that kill many people.

Unikumbuke brings out a lived Christology that puts Christ as the great liberator, a merciful savior, a listener and a healer who is present at every stage of the social and political journey. It presents Christ as a concerned, merciful liberator, in sync with human plights, on whom we can depend when He passes by.

Conclusion

In this chapter, I analyzed Christological expressions through popular African gospel songs, and included those from different Christian denominations, languages, and expressions focusing on West and East African songs in their original languages. In order to gain a real feeling of a lived Christology in sub-Saharan Africa, I endeavored to extend the research to multiple Christian denominations like Catholic, Seventh-Day Adventist, and other Protestant and non-denominational Churches, thus giving this endeavor an ecumenical and multidenominational outlook.

When analyzing these songs and bringing out their Christology, I note how consistent they are with Scripture and Tradition, while remaining so deeply rooted in the local culture from which they spring. One common characteristics is the usage of Christ, God, and the Spirit. It is common to see African songs that express ideas about Christ, using the same terms to express details about God the Father and God the Holy Spirit. It is very common to have songs that refer to the Father in the refrain, while the verses refer to the Son or to the Spirit. It is a witness to the Patristic Trinitarian theology that the persons of the Trinity receive the same adoration and the same glory by virtue of their consubstantial nature. It is a sort of deep-seated, intrinsic communication of idioms in which what can be said of the Father can be said equally of the son and the Holy Spirit. In the final chapter, given the primordial place of motherhood in Africa, I will examine songs that bring out African Mariology in order to deepen our Christological understandings.

· 6 ·

AFRICAN RELIGIOUS CHANTS: UNVEILING A LIVED MARIOLOGY THROUGH MELODIES – A THEOLOGICAL AND PASTORAL PERSPECTIVE

Introduction

The place of Christ in the life of Africans throughout the years has reflected and been strengthened by Africa's strong traditional respect and honor for Mary – the Mother of Jesus. Mary's place in African Christian life has more value because of the key role that motherhood plays in African cultures. In the earlier chapters, I examined not only the different Christological models prevalent and rooted in African culture but also how that Christology is lived and expressed in songs. In this chapter, I will examine a lived Mariology within the African people. It is very important to observe the place of Mary when we talk about Christ in the context of Africa, because of the crucial place that motherhood occupies in the life of children in particular, and in the African society as a whole. First, I will look at the place of motherhood in Africa as it pertains to Mary, and then examine some West African and East African Marian songs which highlight Mary's place in the Christian lives of the people, presenting not only their Mariology but also their cultural significance consistent with Tradition and Scripture.

African Motherhood in Mary: A Mariological Perspective

At Ephesus in 431, exactly 20 providential years before the Council of Chalcedon in 451, Mary was officially defined as the Mother of God-the *theotokos*, to the disapproval of Nestorius. Cyril, Patriarch of the See of Alexandria, was the main protagonist of this fight and it was, thanks to him that Nestorius and his *Christotokos* doctrine was anathemized.

Because he is an ancestor par excellence, it goes without saying that Jesus' mother should also be a topic of deep interest, as was done at Ephesus. Without a proper understanding of the place, role, and dignity of the mother in the African culture, radical truths, such as Jesus' complete human and divine attributes, cannot be fully appreciated in African theology and Christian life. The place of the Mother in African society is indispensable. To insult my mother is to insult me, and to deliberately ignore a mother is an abomination.

The concept of motherhood is therefore of central importance in the African tradition. One cannot talk of mother (Mary) without talking about the son (Jesus), because it is thanks to the son that the woman became mother (of God). "Mary is truly *theotokos* because the body of Christ did not come from heaven but from Mary. Mary bore Emmanuel, God with us, according to the Flesh."[1] Ephesus' focus on *theotokos* and its emphasis on the incarnation was a significant step toward the humanization of God, which Chalcedon later solemnly defined. I use the phrase "humanization of God" in the same sense as Jacques Dupuis did when he defined it as "the divine person, having once become human, has henceforth a divine human personhood, and a divine human person is one who is also truly human."[2]

With motherhood, a woman in the African culture is considered blessed; she acquires a higher status in society, and she is respected and mythologized. The Yoruba people have a proverb that summarizes motherhood in most African cultures: *Iya ni wura. Baba ni dingi*. Literally translated, this means "Mother is gold. Father is a mirror."[3] Motherhood is considered to be very important because the preservation of humanity depends on the role of mothers in

---

1 Davis, *The First Seven Ecumenical Councils (325-787)*, 162.
2 Jacques Dupuis, S.J, *Who Do You Say I Am? Introduction to Christology* (Maryknoll, NY: Orbis, 1994), 90.
3 Taiwo Makinde, "Motherhood as a Source of Empowerment of Women in Yoruba Culture," *Nordic Journal of African Studies* 2, no. 13 (2004): 165.

society.[4] Motherhood is revered among the Yoruba to the extent that most women look forward to motherhood. Mothers are even deified, as is evident in the Yoruba song:

Original Text	Translation
Orisa bi iya ko si	There is no deity like mother
Iya la ba ma a bo	It is the mother that is worthy of being worshipped

What do mothers ordinarily do in relation to their children? What did Mary ordinarily do with Jesus, her son? The answer lies in the lyrics of the Nigerian-Cameroonian musician Nico Mbarga in his song "Sweet Mother."[5]"*If I no sleep, my mother no go sleep, if I no chop, my mother no de chop. She no de taya aa, sweet mother, I no go forget the suffer way you suffer for me eh eh.*" (If I don't sleep, my mother will not sleep. If I don't eat, my mother will not eat. She does not get tired, sweet mother, I will never forget the suffering that she endured for me.)

Regardless of whether a particular society ascribes to a patrilineal or matrilineal kingship, motherhood occupies a special place, for mothers are the indispensable building blocks of social relationships, identities, and society. Mothers represent familial ties, unconditional love, and loyalty, and they are invoked, even in extra-familial situations that call upon these values.[6] It is not uncommon in Yoruba villages, for instance, to hear people call themselves *omoya*, meaning mother's child, to emphasize that fraternal and sororal bonds derive from the mother and the institution of motherhood.[7] The Yoruba also have a saying: *omo k'oni ohun o ye, iya ni ko gba*, translated as "a child survives and thrives only at the mother's will." This reveals the critical role the mother plays in the welfare of the child. This means that at no point in time should details about the child exclude the mother. She is not only the birth-giver but also the

---

4 Lawal Babatunde, *The Gelede Spectacle: Art, Gender, and Social Harmony in an African Culture* (Seattle, WA: University of Washington Press, 1996), 78.
5 "Sweet Mother" is a highlife song by the Nigerian and Cameroonian singer Prince Nico Mbarga and his band Rocafil Jazz. Released in 1976, it remains one of the most popular songs in Africa and is sometimes referred to as *Africa's anthem*. It is a celebration of the primordial place that motherhood occupies in the African society.
6 Oyeronke Oyewumi, "Abiyamo: Theorizing African Motherhood," *Jenda: A Journal of Culture & African Women Studies*, Online edition, 1, no. 4 (2003): 1.
7 Oyewumi, 1.

life-giver, making motherhood a lifelong vocation. There is no greater public institution than motherhood.[8]

Ephesus gave Mary solemn public recognition, consistent with African values, which not only shines the light on Christ but also makes him more real, acceptable, and relatable. Ephesus' emphasis on Mary as the *theotokos* – Mother/bearer of God, as opposed to Mary, the Mother of the human Jesus – *Christotokos*, as espoused by Nestorius, really stressed Christ's full humanity in a unique way. "To become human is to become the child of a mother."[9]

The importance of highlighting the place of motherhood in Africa in relation to Mary is because it represents an effort (conscious or otherwise) to do two related things. First, it helps to retrieve the female/mother experience and its value in the Incarnation. Second, it gives expression to a recurring theme, namely, the incorporation of motherhood in God, emphasizing Christ's human and divine characteristics which resonate with African values. Because the Word became flesh through Mary's agency, the whole event of salvation is exteriorized as God's goodness made accessible to the world. *Theotokos* symbolizes the participation, not only of one Galilean girl but also of motherhood as a whole.

Talking about a Christology in which motherhood is prioritized, Lynette Jean Holness notes:

> A Christology from "within," in which motherhood is a core image, can have profound relevance in the African context. Since motherhood is an integral (perhaps the most basic) part of the reality of most women's lives on this continent, the fact that Christ emerged from the body of a woman accords dignity to this state. Mary's designation as *Theotokos*, bearing in mind the full meaning of the title, can then be understood as a recapitulation of motherhood. . . .[10]

Mary's role at the Incarnation and her unique position as the *theotokos*, in some way, situates motherhood in the scope of redemption, thus helping to mediate a Christ relevant to African pastoral contexts, where motherhood is violated. Mary, as the Mother of God – the God who suffered the excruciating pain of the cross, makes her more relatable to African women. This is particularly true in contexts of hardship and female oppression with which many

---

8 Oyewumi, 3.
9 Balthasar, *The Threefold Garland: The World's Salvation in Mary's Prayer*, 30.
10 Jean Holness Lynette, "Christology From Within: A Critical Retrieval of the Humanity of Christ, with Particular Reference to the Role of Mary" (Doctor in Philosophy Dissertation, University of Cape Town, 2001), 234.

African women identify. It would be problematic for Africans to discuss Jesus in isolation from Mary, for she mediates Christ's humanity, and constitutes the locus of meeting between the human and the divine person of Jesus.

This poem by Alla R. Bozarth is helpful in pushing the place of motherhood in Africa in relation to a lived Mariology and Christology:

> Before Jesus
> was his mother.
>
> Before supper
> in the upper room
> breakfast in the barn.
>
> Before the Passover Feast,
> a feeding trough,
> And here the altar
> of Earth, fair linens
> of hay and seed.
>
> Before his cry,
> her cry.
> Before his sweat
> of blood,
> her bleeding and tears.
> Before his offering, hers.
> Before the breaking
> of bread and death,
> the breaking of her
> body in birth.
>
> Before the offering
> of the cup,
> the offering of her breast.
> Before his blood,
> her blood.
> And by her body and blood
> alone, his body and blood
> and whole human being.
>
> The wise ones knelt
> to hear the woman's word
> in wonder.
> Holding up her sacred child,
> her God in the form of a babe,

> she said, "Receive and
> your hearts be healed
> and your lives be filled
> with love, for
> this is my body,
> is my blood."[11]

The relevance of touching upon the place of motherhood in Africa in relation to Mariology and Christology is very deep. In fact, the use of the word *theotokos* to refer to Mary emphasizes the point that, in accordance with the principle of *communicatio idiomatum*, the purely human attributes can be predicated upon God in his incarnate status as God-man. This makes it easier to say God dies on the cross, or that Mary is the Mother of God. This also applies to the title of ancestor being applied to Christ. Even though ancestorship is purely a human title, it can also be applied to the incarnate Christ as we have seen before, using the same principle of *communication idiomatum*.

Portraits of Mary: West African Popular Gospel Songs

In this section, I am going to analyze three popular West African songs that bring out a Mariology as it is lived in the daily lives of the people. These songs are sung in Churches during Eucharistic celebrations, prayer sessions, and during Marian feast days. Consistent with tradition, grounded in Scriptures, and inspired by the local cultures, these songs reveal a Mariology that is not only unique but also makes Mary part of the daily lives and struggles of the people.

Maria, Maa-Nfor (Mary, Queen-Mother), Cameroon: Divine Maternity: Mariology in the Concept of "Maa-Nfor" (Queen-Mother)

Maria, Maa-Nfor is popularly sung in Catholic Churches in Cameroon during mass and on other Marian feasts. It originated from the Bafut people of northwest of Cameroon. It brings out the unique, powerful place that Mary occupies,

---

[11] Alla Renee Bozarth, *This Is My Body: Praying for Earth, Prayers from the Heart* (San Francisco: Harper, 1996), 169.

not only in our ultimate salvation but also in our day-to-day relationship with her son, Jesus. *Maria, Maa-Nfor* literally means – "Mary, Queen Mother."

Original Lyrics	Translation
Maria, Maa-Nfor	Mary, Queen-Mother.
Maria, oh-oh, Maa-Nfor Mangye.	Oh Mary, Queen-Mother (Mangye = Woman, added for emphasis)
Lo'ge me maa'ne mu fa mbo Nwi, Maria.	Take these offerings and present them to God, Mary

Mariological Analysis

To understand the Mariological concept of Mary as Queen-Mother, one has to fully appreciate the concept of Queen-Mother in the African tradition, as a whole, and in the Bafut culture, in particular. In the Bafut tradition, like in most sub-saharan cultures, polygamy is common. Within polygamy, there is the common practice of wife inheritance, especially for chiefs and titled men. When the Chief or Fon "gets missing,"[12] he has to be replaced immediately either by one of his sons or his brothers. Depending on whether the tribe is matrilineal, such as the case of the Kom tribe in the northwest of Cameroon, nephews on the mother's side could be eligible for chieftaincy.

When a person becomes chief of his village, not only does he move into the royal chambers with all his wives, but he also inherits all the wives of the previous chief who was his father, brother, or uncle. When a man inherits the chieftaincy from his father, his mother automatically becomes the Queen-Mother. He has the right to have sexual intercourse with all the wives, except his own mother, who automatically moves into the Queen-Mother's compound.

The Queen-Mother is the biological mother of the chief. The Queen-Mother can also be a close relation to the chief. At the International Chieftaincy Conference in Accra, Ghana, held in January 2004, a picture of the summary of her role in society is described:

---

12 In the North-West province of Cameroon, like in most African cultures because of the belief that death is not the end, the language used when the Chief "dies" is unique. Bafut people believe that chiefs/fons don't die, they "go missing," they simply disappear.

She is the number one royal in her lineage, can't be the chief's wife and she is the mother of the occupant of the stool, which means that in essence the stool belongs to her. She is a community social welfare officer. She makes sure everyone gets their resources fairly. She is a liaison officer between people and services. She is a role model for women and children and explains policies to them concerning their lives. She is involved in health education and keeps up with her own education in order to serve others. She encourages and helps women to be economically strong and gives advice as to how to raise children. She is a guidance counsellor to chiefs, parents and children. She supervises puberty rites or picks someone to supervise these rights.[13]

Queen-Mothers wield an enormous amount of power. Her role is very extensive and strong and may sometimes extend to the position of Chief Justice in the community. An example would be, according to Owusu-Mensah, because the Akan customs and traditions hold that the land belongs to the dead, the living, and the yet unborn, any proceeds from any sale of any stool property, such as land, must be appropriated to the respective traditional political units within the traditional area. If the chief fails to honor part of the contract, a consequence is often agitations to destool chiefs, led by their Queen-Mother, who will charge the chief with misuse or sale of stool property.[14]

A mother is the epitome of power and influence, specifically because she is a mother.[15] Her role has social, political, and religious aspects to it, and they may help the kings make decisions regarding the ruling of the kingdom. Robert S. Rattray describes the role of the Queen-Mother as "the whisper behind the Stool."[16] The *Maa-Nfor* is revered. It is not just the mother who is revered, it is her womb. According to Orobator, "the womb that gave birth to the king is treated as a sacred object, an object of sacred ritual deference and public devotion."[17] The Benin people of West Africa refer to the womb as the *eko n'bie okhai* which means "the womb that bore the person of dignity and importance."

---

13 Linda Kreitzer, "Indigenization of Social Work Education and Practice: A Participatory Action Research Project in Ghana" (Doctor in Philosophy Dissertation, University of Calgary, Alberta, 2004), 33.
14 Owusu-Mensah, "Queen Mothers: The Unseen Hands in Chieftaincy Conflicts Among the Akan in Ghana: Myth or Reality?" *The Journal of Pan African Studies* 8, no. 6 (September 2015), 6.
15 Carole Fontaine, *Smooth Words: Women, Proverbs and Performance in Biblical Wisdom*, (Sheffield: Sheffield Academic, 2002), 27.
16 *Robert S. Rattray, Ashanti Law and Constitution*, (Oxford: Clarendon Press. 1929), 88.
17 Agbonkhianmeghe E Orobator, *Theology Brewed in an African Pot*, (Nairobi: Paulist Publications, 2008.) 103.

It should be noted that the concept of Queen-Mother was very much alive in Judaic culture.[18] We see evidence of this in Old Testament scriptural passages which emphasize the unique, important role of the mother of the king in monarchy. In 1 Kings 1:11–27, we see Bathsheba (David's mother), the first Queen-Mother of ancient Israel, as she stages a plot, together with the prophet Nathan, to convince David to announce the succession of her son Solomon, the beloved of Yahweh, as king (1 Kgs 1:11–27). She later occupies the role of Counselor (1 Kgs 2:19–20), a position that facilitated Adonijah's request for the concubine Abishag, exposing Adonijah as a threat to the kingship (1 Kgs 2:22). Bathsheba's unique role as Queen-Mother was influential in securing the nation twice, once for David, and once for Solomon, and later ensured the proper choice of Yahweh in Solomon's accession.

Considering Mary as the Queen-Mother is deeply significant, and has implications. It puts Mary into a privilege position in salvation, and while espousing a Mariology that emphasizes, her intermediary role between us and Jesus the king/chief, as well as also her unique traditional position as dispenser of the graces of her son.

The song underlines a fervent plea to the Queen-Mother "*Lo'ge me maa'ne mu fa mbo Nwi.*" (Take these offerings and present them to God.) This is because the *Maa-Nfor* has access to the Fon, even in moments when the King is not available, is sick, or not disposed to receive a particular guest. She is the most trusted person when it comes to relating the words and will of the king. Other intercessors could fail or twist information to their favor, or lie, but the *Maa-Nfor's* assurance is secure. She can see the Fon anytime, whereas the other wives visit the Chief on a calendar basis or by appointment.

This song has particular relevance within the Bafut context. There is the annual ceremony during which people sing and bring gifts to the Fon. The

---

18 In his "The Role of the Queen Mother in Israelite Society," Niels-Erik A. Andreasen underlines the strong influence that the mother of the king had on the day-to-day running of the affairs. In fact, their influence was so strong that the rise and fall on the state was either credited or blamed on her. (See Niels-Erik A. Andreasen, "The Role of the Queen Mother in Israelite Society," Catholic Biblical Quarterly 45 (April 1983), 192. Also see Bruce K. Waltke, *The Book of Proverbs: Chapters 15-31* (Grand Rapids: William B. Eerdmans, 2005), 503. In the book of Kings, we see cases about Maacah (1 Kgs 15), Athaliah (2 Kgs 11), and Nehushta (2 Kgs 24), as wicked and acting in the same manner as the kings who receive a negative or qualified evaluation of their reigns. The books of Jeremiah and Ezekiel depict Nehushta (Jer 13, 22, 29) and Hamutal (Ezek 19) as influential queen mothers, whose presence and power affected their respective kingdoms negatively.

rationale is that since the Fon is the leader of the village, he is the privileged recipient of the first harvest. But the "thanksgiving" to the Fon is brought in terms of some special gifts such as firewood, and grass for the purpose of renewing the *Achum:* (which is a special building at the Palace, roofed by grass and is the venue of the King's prayer encounter with the ancestors). During these ceremonies, it is the Queen-Mother who receives the grass brought by the women, while the Fon and his entourage receive the firewood from the men. In this song, *Maria, Maa-Nfor,* consistent with tradition[19] and Scripture,[20] the Bafut people identify in Mary, a *Maa-Nfor,* the one who is implored to take our offerings to God and intercede on our behalf, as was done at Cana (John 2).

A Nna Maria (O Mother Mary) by Gervais Mendo Ze – Cameroon Mary the
Active Mother: Toward a Dynamic Mariology

A Nna Maria, a song composed by *La Voix de Cenacle* choir headed by Professor Gervais Mendo Ze, talks about the place of Mary as the mediator between us and her son, Jesus Christ. It espouses a Mariology rooted in tradition, and one from the lived experience of the Cameroonian people, which brings out titles/attributes of Mary, thus enriching the field of theology.

---

19   The Fathers of the Church recognized her role as Mediatrix. For example, Saint Ephrem in the fourth century referred to her as the Mediatrix of the whole world (see Saint Ephrem, *Ad Deiparam*, Oratio IV). It should be noted that even though the concept of Mary as mediatrix is not dogmatically defined, yet we glean from the Church's living tradition that she plays such a role. Popes such as: Pope Pius VII, Pope Pius IX, Pope Leo XIII, Pope St. Pius X, Pope Benedict XV, Pope Pius XI, Pope Pius XII, Pope John XXIII, Pope Paul VI, and Pope John Paul II all refer to Mary as mediatrix. (Also See Mark Miravalle, *Introduction to Mary* (Santa Barbara, CA: Queenship Publishing Co., 1993) 74–80.)
20   In Luke 1:41, Mary's physical mediation brings the unborn Jesus to His unborn cousin, John the Baptist, who is still in Elizabeth's womb. John is sanctified by this encounter, making Mary the bringer of grace that John experiences when Elizabeth notes that "the baby in my womb leaped for joy" (Lk.1:42).

A Nna Maria (O Mother Mary)

Original Lyrics	Translation
A nna Maria, ye'elan bi nyo mon (bis)	Ô! Mary our Mother beg your son for us (2x)
Na, azu volô bia minlem Bine be bé a nyia Nde bia zu mbil be wo a nyia Ye'elan bi nyo mon (bis) Na, azu volô bia	So that he brings us consolation We are sinners, Oh Mother We also rush toward you, Oh Mother Beg your son for us (2x) So that he brings us consolation
Na, azu volô bia minlem Bine be bé a nyia Nde bia zu mbil be wo a nyia Ye'elan bi nyo mon (bis) Na, azu volô bia	So that he brings us consolation We are sinners, Oh Mother We also rush toward you, Oh Mother Beg your son for us (2x) So that he brings us consolation
Bine e mvô'ô minjuk si nyu Nde bia fiti ve wo a nyia Ye'elan bi nyo mon (bis) Na, azu volô bia	We are suffering in this valley of tears And we depend on you Beg your son for us So that he brings us consolation
Bine e mvô'ô minjuk si nyu Nde bia fiti ve wo a nyia Ye'elan bi nyo mon (bis) Na, azu volô bia	We are suffering in this valley of tears And we depend on you Beg your son for us So that he brings us consolation
Ônga biaé Nkoté a nyia Yésus ane mon wôé a nyia A bili ngul ése a nyia Ye'elan bi nyo mon (bis) Na, azu volô bia	You gave life to the Redeemer Oh Mother Jesus is, without doubt, your son, Oh Mother He has all power, Oh Mother Beg your son for us (2x) So that he brings us consolation
Mimbôk mise, ône be nyia Minkôkon mise, ône be nyia Minkôkôm mise, ône mie nyia Ye'elan bi nyo mon (bis) Na azu volô bio.	You are the Mother of prisoners You are the Mother of the sick You are the mother of the barren Beg your son for us (2x) So that he brings us consolation

Original Lyrics	Translation
Bejen bisaé, ône be nyia	You are the mother of the unemployed
Bongô be sikôlô, ône be nyia	You are the mother of students
Be tabe nlam, ône be nyio	You are the mother of Peasans
Ye'elan bi nyo mon (bis)	Beg your son for us (2x)
Na azu volô bia.	So that he brings us consolation
Bobenyui bese, ône be nyia	You are the mother of orphans
Minkus mise, ône be nyia	You are the Mother of widows
Ja'a be luk, ône be nyia	Even the husbands, you are their mother
Ye'elan bi nyo mon (bis)	Beg your son for us (2x)
Na, azu vôlô bia.	So that he brings us consolation
Be fata, ône be nyia	You are the Mother of Priests
Ja'a be Pasteur. ône be nyia	Even the pastors, you are their mother
Bebuni bese, ône be nyia	You are the mother of all the faithful
Ye'elan bi nyo mon (bis) Na, azu vôlô bia.	Beg your son for us (2x) So that he brings us consolation
Coda:	Coda:
E a nyia Zambe One njalan o grasia (bis) Nti ane be wo Ye'elan asu dan	Oh Mother of God You are full of grace (2x) The Lord is with you. pray for us
A Mfefé Eva, ye'elan asu dan	New Eve, pray for us
A nyu a nga yebe, ye'elan asu dan	The One who believed, pray for us
A Endun Ngon, y e'lan asu dan	Holy Virgin, pray for us Immaculate
A nyu ane teke aton, y e'lan asu dan	one, pray for us Mother of the Savior,
A Nyia nkote, y e'lan asu dan	pray for us Morning star, pray for
A Ôtété tyé, y e'lan asu dan	us Health of the Sick, pray for us
A Nlet minkôkon, y e'lan asu dan	Protector of Angels, pray for us Queen
A Nkale b'engles, y e'lan asu dan	of apostles, pray for us Mother of the
A Nkukuma Apostel, y e'lan asu dan	Poor, pray for us Refuge of Sinners,
A Nyia Mimbubua, y e'lan asu dan	pray for us Patronness of Cameroon,
A Eke mbil besem, y e'lan asu dan	pray for us
A Nkale Cameroun, y e'lan asu dan	

Original Lyrics	Translation
Ah! (4X)	Ah! (4X)
Refrain:	Refrain:
A nna Maria, ye'elan bi nyo mon (bis)	Oh Mary, our Mother, Beg your son
Na, azu volô bia minlem	for us (2x)
	So that he brings us consolation
Coda:	Coda:
E a nyia Zambe	Oh Mother of God You are full of
One njalan o grasia (bis)	grace(2x) The Lord is with you Pray
Nti ane be wo	for us
Ye'elan asu dan	

Mariological Analysis

A Nna Maria (O Mother Mary) portrays Mary as the best, unique mediator to her son, who is God; the one who is always present and active when we call upon her, especially in times of need and difficulties. The repeated line in the song "*Ye'elan bi nyo mon*" which means "beg your son for us" underlines the important role Mary plays in effecting the answer to our prayers for liberation. It not only reinforces and makes real the biblical words of Elizabeth "you are blessed among women," (Lk 1:42) but it also highlights the trust Africans have in her intercessory and liberating role. This intercessory role is strengthened by the fact that she is the *"nyia Zambe"* (Mother of God) the *theotokos*, the one who, according toMendo Ze, *"Ônga biaé Nkoté"* (gave life to the Redeemer).

In African culture, mothers play a crucial role in influencing the will of their children. That is why Mendo Ze makes notes the relationship that Mary has with Jesus:

Original Lyrics	Translation
Yésus ane mon wôé a nyia.	Jesus is, without doubt, your son, Oh Mother
A bili ngul ése a nyia.	He has all power, Oh Mother
Ye'elan bi nyo mon Na,	Beg your Son for us (2x)
azu volô bia	So that he brings us consolation

The words *"mon wôé"* are translated "your son" in Ewondo. *"Mon"* means "Son" and *"wôé,"* denoting possession, literally means *"of yours."* It is a way of saying, "We all know he is your son, and there is no way He will not listen to you, so beg him for us. We need consolation." Or better still, "We know that he is your son, you alone can beg him on our behalf."

Mary is seen not only as the most reliable intercessor but she is also experienced as the mother of prisoners, the sick, the barren, the unemployed, the students, the peasants, the orphans, the widows, the husband, the priests, and the pastors. She is further described, consistent with tradition as the *"Mfefé Eva"* (The new Eve), the *"nyu a nga yebe"* (the One who believed), the *"Endun Ngon"* (Holy Virgin), the *"nyu ane teke aton"* (Immaculate one), the *"Nyia nkote"* (Mother of the Savior), the *"Ôtété tyé"* (Morning star), the *"Nlet minkôkon"* (Health of the Sick), the *"Nkale b'engles"* (Protector of Angels), *the "Nkukuma Apostel"* (Queen of apostles), the *"Nyia Mimbubua"* (Mother of the Poor), the *"Eke mbil besem"* (Refuge of Sinners), and the *"Nkale Cameroun"* (Patronness of Cameroon).

Hail Full of Grace by Aloysius Fonkeng, Cameroon Radiant Joy: Exploring Mariology and the Resplendence of Mary's Presence

Hail Full of Grace was composed by Aloysius Fonkeng Tindong[21] in Buea – Cameroon 2006. In a bid to honor Mary and to increase local devotion to the Mother of God, Fonkeng composed *Hail Full of Grace*. This song presents a Mariology that not only reiterates the conciliar and biblical notions of Mariology but also the lived experiences of Mary in the African context. Consistent with the 431 Council of Ephesus, *Hail Full of Grace* presents Mary as the Mother of God, the *theotokos*, the unique one who found favor with God and who plays a great indispensable role in our lives.

Refrain

Hail full of grace! Mother of God;
Ark bearing the Light of day, Show us your smiling face.

---

21 "After writing many liturgical songs and other religious songs....I felt it necessary to write at least one song that would inspire devotion to Mary, Mother of God. It took time and plenty of meditation to arrive at this song . . .but she deserved something from me and I had to work hard." (Email response from Mr. Fonkeng about why he wrote *Hail Full of Grace*.)

1. Mother of God the Son, we greet thee;
As we say: Hail, Virgin Mary!

2. Promise of God to sinful Adam;
Second Eve, bearing the Word of God.

3. Spouse of the Spirit, God's chosen one;
Vessel of God the Redeemer.

4. Beacon and hope of the human race;
Pointing the way to heaven above.

5. Virgin most pure, the pride of the Father;
Harbour of mankind's own salvation.

6. Queen of the world adorned up in heaven;
Leading mankind to God's perfect light.

7. Joy of the Saints on earth and in heaven;
God's perfect peace to our hearts bestow.

Mariological Analysis

The title of Mary as Mother of God is very relatable to the African people, because of the high importance of motherhood in the African milieu. There is no greater public institution than motherhood.[22] She is referred to as the ark that contains and carries the light of day. She is also described as having a *smiling face* – an emotion that portrays acceptance, openness, love, and agreement in the African milieu. The description of Mary's face in this song carries particular relevance, especially in the African context, where beauty trends, ideals, and tribal makeup play key roles in conveying vital information. Facial expressions tell stories and provide insights, clues, reminders, and lessons. Sub-saharan African countries put a big emphasis on facial appearance and scarification, and face painting is very common. Vital information or clues about personality, mission, and background can be passed.[23]

---

22 Oyeronke Oyewumi, "Abiyamo: Theorizing African Motherhood," *Jenda: A Journal of Culture & African Women Studies*, Online edition, 1, no. 4 (2003): 3.

23 Face painting can be for identification, health, protection, and decoration. Lauren Cullivan's 1998 research work titled *The Meanings behind the Marks: Scarification and the People*

Consistent with Patristic tradition, Mary is referred to as the new Eve; the bearer of the word of God (Jesus). It was Justin Martyr (d. ca. 165) who was one of the first to make the connection between Mary and Eve.[24] He linked Mary's obedience to Eve's disobedience and Eve's activity in the fall with Mary's activity in salvation; one was disobedient, and one was obedient; one brought the source of death into the world, and one brought the source of life. She is also considered in traditional terms, such as Spouse of the Spirit, Vessel of God the Redeemer, beacon, and hope of the human race, Virgin most pure, Queen of the world, adorned up in heaven, as well as Joy of the Saints on earth and in heaven.

Mary's place in the life of ordinary Christians is so crucial that many consider her indispensable to a full relationship with God. She is considered as "[p]ointing the way to heaven above" and leading mankind to God's perfect light. She is God's perfect peace to our hearts here on earth below.

Portraits of Mary: East African Popular Gospel Songs

In this section, I will discuss three East African songs that espouse a Mariology rooted in the lived experience of the people. Included in this is a prayer composed in the form of a poem/song which highlights the place of Mary in liberating the human race from evil.

Ayi Omutima gwa nyaffe Maria (Oh Heart of Our Mother Mary), Uganda
Mary's Eternal Faithfulness: Analyzing Vows in the Heart of Mariology

This song, *Ayi Omutima gwa nyaffe Maria* is a Lugandan[25] hymn which is popular in religious circles. It is very common among nuns and those who have an affiliation to marian apostolates. It portrays the heart of Mother Mary and

---

of Wa, http://digitalcollections.sit.edu/cgi/viewcontent.cgi?article=1030&context=african_diaspora_isp, accessed on July 17, 2017, is a significant resource in understanding facial appearances/paintings for the Wa people in Ghana.

24 Luigu Gambero, *Mary and the Fathers of the Church* (San Francisco: Ignatius Press, 1991), 46.
25 Luganda, also referred to as Ganda, is one of the major languages in Uganda. It is spoken principally in Southern Uganda, including the capital Kampala. Until the 1960s, Luganda was also the official language of instruction in primary schools in Eastern Uganda.

espouses a Mariology that shows Mary not only as an interceder and supporter but also as the one to whom we can dedicate our lives.

Original Lyrics	Translation
Chorus: Ayi Omutima gwa nyaffe Maria omudabiliza, nzunno nkwekwasiza, Ayi Omutima gwa Nyaffe Marria omudabiliza, nzunno nkwewadde.	Chorus: Oh Heart of our Mother Mary the interceder, I am here and consecrate myself to you Oh Heart of our Mother Mary the interceder, I offer myself to you (*2)
Njagala mu gwe mwemba mbella nga ndi wamu nawentuuse byesubiza. Baptisimu yange gyezilamu mu mutima gwo mange nyamba edde buuto. Omulimu gwe'ssala gwe'noonze mu mutima mange nyamba nga'okwatilako [chorus]	I want to be with you so that I am able to fulfill the promises that I have made. I consecrate my baptismal promises to you; please help me to renew my vows. The life of prayer that I have chosen, in your heart mother, be with me as I live it. [chorus]
Omulimu gwo buweliza mugwe mwemba ngutukiliza kulwabanange, nange Omuka assime.	The ministry that I have, in you mother that I may fulfill it on behalf of my brothers and sisters, so that the Lord may be pleased.
Omulimu gwe essala mugwe mwemba ngutukiliza kulwa banage nangeomukama assime	The work of prayer, that I may fulfill it in you; on behalf of my brothers and sister, so that the Lord is pleased.
Nkwesingila Mange okume nga omwana kumugongo; Nkwesingila Maange onyambe, mumutima gwo mwemba mbela.	I consecrate myself to you mother, like a child on the back of her mother. I consecrate myself to you mother for help, that I may stay in your heart
Maria nzunno mbikilila nno'mulagilo ogwo bulamu, nzunno okumme,mbikilila nno'buzadde bwonina kko	Mary here I am, cover me in your mantel of life; here I am, protect me, cover me in your parental love.

Original Lyrics	Translation
Obulamu obwange mbikilila nno'mulagilo ogwo bulamu, Maama mbukuwade, mbikilila nno'buzadde bwonina kko	My life, cover me in your mantel of life, I give you my life, cover me in your parental love.
Byonna ebyo ebyange mbikilila nno'mulagilo ogwo bulamu, Maama mbikukwasa, mbikilila nno'buzadde bwonina kko	Everything that I have, cover me in your mantel of life, Mother I surrender it to you cover me in your parental love.
Okutengana okwange mbikilila nno'mulagilo ogwo bulamu, Maama nkukukwasa, mbikilila nno'buzadde bwonina kko	My struggles, cover me in your mantel of life, I offer them to you, cover me in your parental love.
Onyamba Maria, mbikilila nno'mulagilo ogwo bulamu, ontuuse gyali, mbikilila no'buzadde boninako	Help me Mary, cover me in your mantel of life, get me to the Lord, cover me in your parental love
Omulokozi Yezu, mbikilila nno'mulagilo ogwo bulamu, Ontuuse gyali, mbikilila no'buzadde boninako	The savior Jesus, cover me in your mantel of life, Get me to where He is and cover me in your parental love
Nkwesigela Mange okume, nga omwana ku mugongo,	I consecrate myself to you mother, like a child on a mother's back.
Nkwesigila Maama onyambe, Mumutima gwo mwemba mbela.	I consecrate myself to you mother, help me, in your heart may I stay.

Mariological Analysis

The verse below from the song *Ayi Omutima gwa nyaffe Maria* is a great indicator of the place Mary occupies in helping people live up to their commitments.

Original Lyrics	Translation
Njagala mu gwe mwemba mbella nga ndi wamu nawentuuse byesubiza.	I want to be with you so that I am can be able to fulfill the promises I have made.
Baptisimu yange gyezilamu mu mutima gwo mange nyamba edde buuto.	I consecrate my baptismal promises to you; please help me to renew my vows.
Omulimu gwe'ssala gwe'noonze mu mutima mange nyamba nga'okwatilako.	The life of prayer that I have chosen, in your heart mother, be with me as I live it.

Mary's role is so crucial that she is called upon to assist in helping Christians keep to their baptismal promises.[26] Consecration to Mary, which is very popular in sub-Saharan Africa, because of the growing rate of Marian spirituality, is taken very seriously. The author of *Ayi Omutima gwa nyaffe Maria* uses very interesting images to describe consecration to Mary, such as: "like a child on the back of her mother." (*okume nga omwana kumugongo*). In Africa, carrying a baby on the back is a way of using a wrapper to strap the baby on the back, with the baby facing his mother's back. It is a very convenient way of bonding with and carrying a baby. It is often a source of great pride and great joy going about with a baby on the back. It brings about societal respect and a proof that one is fertile and contributes to keeping the earth active. This leads some women of childbearing age to go as far as borrowing babies to strap on their backs, especially when going for an outing, as part of their uniform, status, and pride. The Bakoko people of East Cameroon believe that carrying your baby on the back for over two years brings about a lifelong indebtedness to the mother. It creates a situation where the child forever owes the mother. This indebtedness extends right to her old age when the child, in turn, has the obligation to cater to the mother (or parents) when they are not able to. Comparing our consecration to Mary to that of a mother carrying a baby on the back is indeed very interesting and significant in the African context, and brings out a Mariology that is meaningful and consistent with tradition, Scripture, and the lived experience of the people. It underlines not only Mary's love for

---

26 The affirmation to each of the questions establishes the "founded hope" and also serves as an indication of the commitment to the life of Christ that the candidate is about to enter into.

us but also our indebtedness to Mary as well as our willingness to honor her by "taking care of her" out of mutual love.

Mary can protect from evil, which is why asking her to cover us with her mantle is very much in place. Her love, like that of a real African Mother, is parental. That is why staying in her heart is a fervent desire. "*Nkwesingila Maange onyambe, mumutima gwo mwemba mbela*" (I consecrate myself to you, mother, for help that I may stay in your heart).

Ewe Mama Maria (Yes, Mother Mary), Tanzania Divine Motherhood: Mary's Significance in Mariological Reflection

Ewe Mama Maria,[27] a song composed by Paschal Florian Mwarabu, was first sung by the Saint Cecilia Choir in Tanzania. It is part of the album titled *Nakupenda Maria* (I love Mary), dedicated to expressing love for Mary and honoring her for her role in their lives. *Ewe Mama Maria* is a Mariology of love and acceptance of Mary, as the Mother of God and the love and acceptance that she has toward us. She is the "*mama yetu mwema*" (*the Good Mother*) who is worthy of our love.

Original Lyrics	Translation
We mama Maria, mama yetu mwema, Mama wa Mungu *Sisi wanao leo, tunakusalimu, salamu Mama*	Mother Mary, our good mother, Mother of God Today, we greet you, greetings to you, Mom
Ee mama yetu mwema, mama yetu Maria *Sisi tunakupenda, tunakupenda sana*	Our good mother, our mother Mary We love you, we love you very much
Ee mama yetu mpenzi, sikia ombi letu, Katika shida zetu, kwa mwanao tuombee	O my dear mother, hear our petition, In our trouble, Pray for us to your son
Ee Mama mbarikiwa, mama msafi wa moyo *Mama mwenye huruma, uwe nasi daima*	Blessed mother, mother with a pure heart Dear mother, be with us always

---

27 *Ewe Mama Maria* can be found at https://www.youtube.com/watch?v=UhQXhRVc9vE

Original Lyrics	Translation
Na mwisho mama wa ugeni huu,	Lastly, the mother of this stranger,
Tusaidie Mama, tufike juu Mbinguni	Help us Mother, to get to Heaven.

Mariological Analysis

Consistent with Catholic theological tradition, *Ewe Mama Maria* presents Mary as the good mother, who can hear our human petitions and present them to her son, Jesus. She is even considered capable of intervening in times of trouble, on behalf of the people, because she can speak to her son, who alone has all the power to save.

Mary is also associated with purity. In *Ewe Mama Maria*, she is referred to as the *"mama msafi wa moyo,"* that is the "mother with a pure heart." This phrase is of particular significance in black Africa, given the place that purity and purification occupy in the lives of the people. To be considered pure of heart is a privileged position reserved for those whose relationship with the deity is beyond reproach. One is considered pure, either when one stays away from defilement or after one goes through the process or rites of purification.[28] The Zulus consider purification as either a *ukuhlambulula* or a *ukusefa*, both of which mean "making thin," "making a person free, loose, unbound," and is derived from the word *ukuhlamba*, which means "to wash."[29] Mary is pure and undefiled. Biblically speaking, she has found favor with God and that makes her occupy a unique, privileged place in the life of African Christians, recognizing that she can even help us to get to heaven. *"Tusaidie Mama, tufike juu Mbinguni"* (help us Mother, to get to Heaven).

---

[28] Omosade Awolalu notes: "Purification is a positive approach to the cleaning and removal of sin and pollution. It involves an outward act which is consequently believed to have a spiritual inner cleansing. The cleansing may be of the body, or of a thing or of a territory or community" (see J. Omosade Awolalu, "Sin and its removal in African Traditional Religion", JAAR 44/2 (1976), 284). Purification rites in Africa are varied and related to various events and reasons. (See Benjamin C. Ray, *African traditional Religions: Symbol, Ritual and Community* (Englewood Cliffs: NJ: Prentice Hall, 1976), 90–100.) It is important to note that not all purification rites are for religious purposes. There are basically three major grounds for purification, namely, taboos, the holiness of God, and relationship with the deity (God).

[29] Bengt G. M. Sundlker, *Bantu Prophets in South Africa*, 2nd ed. (London: Oxford University Press, 1961), 210.

Mama Maria, Mother of All Mothers (Mother Mary, Mother of All Mothers), Kenya Liberating Love: Toward a Mariology of Liberation

In his *Theology Brewed in an African Pot*, Orobator composed a prayer in the form of a poem, which to an extent summarizes a lived expression of Mariology in the African context. It presents a lived Mariology that shows Mary at the forefront of liberation – a liberation Mariology.

Mama Maria, Mother of all Mothers (Mother Mary, Mother of all Mothers)

> Mary, a mother in labor is not ashamed of nudity;
> help us to overcome all forms of injustice and abuse of women.
>
> Mary, when a father punishes a child it seeks refuge in its mother's hut;
> draw us closer to the mercy and compassion of your son Jesus.
>
> Mary, a child on its mother's back does not care if the journey is long;
> by your prayers carry all refugees to safety and peace as you carried
> the infant Jesus to safety in Egypt.
>
> Mary, a child cannot pay for its mother's milk;
> by your prayers may we find constant nourishment for our faith in your son, Jesus.
>
> Mary, a child does not laugh at the ugliness of its mother;
> by your prayers may we treat all women and men with respect and
> dignity.
>
> Mary, a person who has not traveled thinks his or her mother is the best
> cook; by your prayers may we free our minds from all forms of
> tribalism, discrimination, and ethnic violence.
>
> Mary, if a calf sucks greedily, it tears away its mother's udder;
> by your prayers help us to overcome greed and selfishness.
>
> Mary, the earth is the mother of all;
> by your prayers help us to use the resources of the earth with prudence and care.
>
> Mary, the mother of a great person has no horns;
> by the example of your life may we grow in humility and selfless service to all women
> and men.

Mary, we are born from the womb of our mothers, we are buried in the womb of the earth; by your prayers may we know the joy of a peaceful death and come to the eternal happiness of heaven together with our ancestors in faith. Amen.[30]

Mariological Analysis

In a Mariological nuance, this prayer addresses the problems that bewail the African continent: such as the abuse of human and women's rights, refugee problems, food insecurity, crises of faith, peace, security, tribalism, and anthropological poverty.

It is quite interesting to notice how in this poem/prayer, as in the Marian song – A Nna Maria (O Mother Mary), Orobator, ascribes to Mary roles that are liberating in all aspects of human life. This, of course, shows a shift from the traditional portrayal of Mary, as the gentle Jewish girl from Nazareth, who does nothing but obey the angel, follow her son, Jesus, and espouse virtues of humility, peace, and gentleness for humanity. Mary is seen not only as the one who can "help us to overcome all forms of injustice and abuse of women" but also as the one who can carry all refugees to safety and peace in the same way as she carried the infant Jesus to safety in Egypt. In the face of sociocultural ills, such as tribalism, discrimination, and ethnic violence present in Africa, and the greed and selfishness exhibited by political leaders with their high level of corruption and abuse of state resources, Mary provides hope for the African continent. She is an integral participant of liberation in the concrete daily lives of the people. Tissa Balasuriya, in his *Mary and Human Liberation*, first published in 1997, reflects on Mariology from the standpoint of third-world realities, with a prevalence of poverty, women's exploitation, and social injustice. He engages in a reflection of Jesus' liberative message, with Mary as a prime participant, showing how such an endeavor deepens women's consciousness of their rights and dignity. This reflection not only deepens our understanding but also inspires us, as disciples of Jesus, to actively participate in the crucial fight for women's rights and dignity.[31]

In his *Mary-Mother of the African Church: A Theological Inculturation of Mariology*, Ferdinand Nwaigbor argues that the theology of Mary as the mother of the African race is based on the divine words on the cross, as recounted by John the Evangelist:

---

30 Orobator, 106–107.
31 Tissa Balasuriya, *Mary and Human Liberation*, (Harrisburg, PA, Trinity Press International, 1997). As much as his enterprise to bringing out Mary's role in liberation struggles could

> Near the cross of Jesus stood his mother's sister, Mary the wife of Cleopas, and Mary of Magdala. Seeing his mother and the disciple he loves standing near her, Jesus says to his mother "Woman, behold your Son" Then to the disciples he said "Behold your mother" And from that moment the disciple made a place for her his home. (Jn 19:25–27)

He interprets Jesus' words to mean that at the foot of the cross, the woman, Mary, became not only the mother to the disciples but also the mother of the community itself, the Church.[32] This passage of St. John's Gospel speaks not only about how Mary established a communication of her maternity with the Church, as its mother and model, but also speaks to us personally about how Mary is related to the African race as mother. As a mother of the African race, she is not tied only to the African folk, but has with each race a particular relationship, stemming from the human situation and condition of the people. Socially and economically, Africa is poor and in need. Mary, as a mother of the African race, shares with them in their sufferings and wants, attending to their requirements and replenishing the hollow of their poverty and wounded identity. As a model, she is a mirror on which Africa is to see herself.[33]

In addition to the social and economic connection that Africa has with Mary, Ferdinand Nwaigbor also makes a case for political connection. For him, Mary mirrors the frame of mind that all African nations need to have. This is seen in the fact that she is law-biding, never transgressing any of the laws of God or of the land. She faithfully carried out the purification law by taking Jesus to be circumcised. (Lk 2:22–23) "The person of Mary can fill African nations afresh with the source of her hope, which will enable us to continue in our struggle for social justice, peace and good neighborliness with a renewed

---

be considered praise worthy, in general, Tissa Balasuriya's book did not find favor in the sight of the Church authorities who found his underlying Christological principles to be extremely wanting in terms of the dogmas. He was accused of denying not only the dogma of original sin but also the *marian dogmas* such as Mary's divine motherhood, her Immaculate Conception and virginity, and her bodily Assumption into heaven. (See notification concerning the Text "Mary and Human Liberation" by Father Tissa Balasuriya, OMI issued by the Sacred Congregation of the Doctrine of the Faith at http://www.vatican.va/roman_curia/congregations/cfaith/documents/rc_con_cfaith_doc_19970102_tissa-balasuriya_en.html, accessed on December 2017.)

32 Ferdinand Nwaigbor, *Mary-Mother of the African Church: A Theological Inculturation of Mariology* (Frankfurt: Peter Lang, 200), 39.
33 Ferdinand Nwaigbor, 39.

vision and vitality."[34] In the words of Megan McKenna, Mary "stands in solidarity with us, and she is still given to all the disciples, the beloved of God."[35]

Conclusion

The ecclesiological image of the "Family of God," with its newness and its richness, attests to a renewed vitality of the theological reflection in Africa, and in particular about Mary. The sociopolitical context of African ecclesiology and Christology has promoted the opening of new theological visions for marian theology in Africa, especially in the dimension of the concept of *Mama Maria* of Africa. The Church of God in Africa is made up of Mary and the African race, with Christ as the head of the body. This unique family has as its ultimate goal to foster justice, non-violence, and rights and privileges of individuals and groups, rather than condone oppression and discrimination. This family, to which Mary is the mother, embraces everyone, from the baptized to the just ancestors of old. She, therefore, like a faithful mother, brings people under the one family of God, just as a hen gathers her young beneath her wings. The ecclesiological image of the "Family of God," with its newness and its richness, attests to a renewed vitality of theological reflection in Africa, and in particular about Mary.

Far from being an abstract reality in Africa, Mariology is lived out by the everyday Christian in their walks of faith. I have specifically analyzed songs that highlight and portray the place of Mary in African Christian life. I have also demonstrated how, consistent with Scripture and tradition, cultural images present Mary with titles such as Mother, Queen-Mother, Intercessor, Mediator, patroness, Ideal Believer, Health of the Sick, Protector of Angels, Queen of Apostles, Mother of the Poor, and Refuge of Sinners, as well as the Lady with the Smiling face, the Bearer of the Word of God, Beacon, and Hope of the Human Race. She is also revered as the Virgin most pure, Queen of the World Adorned up in Heaven, Joy of the Saints on Earth and in Heaven, and Pointer of the Way to Heaven above, with each portrayal, having some cultural significance.

It should be noted that among all the images of Mary prevalent in Africa, that of Mary as "Mother" is the most popular. She is definitely *"Mama Maria."*

---

34   Ferdinand Nwaigbor, 39.
35   Megan McKenna, *Mary: Shadow of Grace* (Bangladesh: Orbis, 1995), 113.

In Chapter 2, we discussed African ecclesiology, looking at various major African ecclesiological models, paying special attention to the Church in Africa as the Family of God." It is interesting to note that in Africa, it is possible to imagine a family without a father, but it is unthinkable to envision one without a mother. This is because the mother is the pillar of the family, and whoever says "family," says "mother." In this light, if I assert that in Africa, the Church is the family of God, I am also asserting that God is the Father. Who therefore is the mother? It is indeed safe to assert that, for many Catholic faithful, Mary is the Mother of the Church, not in the ordinary sense of the word. In following this logic, however, it is necessary to avoid one danger, that is – the danger of thinking that because the first person of the Trinity is the Father, and Mary is the mother of Jesus, the father and the mother are more or less on the same level, as it is in a human family. It is thanks to the graces of the three persons of the Trinity that Mary is who she is for us.

GENERAL CONCLUSION

By conclusion, I do not in any way imply an exhaustion of this subject. I simply want to impose a break, quite aware, along with Leonardo Boff, that "no concrete historical reality can exhaust the richness of Christ. Hence, no title conferred on Christ can be absolutized."[1] This research has analyzed only a few of the rich values which exist when sub-Saharan African Christology engages in this urgent, dynamic dialogue with Patristic Christology. It served to show how Africa's unique anthropology informs the articulation of its Christology in the same way that Patristic anthropology did for its Christology. This reveals the primordial role that anthropology has in Christological endeavors. Moreover, it removes African Christology from its perceived isolation, highlighting its consistency with Scripture and Patristic Christology, and revealing by its Lived Christology, what Pope John Paul II terms "the wealth of cultural values and priceless human qualities which Africa can offer to the Churches and to humanity as a whole" (*Ecclesia in Africa*, 42).

This work begins with a discussion on the development of Patristic Christology between the two ancient schools of Alexandria and Antioch, which culminated at Chalcedon. It sets the dialogue between Patristic Christology

---

1 Boff, *Jesus Christ Liberator: A Critical Christology for Our Time*, 230.

with African Christologies articulated through the examination of Christological models and expressed through popular daily gospel songs, noting how various anthropological understandings informed Christological titles and notions. With this dialogue comes a greater awareness, clarity, and understanding of the two Christologies. It weakens prejudice, and enables a better understanding of differences and a greater appreciation for others' spiritual, social, and cultural values. A continuous Christological dialogue is absolutely necessary given that Christianity was brought to Africa at a time when the colonial system of injustice and oppression was very much active. This research is an added voice to dispel that apparent discontinuity, showing anthropology as common, determinant factor in the articulation of different Christologies. Moreover, representing a pivotal exploration of the intersections between African cultural identity and Christian theological thought, this study has navigated through complex layers of Patristic traditions and vibrant African spiritual landscapes, uncovering the profound ways in which African Christology not only resonates with, but also enriches, global theological discourse. By interweaving the rich tapestry of African anthropology with the foundational doctrines of Christianity, this work has laid down a formidable challenge to the conventions of Eurocentric theological narratives, advocating for a more inclusive approach that honors and integrates the diverse cultural expressions of faith.

The various Christological titles or models or chants that I analyzed in this work are analogous to the title Christologies that characterized the early centuries of the Church. These chants and titles are based on the needs and experiences of the local people. What Jesus is for someone is determined by that person's life experiences, which helps instill a parochial mentality about Jesus Christ. This is a sort of functional Christology. African Christological models, despite their limitations, help set a platform for a fuller understanding of the role and person of Jesus Christ, going beyond the concerns of Chalcedon.

While no image or title is superior to the other, some images or titles may address a specific situation more than others. I place the ancestor model at the center of African Christology. In African tradition, ancestors are related to the communication of life, and good relations with them are essential to the wellbeing of their descendants. The title of ancestor enjoys a priority of place from other titles like chief, king, liberator, and master of initiation, for they are all mediatory figures between the human and the divine. "The chief and the master of initiation has a role which is played in this world; the ancestors to some degree transcends the community. They belong to the other world, but at the same time are present in this world."[2] In the future, as I further explore the concept of lived Christology as found in indigenous traditional dance and proverbs, I also hope to explore in detail the African Christological title and research concrete ways in which ancestral divine qualities could be juxtaposed with their human qualities.

Unfortunately, oftentimes, theological dialogues are dominated by the "gatekeeper elites" (usually men), who claim to speak for everyone. This research brought in the voices of the ordinary, often-unheard people (women and children) through a common channel – popular religious songs or chants. In Africa, songs serve as mediums through which the erring and ignorant, the malicious and the corrupt could be shocked back into awareness of inherent norms, values, and beliefs. Analyzing popular African religious songs with the aim of bringing out their inherent Christology and Mariology, and presenting their consistency with Scripture and tradition shows how a people can appropriate foreign values, making them their own, without abandoning their rich traditional culture to settle for rot repetition in a bid to practice Christianity. It is in this light that they can be referred to as chants of Christological continuity. Indeed, all Christological and Mariological chants (even theology in general) must feed and draw strength both from tradition and also from its rich and mutating culture.

Far from being inspired by a theological inferiority or superiority complex, this work stems from an ardent desire to make a contribution to Christian theology through the African culture, by bringing out the place of popular religiosity in theological endeavors. These chants of Christological continuity do serve as a form of enrichment of the universal Church through its active members. In fact, "[a]ll Church reforms remain theologically shallow and pastorally ineffective unless it clearly bases itself on the founder of Christianity and on our faith in him as the Son of God and saviour."[3]

In writing this book, I grew in my appreciation of the role of anthropology and Mariology in African Christological matters. In fact, by looking at early conciliar Christology with African cultural eyes, it makes absolute sense that issues regarding the mother are dealt and concluded with before those of the son. In other words, it makes absolute sense that Mariological matters were discussed in 381 and settled, before the Council of Chalcedon could deal with the

---

2 Kuster, *The Many Faces of Jesus Christ*, 66.
3 Gerald O'Collins, *Interpreting Jesus* (Eugene, OR: Wipf & Stock Publishers, 2002), 3.

question of the natures of Christ in 451. If Ephesus did not exist, it would have been necessary to invent it for the sake of a fuller understanding of African Christology. Inspired by my own epistemological location of motherhood of Mary in the African context, I have honed my sensitivity to issues that need to be recovered for my understanding of the person of Christ. Among the insights contained in this work is the central place of Mary in the understanding of the person of Christ as a mediator of Christ's humanity.

In crafting a future where theology is as diverse as the church it seeks to represent, "Chants Of Christological Continuity" serves as a call to theologians, church leaders, and believers worldwide to engage in a continuous dialogue that cherishes and learns from the unique theological contributions of every culture. As we move forward, we carry with us the lessons that Christological expressions are based on anthropological understandings and that they must mirror the multifaceted faces of its followers. Thus, this book is not merely a conclusion of a study but a beacon guiding us towards a more equitable and holistic understanding of our faith in the modern world.

The Patristic Christological articulations were attempts by the Church Fathers, using their philosophical background and culture to interpret the mystery of Christ, by being faithful to Scripture and to other previous ecumenical councils. This research, using Patristic Christology as a springboard, aimed at expressing the never-changing word of God in ever-changing modes for relevance.

Constructing a contextual Christology as I have done in this book does not imply that the Patristic or African Christology can be determined entirely and solely by any given culture. In the words of Penoukou, the goal is "not to reduce the content of faith in Christ to human questions, but rather to begin with the latter in a concrete enterprise of conversion of actual questioning, of these human questions."[4] Since the Gospel's message is divinely inspired, yet the manner of its expression is not, it is both necessary and urgent to contextualize how we express this message.

---

4 Penoukou Efoe Julien, "Christology in the Village" in *Faces of Jesus in Africa*, ed. Robert Schreiter (Maryknoll, NY: Orbis, 1991), 28.

BIBLIOGRAPHY

Achebe, Chinua. *Things Fall Apart*. Ibadan: Anchor, 1956.
Adamolekun, Taiye. "Christ as a Social Liberator: A Challenge for African Christianity." In *Christology in African Context*. Ibadan: University of Ibadan Publishers, (2003): 389–399.
Agwu, Christopher. *Ipu Ogo: Traditional Rites of Initiation into Manhood in Edda*. Owerri: Nnamdi Printing Press, 1994.
Amadi, Elechi. *Ethics in Nigerian Culture*. Ibadan: Heinemann Educational Books, 1982.
Andreasen, Niels-Erik A. "The Role of the Queen Mother in Israelite Society," *Catholic Biblical Quarterly* 45 (1983): 179–194.
Apollinarius of Laodicea. "Fragment 25." Trans. and ed. Richard A. Norris Jr. Minneapolis: Fortress Press, 1980.
———. "Fragment 89." In *The Christological Controversy*. Trans. and ed. Richard A. Norris Jr. Minnesota: Fortress Press, 1980.
———. "On the Union in Christ of the Body with Godhead." In *The Christological Controversy*, Trans. and ed. Richard A. Norris Jr. Minneapolis: Fortress Press, 1980.
Arendzen, John. "Docetae." *The Catholic Encyclopedia*. New Advent, Online edition. http://www.newadvent.org/cathen.
Athanasius. "De Synodis." In Nicene and Post Nicene Fathers. Buffalo, NY: Christian Literature Publishing Co., 1892. http://www.newadvent.org/fathers/2817.htm.
———. "Orationes Contra Arianos." In *Nicene and Post Nicene Fathers*, Ed. Philip Schaff and Henry Wace. Vol. IV. 2nd. ed. Grand Rapids, MI: Eerdmans Publishing Co, 1975.
Augustine. *The City of God*. I, 35. New York: The Modern Library, 1950.

Austryn, Harry. *The Philosophy of the Church Fathers I: Faith, Trinity, Incarnation, His Structure and Growth of Philosophic Systems from Plato to Spinoza*, vol. I. Cambridge, MA: Harvard University Press, 1956.

Ayandele et al. *The Growth of African Civilization: The Making of Modem Africa*. Vol. 2. London: Longman, 1968.

Ayittey, George. *Betrayed*. New York City, NY: St. Martin's Press, 1992.

Azombo-Menda, S. *Precis de Philosophie Pour l'Afrique*. Paris: F. Nathan, 1981.

Babatunde, Lawal. *The Gelede Spectacle: Art, Gender, and Social Harmony in an African Culture*. Seattle, WA: University of Washington Press, 1996.

Balasuriya, Tissa. *Mary and Human Liberation*. Harrisburg, PA: Trinity Press International, 1997.

Balthasar, Hans Urs Von. *The Threefold Garland: The World's Salvation in Mary's Prayer*. San Francisco: Ignatius Press, 1982.

Banks, Robert. *Paul's Idea of Community*. Peabody, MA: Hendrickson Publishers, Inc., 1998.

Battle, Michael. *Reconciliation: The Ubuntu Theology of Bishop Desmond Tutu*. Cleveland, OH: Pilgrim's Press, 1997.

———. *Ubuntu, I in You and You in Me*. New York: Seabury Books, 2009.

Benedict XVI, *Africae Munus. Post Synodal Apostolic Exhortation to the Bishops, Clergy, Consecrated Persons and the Lay Faithfulon the Church in Africa in Service to Reconciliation, Justice and Peace*. Nairobi, Kenya: Paulines Publications, 1995.

Bennett, Thomas W. *Customary Law in South Africa*. Cape Town: Juta Legal and Academic Publishers, 2004.

Bevans, Stephen B. *Models of Contextual Theology*. Maryknoll, NY: Orbis, 1996.

Boff, Leonardo. *Jesus Christ Liberator: A Critical Christology for Our Time*. Maryknoll, NY: Orbis, 1995.

Bohannan, Paul, and Philip Curtin. *Africa and Africans*. Garden City, NY: Waveland Press inc, 1971.

Bonn, Martha. "Children's Understanding of *Ubuntu*." *Early Child Development and Care*. 177, no. 8 (2007): 863–873.

Bozarth, Alla Renee. *This Is My Body: Praying for Earth, Prayers from the Heart*. San Francisco, CA: Harper, 1996.

Branick, Vincent. *The House Church in the Writings of Paul*. Wilmington, DL: Michael Glazier, 1989.

Bray, Gerald. *Biblical Interpretation: Past and Present*. Downers Grove, IL: Intervarsity Press, 1996.

Broodryk, Johann. *Ubuntu: Life Lessons from Africa*. Pretoria: *Ubuntu* School of Philosophy, 2002.

Brueggemann, Walter. *To Act Justly, Love Tenderly, Walk Humbly*. Eugene, OR: Wipf & Stock Publishers, 1986.

Bujo, Benezet. *African Theology in Its Social Context*. Trans. John O'Donohue. Eugenge, OR: Wipf & Stock Publishers, 2006.

———. "Pour Une Ethique Africano-Christocentrique." *Bulletin de la Theologie Africaine* 3, no. 5 (1981): 41–52.

Byarugaba, George William. "The Response of the Roman Catholic Church in South Africa to the Problems of HIV/AIDS in Light of the Modern Catholic Social Teaching." Licentiate in Sacred Theology Thesis, Jesuit School of Theology of Santa Clara University, 2009.

Cahil, Lisa Sowle. *Theological Bioethics: Participation, Justice, Change.* Washington D.C.: Georgetown University Press, 2005.

Carson, Donald A. *The Gagging of God: Christianity Confront Pluralism.* Grand Rapids, MI: Zondervan, 1996.

Chafer, Lewis S. "Trinitarianism: Part 7." *Bibliotheca Sacra.* no. 98 (1941): 264–75

Crowder, Michael. *The Story of Nigeria.* London: Faber and Faber, 1962.

———. *West Africa Resistance: The Military Response to Colonial Occupation.* Teaneck, NJ: Holmes & Meier Publishing, 1971.

Curtin, Philip et al. *African History Earliest Times to Independence.* 2nd ed. London & New York: Longman, 1995.

Cyril of Alexandria. "Commentary on Luke." Online edition, Trans. Roger Pearse, 1996. http://www.tertullian.org/fathers/cyril_on_luke_01_sermons_01_11.htm#C1.

———. "Five Tomes Against Nestorius." Online edition, Trans. Roger Pearse, 2005. http://www.tertullian.org/fathers/cyril_against_nestorius_00_intro.htm.

———. "A Defense of the Twelve Anathemas against Theodoret." Trans. Daniel King. In Daniel King, *St. Cyril of Alexandria: Three Christological Treatises.* Washington, D.C.: The Catholic University of America Press, 2014.

———. "Cyril's Letter to the Monk of Egypt." Trans. John A. McGuckin. In John A. McGuckin, *St. Cyril of Alexandria: The Christological Controversy.* 245–162. New York: St. Vladimir's Seminary Press, 2004.

———. "Scholia on the Incarnation of the Only Begotten." Trans. John A. McGuckin. In John A. McGuckin, *St. Cyril of Alexandria: The Christological Controversy.* 294–135. New York: St. Vladimir's Seminary Press, 2004.

———. "The Second Letter of Cyril to Nestorius." Trans. John A. McGuckin. In John A. McGuckin, *St. Cyril of Alexandria: The Christological Controversy.* 262–65. New York: St. Vladimir's Seminary Press, 2004.

———. "Festal Letter 17," in *Festal Letters 13-30.* Trans. Philip R. Amidon Washington, D.C.: The Catholic University of America Press, 2013.

———. "Second Letter of Cyril to Succensus." Trans. John A. McGuckin. In John A. McGuckin, *St. Cyril of Alexandria: The Christological Controversy.* 259–63. New York: St. Vladimir's Seminary Press, 2004.

———. "Third Letter of Cyril to Nestorius." Trans. John A. McGuckin. In John A. McGuckin, *St. Cyril of Alexandria: The Christological Controversy.* 266–75. New York: St. Vladimir's Seminary Press, 2004.

Dabire, Kusiele J. M. "Eglise-Famille de Dieu." *Revue de l'Institut Catholique de l'Afrique de l'Ouest,* Vol. 25. no. 14–15 (1996): 81–119.

Davis, Leo D. *The First Seven Ecumenical Councils (325–787): Their History and Theology.* Minnesota: Liturgical Press, 1990.

Diop, Cheikh Anta. *L'Unite Culturelle de L'Afrique Noire.* 2nd ed. Paris: Presence Africaine, 1982.

Douglas, John Hall. *Thinking the Faith: Christian Theology in a North American Context.* Minneapolis: Fortress Press, 1991.
Driver, G. R, and Leonard Hodgson. "Commentary to Nestorius, Bazaar of Heracleides." In *The Bazaar of Heracleides*, Trans and ed. G. R. Driver and Leonard Hodgson. Oxford: The Clarendon Press, 1925.
Dupuis, S.J, Jacques. *Who Do You Say I Am? Introduction to Christology.* Maryknoll, NY: Orbis, 1994.
Ela, Jean-Marc. *African Cry.* Maryknoll, NY: Orbis, 1986.
―――. "De l'assistance á La Liberation: Les Taches Actuelles de l'église En Milieu Africain." In *Foi et Dévelopement.* Paris: Centre Lebret, 1981.
―――. *My Faith as an African.* Maryknoll, NY: Orbis, 1988.
Elenga, Yvon Christian. "Engelbert Mveng (1930-1995), l'invention d'un Discour Theologique." In *Recoil d'homages.* Kinshasa: Editions Loyola-Canisius, 2005.
Erickson, Millard J. *The Word Became Flesh: A Contemporary Incarnational Christology.* Grand Rapids, MI: Baker Books, 1906.
Esler, Philip F. "Family Imagery and Christian Identity in Galatians 5:13 to 6:10," In *Constructing Early Christian Families.* Ed. Halvor Moxnes, London: Routledge,1997.
Ezeh, Uchenna A. *Christ the Ancestor, An African Contextual Christology in the Light of the Major Dogmatic Christological Definations of the Church from the Council of Nicaea (325) to Chalcedon (451).* Berne: Peter Lang AG, European Academic Publishers, 2003.
Ezukwu, Eugene E. "Towards an African Christology." *Foundation of African Theology* 3, no. 2 (1992):51–62.
Fairbairn, Donald. "Patristic Exegesis and Theology: The Cart and the Horse," *Westminster Theological Journal* 69, no. 1 (2007): 1–19.
Freire, Paulo. *Pedagogy of the Oppressed.* New York: Continuum, 2002.
Froehlich, Karlfried. *Biblical Interpretation in the Early Church.* Philadelphia: Fortress Press, 1984.
Gade, Christian B. N. "The Historical Development of the Written Discourses on *Ubuntu*" *The South African Journal of Philosophy* 30, no 3, (2011): 302–229.
Gann, L. H, and P Duignan. *The Rulers of British Africa, 1870–1914.* Stanford, CA: Standford University Press, 1978.
Gehman, Richard J. *African Traditional Religion in Biblical Perspective.* Kijabe: Kesho Publications, 1989.
Green, Joel B., and Mar Turner. *Jesus of Nazreth: Lord and Christ.* Grand Rapids, MI: Eerdmans Publishing Co, 1994.
Gregory of Nazianzen. "Letter to Cledonius." In *St. Cyril of Alexandria: The Christological Controversy,* Trans. John A. McGuckin. New York: Vladimir's Seminary Press, 2004.
Grillmeier, Aloys. *Christ in Christian Tradition: From the Apostolic Age to Chalcedon (451).* 2nd ed. Vol. I. Louisville, KY: Westminster John Knox Press, 1975.
Haigh, Roger. *Symbol of God.* Maryknoll, NY: Orbis, 1999.
Harries, Jim. "Western Theology in Africa: Christian Mission in the Light of the Undermining of Scientific Hegemony" *International Review of Mission* 106, no. 2 (2017): 241–260.
Hastings, Adrian. *Church and Mission in Modern Day Africa.* London: Burns & Oates, 1967.

Hebga, Meinrad P. *Sorcellerie et prière de délivrance*, Paris, Présence Africaine; Abidjan: inades Éditions. 1986.

———. *La Rationalite d'un Discours Africain Sur Les Phenomenes Paranormaux*. Paris: Harmattan, 1998.

Hinga, Teresa. "Jesus Christ and the Liberation of Women in Africa." In *The Will to Arise: Women, Tradition, and the Church in Africa*. Maryknoll, NY: Orbis, 1997.

Hodge, Charles. *Systematic Theology*. Vol. 2. Peabody, MA: Hendrickson Publishers, 1999.

Hough, Lynn Harold. *Athanasius: The Hero*. Cincinnati, OH: Jennings and Graham, 1906.

Ignat, Adrian. "The Spread Out of Arianism. A Critical Analysis of the Arian Heresy." *International Journal of Orthodox Theology* 3, no. 3 (2012): 105–129.

Imasogie, Osadolor. "The Church and Theological Ferment in Africa." *Review and Expositor* 82, no 1. Spring (1985): 225–36.

Isichei, Elizabeth. *A History of Christianity in Africa: From Antiquity to the Present*. Grand Rapids, MI: Eerdmans, 1995.

Iwe N. S. S. Christianity, *Culture and Colonialism in Africa*. Port Harcourt: COE, 1985.

Jenson, Robert W. *Systematic Theology*. vol. 2. New York: Oxford University Press, 1997.

John Paul II. "Ecclesia in Africa: Post Synodal Apostolic Exhortation," September 1995. http://w2.vati can.va/cont ent/john-paul-ii/en/apo st_e xhor tati ons/docume nts/hf_jp-ii_ex h_14 091995_ecclesia-in-africa.html.

———. "Ecclesia in Africa, Post Synodal Apostolic Exhortation to the Bishops Priests and Deacons, Men and Women Religious and All the Lay Faithful on the Church." In *Africa and Its Evangelizing Mission Towards the Year 2000*. Nairobi, Kenya: Pauline Publications, 1995.

———. *Familiaris Consortio*. Apostolic Exhortation on the Role of the Christian Family in the Modern World. Homebush, NSW: St Paul's Publications, 1982.

Jones, Rufus M. *The Church's Debt to Heretics*. London: James Clarke & Co. Limited, 1925.

K. Sarpong, Peter. "Asante Christology." *Studia Missionalia* 45, no. 45 (1996): 189–205.

Kabasele, Francois. *Celebrating Jesus Christ in Africa: Liturgy & Inculturation*. Maryknoll, NY: Orbis, 1998.

———. "Christ as Ancestor and Brother." In *Faces of Jesus in Africa*. Ed. Robert J. Schreiter. Maryknoll, NY: Orbis, 1991.

———. "Christ as Chief." In *Faces of Jesus in Africa*, Ed. Robert J. Schreiter. Maryknoll, NY: Orbis, 1991.

———. "Le Christ comme chef," Chemins de la Christologie africaine. éd. F. Kabasélé, J. Doré, and R. Luneau. Paris: Desclée, 1986.

Kannengiesser, Charles. "A Key for the Future of Patristics: The 'Senses' of Scripture." in *In Dominico Eloquio—In Lordly Eloquence: Essays on Patristic Exegesis in Honor of Robert Louis Wilken*. Ed. Paul M. Blowers et al. Grand Rapids: MI, Eerdmans, 2002.

Kasper, Walter. *Jesus Christ*. Trans. V. Green. Mahwah, NJ: Paulist Press, 1977.

Khaldun, Ibn. *An Arab Philosopher of History*. London: John Murray, 1950.

Kuster, Volker. *The Many Faces of Jesus Christ: Intercultural Christology*. Maryknoll, NY: Orbis, 1999.

Lubac, Henri de. *The Motherhood of the Church*. San Francisco: Ignatius Press, 1982.

Lumen Gentium. Dogmatic Constitution on the Church. 1964. http://www.vati can.va/arch ive/hist_councils/ii_vatican_council/documents/vat-ii_const_19641121_lumen-gentium _en.html.

Lynette, Jean Holness. "Christology from Within: A Critical Retrieval of the Humanity of Christ, with Particular Reference to the Role of Mary." Doctor in Philosophy Dissertation, University of Cape Town, 2001.

Magesa, Laurenti. "Christ the Liberator and Africa Today." In *Faces of Jesus in Africa*. Maryknoll, NY: Orbis, 1991.

Makinde, Taiwo. "Motherhood as a Source of Empowerment of Women in Yoruba Culture." *Nordic Journal of African Studies* 2, no. 13 (2004): 164–74.

Mayemba SJ., Bienvenu. "Reviving a Church of the Poor and for the Poor, And Reclaiming Faith Doing Justice and Seeking Liberation Convergence between Pope Francis and Jean-Marc Ela." *The Church We Want: African Catholics Look to Vatican III*. Ed. Agbonkhianmeghe E. Orobator. Maryknoll, NY: Orbis, 2016.

Mbiti, John. *African Religions and Philosophy*. London: Heinemann, 1969.

McDonald, H. D. "Development and Christology." *Vox Evangelica*, 51, no. 9 (1975): 5–27.

McGuckin, John. *Saint Cyril of Alexandria and the Christological Controversy: Its History, Theology, and Texts*. New York: St. Vlademir's Seminary Press, 2004.

McKenna, Megan. *Mary: Shadow of Grace*. Hyde Park, NY: New City Press, 1995.

Meijering. "Cyril on the Platonists and the Trinity." In *God, Being, History: Studies in Patristic Philosophy*. Amsterdam/Oxford: North Holland Publishing, (1975): 114–27.

Menanga, SJ., and Yves Kizito. "Meriter Notre Bonheur: Deux Meditation Philosophiques Sur La Pensée du Père Engelbert Mveng." In *Recuil d'Hommages*. Kinshasa: Editions Loyola-Canisius, 2005.

Mercy Amba E, Oduyoye. *Hearing and Knowing: Theological Reflections on Christianity in Africa*. Maryknoll, NY: Orbis, 1985.

Milingo, Emmanuel. *The World in Between*. Maryknoll, NY: Orbis, 1984.

Mnyaka, Mluleki, and Mokgethi Motlhabi. "The African Concept of Ubuntu/Botho and Its Socio-Moral Significance." *Black Theology* 3, no. 2 (2005): 215–37.

Muzorewa, Gwiny. "Christ as Our Ancestor: Christology from an Africa Perspective by Charles Nyamiti: A Review Essay." *Africa Theological Journal*. 17, no. 3, (1988): 255–64.

Mveng, Engelbert. *L'Afrique dans l'Eglise, Paroles d'un Croyant*. Paris: L'Harmattan, 1985.

———. "Impoverishment and Liberation: A Theological Approach for Africa and the Third World." In *Paths of African Theology*. Ed. Rosino Gibellini. Maryknoll, NY: Orbis, (1994) 154–65.

Mveng, Engelbert, and Benjamin Lipawing. *Theologie, Liberation et Culture Africaine. Dialogue Sur l'anthropologie Negro Africaine*. Yaounde: Presence Africaine, 1996.

Nasimiyu Wasike, Anne. "Witnesses to Jesus Christ in the African Context." Propositum, 1, no. 3, (June 1998): 17–29.

Need, Stephen W. *Truly Divine & Truly Human: The Story of Christ and the Seven Ecumenical Councils*. Peabody, MA: Hendrickson Publishers, 2008.

Ngussan, Julien. "Conversion to Jesus Christ in the Context of Anthropological Poverty of Africa: A Case Study of Cote D'Ivoire." Doctoral dissertation, Jesuit School of Theology of Santa Clara University, 2015.

Niebuhr, Richard. *Christ and Culture*. New York: Harper and Row, 1975.

Njoku, Francis O. C. *Essays in African Philosophy, Thought & Theology*. Owerri: Claretian Institute of Philosophy & Clacom Communication, 2002.

Noll, Mark. *Turning Points: Decisive Moments in the History of Christianity*. Grand Rapids, MI: Baker Books, 1997.

Norris, Richard A. *Manhood and Christ: A Study in the Christology of Theodore of Mopsuestia* Clarendon Press: Oxford, 1963.

Nothomb, Dominique. *Un Humanisme Africain: Valeurs et Pierres Dattente / Dominique Nothomb; Preface de M. LAbbe A. Kagame*. Bruxelles: Lumen Vitae, 1965.

Ntetem, Marc. *Initiation: Traditional and Christian. A Reader in African Christian Theology*. London: SPCK Publisher, 1997.

Nyamiti, Charles. "African Ancestral Veneration and Its Relevance to the African Churches." *The Journal of African Christian Studies*. 9, no. 3 (1993): 14–37.

———. *Christ as Our Ancestor*. Gweru: Mambo Press, 1984.

———. "Jesus Christ, the Ancestor of Mankind, Methodological and Trinitarian Foundations." *Studies in African Christian Theology* Vol. I. Nairobi: CUEA Publications, 2005.

Nwaigbor, Ferdinand. *Mary - Mother of the African Church: A Theological Inculturation of Mariology*. Frankfurt: Peter Lang, 2000.

Ocitti, Jimmy. "Media and Democracy in Africa: Mutual Political bedfellows or Implacable Arch-foes." Fellows Program, Weatherhead Center for International Affairs. Harvard University. July 1999. https://scholarsprogram.wcfia.harvard.edu/sites/projects.iq.harvard.edu/files/fellows/files/ocitti.pdf.

O'Collins, Gerald. *Interpreting Jesus*. Eugene, OR: Wipf & Stock Publishers, 2002.

Oduyoye, Mercy A. *Daughters of Anowa: African Women and Patriarchy*. Maryknoll, NY: Orbis, 2003.

———. *Hearing and Knowing: Theological Reflections on Christianity in Africa*. Maryknoll, NY: Orbis, 1986.

Ogbu, Kalu. "The Formulation of Cultural Policy in Colonial Nigeria." *African Humanities: Traditional and Modem Culture*, Vol 33. no. 2. Enugu: Fourth Dimension (1985): 125–38.

———. *The History of Christianity in West Africa*. Essex. Longman. London, 1980.

Okeke, Hilary O. "From 'Domestic Church' to 'Family of God': The African Christian Family in the African Synod." *Nouvelle Revue de Science Missionnaire*, no. 52 (1996): 193–94.

Oladipo, Caleb O. *African Christianity: Its Scope in Global Context*. in *Development, Modernism and Modernity in Africa*. Ed. Augustine Agwuele. New York & London: Routledge (2012): 212–29.

Olbricht, Thomas H. "Greek Rhetoric and the Allegorical Rhetoric of Philo and Clement of Alexandria." In Rhetorical Criticism and the Bible. Ed. Stanley E. Porter and Dennis L. Stamps, *Journal for the Study of the New Testament Supplement*, no. 1. 195, 2002.

Onwubiko, Oliver. *African Thought, Religion and Culture*. Enugu: Snaap Press, 1991.

Origen. "Comm. John 10. 37. 212." In Origen, Commentary on the Gospel According to John, Books 1–10, Trans. Ronald E. Heine. Washington, D.C.: The Catholic University of America Press, 1989.

———. *De Principiis*. Revised and edited for New Advent by Kevin Knight. Buffalo, NY: Christian Literature Publishing Co., 1885. http://www.newadvent.org/fathers/0412.htm.

Orobator, Agbonkhianmeghe E. *The Church as Family: African Ecclesiology in Its Social Context*. Nairobi: Pauline Publications, 2000.

———. "The Quest for an African Christ: An Essay on Contemporary African Christology." *Hekima Review*, no. 11 (September 1994): 75–99.

———. *Theology Brewed in an African Pot*. Nairobi: Paulist Publications, 2008.

———. "Reading the Signs of the Future." In *The Church We Want: African Catholics Look to Vatican III*. Ed. Agbonkhianmeghe E. Orobator. Maryknoll, NY: Orbis, 2016.

Oyewumi, Oyeronke. "Abiyamo: Theorizing African Motherhood." *Jenda: A Journal of Culture & African Women Studies*, Online edition, 1, no. 4 (2003).

Parratt, John. *Reinventing Christianity: African Theology Today*. Grand Rapids, MI: Eerdmans Publishing Company/Trenton Africa World Press, 1995.

Penoukou, Efoe Julien. "Christology in the Village." In *Faces of Jesus in Africa*. Ed. Robert Schreiter. Maryknoll, NY: Orbis, 1991.

Pobee, John. S. *Christ Would Be an African Too*. Geneva: WCC Publications, 1996.

———. *Skenosis: Christian Faith in an African Context*. Gweru, Zimbabwe: Mambo Press, 1992.

———. *Towards an African Theology*. Nashville, TN: Abingdon, 1979.

Pohle, Joseph. *Christology: A Dogmatic Treatise on the Incarnation*. London: Herder, 1946.

Ponti, Merleau. *Phénoménologie de La Perception*. Paris: Librairie Gallimard, 1945.

Price, Richard and Michael Gaddis. *The Acts of the Council of Chalcedon*. Liverpool: Liverpool University Press, 2007.

Quash, Ben and Michael Ward. *Heresies and How to Avoid Them: Why It Matters What Christians Believe*. Peabody, MA: Hendrickson Publishers, 2007.

R. McL., Wilson. *The Gnostic Problem*. London: A.R. Mowbray & Co. Limited, 1958.

Rahner, Karl. *Theological Investigations*. Vol. I. Baltimore: Helicon Press, 1961.

———. *Theological Investigations*. Vol. IV. Baltimore: Helicon Press, 1961.

Ramose, Mogobe B. *African Philosophy through Ubuntu*. Harare: Mond Books, 1999.

Rays, Benjamin. *African Religions Symbol, Ritual, and Community*. Englewood Cliffs, New Jersey: Prentice-Hall, 1976.

Rodney, Walter. *How Europe Underdeveloped Africa*. London: L'ouverture, 1972.

Sanon, Anselme T. *Enraciner l'évangile: Initiations Africaines et Pédagogie de La Foi*. Paris: Cerf, 1982.

———. "Jesus Master of Initiation." In *Faces of Jesus in Africa*, Ed. Robert J. Schreiter. Maryknoll, NY: Orbis, 1991.

Schaff, Philip. "Ebionites." *The New Schaff-Herzog Encyclopedia of Religious Knowledge*. Grand Rapids, MI: Baker Books, 1953.

Schoepf, Brooke Grundfest. "AIDS." In *A Companion to the Anthropology of Politics*. Ed. D. Nugent and J. Vincent. Malden: Blackwell Publishers, 2004.

Schor, Adam M. "Theodoret on the 'School of Antioch': A Network Approach."

Journal of Early Christian Studies 15, no. 4 (2007): 517–62.
Schreiter, Robert J., *Faces of Jesus in Africa*. Ed. Robert Schreiter. Maryknoll, NY: Orbis, 1991.
Severus. "Letter to Eusebius." Online edition. Accessed May 22, 2016. http://www.newadvent.org/fathers/3502.htm.
Shelley, Bruce L. *Church History in Plain Language*. Dallas, TX: Word Publishing, 1995.
Shutte, Augustine. *Ubuntu: An Ethic for a New South Africa*. Pietermaritzburg: Cluster Publications, 2001.
Simon Ottenberg. *Boyhood Rituals in an African Society: An Interpretation*. Seattle, WA: University of Washington Press, 1989.
Smulders, Pieter Fran. *The Fathers on Christology: The Development of Christological Dogma from the Bible to the Great Councils*. De Pere, WI: St. Norbert Abbey Press, 1968.
Stafford, Glass. *The Matabele War*. London: Longmans, 1968.
Stinton, Dianne B. *Jesus of Africa: Voices of Contemporary African Christology*. Nairobi, Pauline Publications Africa, 2004.
Sundlker, Bengt G. M. *Bantu Prophets in South Africa*. London: Oxford University Press, 2nd ed, 1961.
Taylor, John V. *The Primal Vision: Christian Presence Amid African Religion*. London: SCM Press, 1963.
Tiénou, Tite "Christian Theology: African Realities and African Hope." *International Bulletin of Mission Research* 41, no. 4 (2017): 294–95.
The International Theological Commission. "Theology, Christology, Anthropology," 1981.https://www.vatican.va/roman_curia/congregations/cfaith/cti_documents/rc_cti_1982_teologia-cristologia-antropologia_en.html.
Thomas, Louis-Vincent and René Luneau. *La Terre Africaine et Ses Religions*. Paris: Larousse, 1975.
Tutu, Desmond. *No Future without Forgiveness*. New York: Doubleday, 1999.
Uzukwu, Eluchukwu. *A Listening Church: Autonomy and Communion in African Churches*. Maryknoll, NY: Orbis, 1996.
Vine, Aubrey R. *An Approach to Christology: An Interpretation and Development of Some Elements in the Metaphysic and Christology of Nestorius as a Way of Approach to an Orthodox Christology Compatible with Modern Thought*. London: Independent Press, 1948.
Wace, Henry. *A Dictionary of Christian Biography and Literature to the End of the Sixth Century A.D., with an Account of the Principal Sects and Heresies*. Peabody, MA: Hendrickson Publishers, 1994. https://www.documentacatholicaomnia.eu/03d/20012001,_Wace_and_Piercy_Eds,_A_Dictionary_Of_Early_Christian_Biography,_LT_EN.pdf.
Waltke, Bruce K. *The Book of Proverbs: Chapters 15–31*. Grand Rapids, MI: William B. Eerdmans, 2005.
Watney, Simon. *Practices of Freedom: Selected Writings on HIV/AIDS*. Durham, NC: Duke University Press, 1994.
Wilhite, David E. *The Gospel According to Heretics: Discovering Orthodoxy through Early Christological Conflicts*. Ada, MI: Baker Academic, 2015.
Wolfson, Harry Austryn. *The Philosophy of the Church Fathers I: Faith, Trinity, Incarnation*. Vol. I. His Structure and Growth of Philosophic Systems from Plato to Spinoza. Cambridge, MA: Harvard University Press, 1956.

Bible & Theology in Africa

Knut Holter, *General Editor*

The twentieth century made sub-Saharan Africa a Christian continent. This formidable church growth is reflected in a wide range of attempts at contextualizing Christian theology and biblical interpretation in Africa. At a grassroots level ordinary Christians express their faith and read the bible in ways reflecting their daily situation; at an academic level, theologians and biblical scholars relate the historical traditions and sources of Christianity to the socio- and religio-cultural context of Africa. In response to this, the Bible and Theology in Africa series aims at making African theology and biblical interpretation its subject as well as object, as the concerns of African theologians and biblical interpreters will be voiced and critically analyzed. Both Africans and Western authors are encouraged to consider this series.

Inquiries and manuscripts should be directed to:
    Professor Knut Holter
    NLA University College
    Amalie Skrams vei 3
    5036 Bergen
    Norway
    prof.knut.holter@gmail.com

To order other books in this series, please contact our Customer Service Department:
    peterlang@presswarehouse.com (within the U.S.)
    orders@peterlang.com (outside the U.S.)

Or browse online by series
    www.peterlang.com